Country Inns
& Back Roads

"Why should not the New Englander
be in search of new adventures?"
THOREAU: *Walden*

Country Inns and Back Roads

VOLUME IX

BY THE BERKSHIRE TRAVELLER

Norman T. Simpson

THE BERKSHIRE TRAVELLER PRESS
Stockbridge, Massachusetts 01262

THE BERKSHIRE TRAVELLER TRAVEL SHELF

Country Inns and Back Roads
Very Special Resorts
Farm, Ranch and Countryside Guide
Adventure Trip Guide

COVER PAINTING Sheila Granda

This time Sheila has given us a Massachusetts Colonial village near sundown. It is early April 1775. Perhaps Samuel Adams or John Hancock has just arrived at the inn to enjoy dinner and greet old friends before adjourning to the church, which also served as a meeting house, to speak about Parliament's most recent Intolerable Act. Soon the men of this village will heed the call to arms, and the Great Revolt will be under way. The inn may well have survived 200 years and still be thriving today.

BOOK DESIGN Janice Lindstrom

SCRATCHBOARD DRAWINGS Janice Lindstrom, Jane McWhorter, Linda Winchester

Library of Congress #75-2519
ISBN #0-912944-28-5
Copyright 1975, Berkshire Traveller Press

PREFACE

WHILE the American Bicentennial is on our minds it occurs to me that there are few institutions that have endured since 1775 like the American country inn. Fundamentally, they've remained the same for 200 years and more. Now, as then, most of them are family owned and operated. They're highly individualistic, expressing the innkeeper's style and personality. They take pride in getting to know their guests and anticipating their wants. The inns themselves are very often community meeting places, looked upon with pride by local people as "their inn."

Furthermore their appearance is inviting. No need for multicolored roofs that clash with the scenery or garish neon lights that are offensive to gentle sensibilities. Very often the food is prepared from scratch and features dishes of local and regional origin. Pride begins in the kitchen.

At a time when it's so much easier to make a dollar by computerizing and systematizing everything from lodging room furniture to fried chicken, I extend my deep gratitude to the keepers of country inns for maintaining their integrity and keeping their doors open in the face of rising food, labor and gasoline costs.

VOLUME IX — It hardly seems possible.

In this volume I've included visits to 126 country inns in Eastern and Maritime Canada (including Newfoundland and Prince Edward Island) and all of the United States. Seventeen inns in our previous edition have been replaced by seventeen newly-discovered inns. Almost without exception I have visited and revisited every inn between June 1974 and January 1975. This book is completely rewritten every year. It's the only fair way I know of to keep our readers truthfully informed.

In this edition I've also tried to orient the reader to the stirring events of 1775, suggesting country inns that are located near these scenes.

I would like to thank my staff through art director Jan Lindstrom who designed this book and made the scratchboard drawings, and editor Nancy O'Reilly who patiently read and rechecked every word. It is only through dedicated teamwork, that a book like this can be written and published every year. Recognition should also go to the Studley Press in Dalton, Massachusetts, who worked overtime, holidays, early and late, to meet our deadlines.

Thank you everyone.

CONTENTS

A TRAVELLER'S-EYE VIEW OF 1775

ONE of my favorite movies is *Berkeley Square*. In it Leslie Howard, a modern young man, is transported to an early period in time when he steps inside an old English mansion. I'm inviting all of you to take such a step backward in time and we shall briefly retrace the events of 1775, events which changed the course of history and eventually resulted in the formation of the New Republic.

I would be remiss if I did not point out that it is possible for the traveler of 1975 to visit the locale of many of these stirring events, and find personal accommodations nearby at country inns mentioned in this volume. I've included an asterisk (*) next to those historic sites which can still be visited today.

But first let's set the stage. For 300 years the continent of North America had been fought over by European countries. England emerged more or less victorious around 1760, after breaking the French rule in Canada. The English, however, viewed their American Colonies with a somewhat feudal eye, and attempted to keep them in line using various Parliamentary and Royal decrees which the Colonists found increasingly abusive.

Men of reason on both sides of the Atlantic attempted to conciliate the hostile factions, but some extremists among the Colonists were already running with the bit in their teeth. They wanted complete separation.

Resistance was dramatized by the Boston Massacre* of March 5th, 1770, when British troops fired on a mob. On December 16th, 1773, in an overt response to the tax on tea, some firebrand Bostonians dressed as Indians threw the tea, which had arrived in ships from England, into the Boston Harbor at the Boston Tea Party.*

King and Parliament kept imposing more regulations which fanned the tempers of such dissident groups as the Sons of Liberty. Since a great deal of the opposition seemed to be centered in Boston, Parliament passed the Boston Port Bill closing the port. The other Colonies rallied around Boston and sent money and food.

Meanwhile the Colonies sent representatives to the First Continental Congress on September 17th, 1774, which sent courteous letters to England suggesting a more moderate course.

Now we're ready to step back into time and watch the events of 1775 unfold.

Early in the year, General Gage, the British Commander in

Boston took steps to re-acquire some of the purloined Royal stores, arms, and powder that had been hidden in various Massachusetts towns. "Yankee Doodle" a song by Edward Barnes that was to carry the Spirit of the Revolution, began to appear in broadsides.

In Parliament, William Pitt put forth a "plan for conciliation with the colonies," which was rejected. In May his speech for recommending the withdrawal of British troops from Boston was distributed widely in the colonies and he became the principal Colonial spokesman in Parliament.

On March 23rd, 1775, Patrick Henry, a young lawyer from Virginia, spoke out publicly choosing liberty rather than death.*

In mid-April, Gage sent troops toward Lexington and Concord. Apparently the purpose of this mission was not only to gather the stores but to arrest Samuel Adams and John Hancock, two of the more prominent of the dissidents. However, word was sent on ahead and the populace was roused by Paul Revere and other riders. Incidentally, Revere was captured on that ride, although released after being held for a very short time.

The fat was in the fire and the local militiamen who had been drilling in various village squares and gathering in various village taverns, began to assemble on the Lexington Green.* When the skirmish was over, the redcoats went on toward Concord, leaving eight American militiamen dead.

At North Bridge in Concord* still another skirmish took place. It was here that the legendary first shot was fired. This time the British retreated.

The withdrawal route* to Boston where the farmers and militiamen took potshots at the redcoats is renowned. It continued through the small towns and finally ended under the safety of the guns of the Royal Navy.

Meanwhile the Second Continental Congress assembled in Philadelphia* in May. Also in that month Colonel Ethan Allen and Colonel Benedict Arnold captured Fort Ticonderoga* on Lake Champlain, and acquired a considerable supply of artillery.

The situation was brought to a climax at the Battle of Breed's Hill (Bunker Hill) in June 1775.* General Gage, apparently nervous about the fact that Americans were occupying this height of land, sent seasoned troops to dislodge them. The raw, untrained militia were able to withstand superior fire power and keep their heads. The British charged twice without taking the height. However, on the the third attempt the Americans retreated.

Shortly after the Battle of Bunker Hill the Second Continental Congress made a number of decisions. First, they decided to accept the main body of the various state militia at Boston as the principal army, and on June 16th they chose George Washington of Virginia as their Commander-in-Chief. Conciliation was still in the air as they sent the Olive Branch Petition to England, although they had rejected earlier British proposals.

On the 23rd of August, 1775, George III issued a Royal Proclamation saying officially that the Americans were in rebellion and in September, 1775, the French, still smarting from earlier defeats by the British, decided to throw in with the rebels, because they figured they were going to win anyway.

Meanwhile, the British in Boston, no doubt considerably agitated and frustrated by recent events, sent several elements of the fleet and bombarded the town of Falmouth, Maine.*

On October 5th, 1775, the Continental Congress ordered the arrest of "all dangerous loyalists." On October 13th they also voted to outfit two ships of ten guns each and thus established the Navy.

George Washington also sent General Knox to be in charge of the tremendous feat of dragging, pulling, pushing and shoving the Fort Ticonderoga cannon from Lake Champlain through the Berkshires* to Dorchester Heights overlooking Boston. This was accomplished during the winter of 1775-76.

In the two-pronged invasion of Canada, Washington sent General Montgomery north using the Lake Champlain* and Richelieu River* waterways. On November 13th, the Americans were successful in occupying Montreal.* Montgomery led his forces toward Quebec City* where a rendezvous had been planned with Benedict Arnold who had led another army through Maine, using the waters of the Kennebeck River.

Although success seemed certain, the combination of staunch resistance by the British and Canadian militiamen, plus a violent snowstorm and Montgomery's death in the first attack broke the spirit of the Americans and they retreated.

Practically all hope of conciliation ended when all trade with the Colonies was prohibited by Parliament on December 22nd.

So the year 1775 ended. Skirmishes gave way to battles, and the Americans had seen both success and failure. The smoldering fires of discontent which might well had been handled had wiser heads prevailed, broke into open warfare.

It was a time of accusation and counter-accusation. Households were divided, loyalties confused. General Washington had emerged as Commander-in-Chief, and the British declared war on the Colonies. However, the Colonies would not declare their independence until July, 1776.

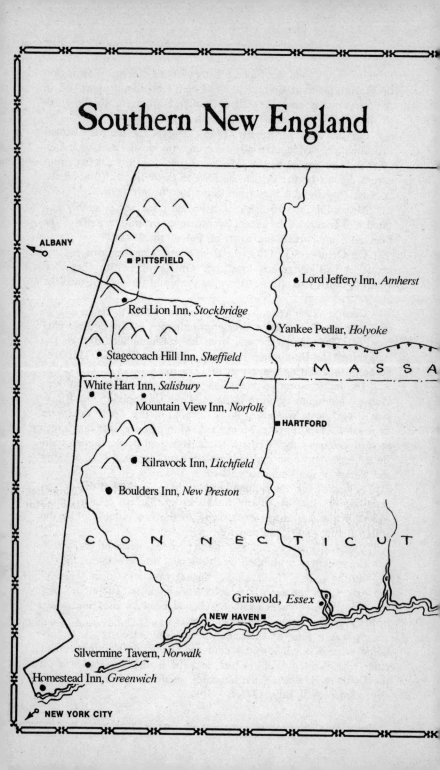

Southern New England

ALBANY

■ PITTSFIELD

● Lord Jeffery Inn, *Amherst*

● Red Lion Inn, *Stockbridge*

● Yankee Pedlar, *Holyoke*

MASSACHUSETTS

M A S S A

● Stagecoach Hill Inn, *Sheffield*

White Hart Inn, *Salisbury*
●

Mountain View Inn, *Norfolk*

■ HARTFORD

● Kilravock Inn, *Litchfield*

● Boulders Inn, *New Preston*

C O N N E C T I C U T

Griswold, *Essex* ●

■ NEW HAVEN

Silvermine Tavern, *Norwalk*
●

Homestead Inn, *Greenwich*
●

NEW YORK CITY

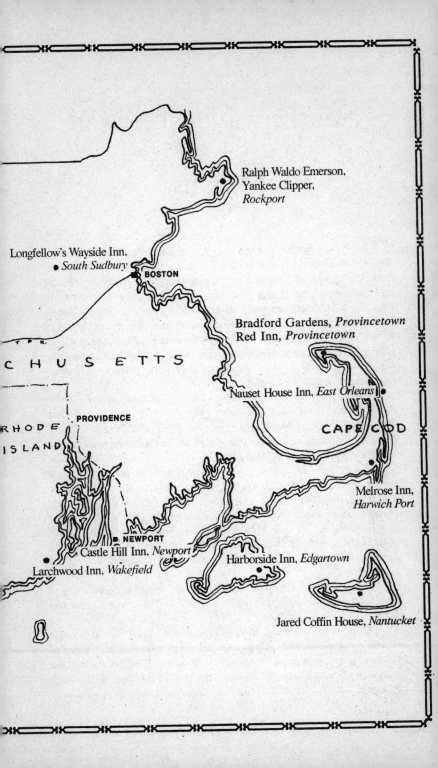

Ralph Waldo Emerson,
Yankee Clipper,
Rockport

Longfellow's Wayside Inn,
● *South Sudbury*

BOSTON

Bradford Gardens, *Provincetown*
Red Inn, *Provincetown*

Nauset House Inn, *East Orleans*

MASSACHUSETTS

PROVIDENCE

RHODE
ISLAND

CAPE COD

Melrose Inn,
Harwich Port

NEWPORT

Castle Hill Inn, *Newport*

Larchwood Inn, *Wakefield*

Harborside Inn, *Edgartown*

Jared Coffin House, *Nantucket*

Mass'tts

Here, on Boston's Freedom Trail, was the house of Paul Revere. Paul Revere—just saying his name over to myself I could hear the sound of muffled oar locks on the Charles River and the thunder of hoofbeats. I could see a galloping figure racing into the hinterland, stopping at crossroads, hammering on doors. I imagined men grabbing flintlocks with one hand and breeches with the other, hurriedly kissing their wives and dashing off to join other men, cursing the chill morning and at the same time feeling a tightness in their throats as they anticipated a confrontation with the hated redcoats.

Today, this is the oldest house in Boston, built around 1677. Paul Revere lived here for thirty years, during the Boston Tea Party in 1773, and the historic ride to Lexington in April, 1775. Silversmith, activist and patriot—from all accounts he was one of the Renaissance men of his day.

It's easy to experience the events of two hundred years ago on the Freedom Trail. It runs from the Boston Common to the U.S.S. Constitution. There are sixteen numbered historic sites and several other interesting landmarks along its course. It can be covered on foot, on the MPTA Freedom Trail Shuttle Bus, or on a sightseeing bus. It is about one and a half miles in length and can be followed by a red brick path and footprints at street crossings.

Fortunately, the trail is well annotated in a very easy-to-read booklet available at the Freedom Trail Information Center on Boston Common.

Along with the Paul Revere House, the Trail includes some of the most historic buildings and places of Colonial and Revolutionary War interest in the country. There's King's Church, the first Episcopal Church in Boston, and the Statehouse, which was designed by Charles Bullfinch. The Trail passes the statue of Ben-

jamin Franklin, the Old Corner Bookhouse and the Old South Meeting House where Adams acted as deacon and town clerk.

It also takes in the site of the Boston Massacre and the famous Old North Church. There are several other places of interest off the Freedom Trail including the Bunker Hill Monument and Copps Hill Burying Ground.

Visitors, at any time, will find it rewarding to go to Lexington and Concord, as well as the historic North Shore. Plymouth and Cape Cod are just a few miles south of Boston and visitors can see the Plymouth Rock, Mayflower II, and the Plimouth Plantation.

There are country inns in this book on the North Shore, near Lexington and Concord, and on Cape Cod.

LONGFELLOW'S WAYSIDE INN, South Sudbury

Francis Koppeis, who is the absolute personification of a country innkeeper of today, was explaining some of the heritage of Longfellow's Wayside Inn.

"Around 1702, one of Sudbury's earliest settlers, David How built a two-room stopping place here. It was on the direct road from Boston to Albany. It was expanded into four rooms a few years later. In 1716, How took out the first innkeeper's license of record for the inn at the Concord Courthouse.

"How's son, Ezekiel, a man of many resources, became innkeeper in 1746. He built four more rooms and added an "e" to the family name. It was first known as Howe's Tavern, then The Red Horse.

"He was a lieutenant colonel in the Massachusetts *Minutemen and Militia* and was very influential at the Sudbury town meeting in January 1774 when the Tea Tax Resolution was unanimously passed.

"I can well imagine the fiery meetings held at the inn in the days leading up to April 19, 1775, when Colonel Howe led two companies of Sudbury men to the historic skirmish at North Bridge in Concord.

"The re-enactment of this event takes place every year at the inn. By the way, all musters of Minutemen and Militiamen take place right here, as well."

At this point the waitress in Colonial dress brought our dinner. I had chosen Yankee Pot Roast and Frank ordered baked scrod.

"So you see," Frank went on, "there've been accommodations for man and beast here in these woods for more than 275 years. Presidents and congresses have replaced kings and Parliaments; wars have been fought; good and bad times have come and gone; horses have been replaced by stagecoaches; and stagecoaches, by trains and automobiles. Through all of this I hope that we have managed to preserve not only Colonial times, but also Victorian and 19th century days as well."

Indeed all of these epochs in our country's history have been part of Longfellow's Wayside Inn. It's had its own share of turbulence and disaster, as well, but it still goes on. I've written about it many times in the past and it's been visited by literally thousands of the readers of *Country Inns and Back Roads*.

The dessert arrived, deep dish apple pie for me and, Indian pudding for Frank—both of them traditional at the inn. As we finished our delicious dinner, Frank had one piece of advice for all of us:

"If any of your readers are planning to come and stay with us either for dinner or overnight during the next few years, considering the interest in the Bicentennial in this section, I hope all of them will make reservations well in advance."

LONGFELLOW'S WAYSIDE INN, Wayside Inn Rd., off Rte. 20, South Sudbury, Mass. 01776; 617-443-8846. A 10-room historic landmark inn, midway between Boston and Worcester. Within short distance of Concord, Lexington, and other famous Revolutionary War landmarks. European Plan. Lunch and dinner served daily except Christmas. Breakfast to overnight guests. For history and antique lovers. Francis Koppeis, Innkeeper.

Directions: From the west, take Exit 11A from I-95 to Rte. 495 N. Proceed north on 495 to Rte. 20. Follow Rte. 20 east to inn. From the east, take Exit 49 from Rte. 128. Follow Rte. 20 west to inn.

THE RALPH WALDO EMERSON, Rockport
YANKEE CLIPPER, Rockport

Here's the true story about one of New England's most picturesque seacoast towns and two inns, each of which extends its own individual hospitality.

Rockport is well named, for indeed it has rocks galore. They are flung about with glorious abandon, around sandy beaches, capricious inlets and snug harbors. Here are to be found fishing boats and luxury yachts cheek-by-jowl with fishermen's dinghies, dories and lobster boats.

The town boasts many late 18th and early 19th century homes with narrow clapboards, wooden shutters and fan doorways which are to be found on beguiling lanes and winding elm-shaded streets.

All this is placed against the backdrop of the many moods of ocean and sky. It has been all of these elements that have drawn artists to Rockport for over a hundred years. It is that

The Clipper

19

indefinable quality of "paintableness." The painters with their watercolors and oils were followed in due time by photographers. Today Rockport has a plethora of galleries and studios both large and small, and the artistic media have grown to include pottery, weaving, basketry, gems and jewelry, and sculpture soft and hard. Almost all types of handicrafts are represented among Rockport shops. One of the best features is that for the most part these shops are open year-round.

Now to the two inns. They present an interesting study in contrasts. Both are operated by members of the Wemyss family with Fred and Lydia, father and mother, being innkeepers at the Yankee Clipper, and son, Gary, the innkeeper at The Ralph Waldo Emerson.

The three-story gleaming white Emerson with its 36 rooms is a traditional north shore resort-hotel, with a direct view of the ocean.

On the other hand, the Yankee Clipper sits back in the shelter of some great rocks. The main building was once a late 19th century mansion and is hidden among the trees. One of the buildings is a jewel, originally designed by Boston architect Bullfinch who flourished during the early 19th century. Bullfinch homes are highly prized in New England. There is a fine group of them in Orford, New Hampshire.

Both inns have swimming pools but the grounds of the Emerson also provide the opportunity to play croquet, horseshoes and badminton. The Clipper has less emphasis on active sports.

Activity at the Emerson provides a great deal of opportunity

The Emerson

for families with children. Children are welcome at the Clipper but I've always seen more of them at the Emerson.

It's possible to sit on the big terrace at the Emerson and gaze at the ocean for hours on end. At the Clipper you can either sit on the grassy section on the low cliffs and watch the boats in Rockport harbor or climb to the top of the great granite boulders and find your own private vantage point.

Both inns have a profusion of flowers including roses, tulips, pansies, rhododendron, spirea, dahlias, snapdragons, petunias, and other flowers that flourish in New England. The swimming pool at the Clipper nestles among pines, elms, maple and mulberry trees.

As far as the food is concerned, the Emerson, on the American Plan in summer, has Yankee pot roast, native lobster, and fried filet of sole. The Clipper features fish chowder, steamed lobster, a delightful dish poached in milk, chicken Yankee Clipper, and blueberry pancakes, among others.

For the sports-minded, there are fishing, golf, and tennis near both inns and there's also a power boat in which guests of both inns are frequently treated to trips around the harbor.

That's the word picture of these two Rockport inns. During the summertime, when both are open, I'd say that perhaps the Clipper is more intimate, a little more quiet. Both of them are favorites of mine and I savor the individual features of each.

RALPH WALDO EMERSON, 1 Cathedral Ave., Rockport, Mass. 01966; 617-546-6321. A 36-room oceanside inn, 40 mi. from Boston. Mod. American and European Plans. Breakfast and dinner served to travelers daily. Snack bar luncheon in season. Season: July 1 through Labor Day. Open Memorial Day through Nov. 1. No pets. Pool and sailing. Tennis, golf nearby. Courtesy car. Gary Wemyss, Innkeeper.

YANKEE CLIPPER, Rockport, Massachusetts 01966; 617-546-3407. An intimate 26-room inn on the sea, 40 mi. from Boston. European Plan available year-round; Mod. American Plan from May 15 to June 15 and September 15 to Veteran's Day. Breakfast and dinner served daily. Lunch served during July and August. Meals served to travelers by reservation only. No pets. Ocean view, shoreline walks, many antique shops and other stores nearby. Fred and Lydia Wemyss, Innkeepers.

Directions: Take I-95 to Rte. 128 to 127 (Gloucester). Proceed 6 mi. on Rte. 127 to Rockport and continue to Pigeon Cove.

Cape Cod

Like a bold bent arm, Cape Cod thrusts some seventy miles into the Atlantic Ocean from the Massachusetts mainland. For three centuries, the "Cape" with its magnificent shoreline was spared the considerable industrial buildup of the eastern coast. Its seafaring way of life and proud heritage, combined with a natural isolation, produced a picturesque scene which included weathered-grey cottages, cloistered villages, windmills and lighthouses.

Fortunately, a great deal of this environment has been preserved by the establishment of the Cape Cod National Seashore. Beaches, forests and ponds are no longer threatened in one of the last expanses of uninterrupted natural lands along the Atlantic. Historical houses still can be seen in their natural surroundings.

At the Visitor's Center in Salt Pond off Route 6 in Easton, information, exhibits, maps and illustrated programs about the history and natural history of the Cape are provided. There are also self-guided nature trails and illustrated talks to orient the traveler with the natural and human history of this beautiful area.

We have discovered several inns scattered along the south coastline and the islands that should further enhance any traveler's trip to Cape Cod.

BRADFORD GARDENS INN, Provincetown

It was breakfast time at the Bradford Gardens with John Venner and Jim Logan in the big, friendly kitchen overlooking the orchard. This morning we were having flippers, and this is the way John described them:

"I use a very fine Portuguese bread dough, warm it to room temperature and then sort of play around with it like you would a pizza, to get it nice and thin. Then I pop it into hot corn oil and float it about an inch deep, turning it just once. I butter it and top it with good things like maple syrup, fruit, honey or powdered sugar. The Portuguese way of serving it is with hot Portuguese sausage."

Still on the subject of breakfast which is the only meal served at the Bradford Gardens, Jim continued, "Eggs King Oscar

is our fanciest dish. This consists of toasted English muffins, buttered, with a slice of American cheese, one poached egg, two long spears of fresh asparagus and two strips of bacon crisscrossed, with hollandaise on top of everything."

Breakfasts are very important at this inn far out on the tip of Cape Cod. They provide the nutritional lift one needs to start a day in Provincetown. A typical Provincetown day can include active sports such as swimming, riding, tennis, and dune buggying as well as a complete tour of the shops which by this time number well into the hundreds.

Two words I think best describe the Bradford Gardens: "informal and intimate." It's an old Provincetown house that has been tastefully redecorated and furnished to provide casual comfort.

The informality comes into play at breakfast time in the kitchen because there is always a lot of conversation as more guests drift in to enjoy the morning meal. This same easy informality in the kitchen continues as the guests take their coffee out into the orchard and the morning sunshine. Many people, glad to be away from the strife of urban living, spend the whole day there, reading, napping and talking. The flowering fruit trees, lilac bushes and roses provide a home for many songbirds. During the wintertime the three bird feeders are very busy with the grosbeaks, jays and cardinals.

The inn has nine rooms in the main house, six of which have fireplaces and are quite cozy. There are also some large, airy modern apartments just across the road commanding an excellent view of Provincetown harbor.

Jim and John are very enthusiastic art collectors and they have recently acquired nine of the original Fletcher Martin illustrations for Jack London's book, "The Sea Wolf." These have been added to the inn's collection of original paintings which includes Picasso, Chagall, Edward Paine and Eugene Sparks.

A word to the wise—be certain to have reservations well in advance of visiting in July and August.

BRADFORD GARDENS INN, 178 Bradford Street, Provincetown, Mass. 02657; 617-487-1616. A small 9-room village inn overlooking Provincetown Bay. European Plan includes complimentary gourmet breakfast. No other meals served. Open year-round. Within walking distance of Provincetown harbor and shops. Bicycles, swimming, riding, tennis, golf and dune buggies nearby. John Venner and Jim Logan, Innkeepers.

Directions: Follow Rte. 6 to Provincetown.

THE RED INN, Provincetown

Ted Barker was talking about the first landing of the Pilgrims in the New World. "Actually it's just within walking distance of where we are now," he said. "They came here on November 11, 1620, and signed the Mayflower Compact. The monument in the middle of town on the top of Monument Hill commemorates their landing.

"Well, we still have a lot of fishermen here, thank heavens. They're the ones that supply us with our fresh fish everyday. But I think they're getting outnumbered by resident artists who enjoy painting the dunes and the old buildings in town."

The Red Inn is a restaurant that is open year-round and serves just one meal every day in the year, except Christmas night. Some of the fish dishes which are available in the summer and early fall are striped bass, swordfish and bluefish. There's also native cod scrod or haddock scrod during most months of the year. They have a special baked stuffed fillet of sole and always get many compliments on the sauce—a seafood bisque with bits of shrimp. There are shrimp and scallops in the stuffing, also.

I always order seafood when I'm near the sea, as I like to sample foods of the region in all parts of the country. That particular night I had Shrimp Champignon a la Black Bart, which has a delicious mushroom sauce and is served on a bed of rice. But the Scallops a la Pierre looked very good as did the lobsters

which Ted said were delivered right from the Provincetown wharf.

The dessert list at the Red Inn is printed on a series of little cards which are made up with a generous dollop of good humor. Some of the more frequently served desserts include Strawberries Romanoff, a combination of strawberries, ice cream and fresh whipped cream, mingled with a complementing liqueur; baked apples filled with brown sugar and cranberries and topped with vanilla ice cream; chocolate Bavarian pie; Indian pudding which is a Cape Cod tradition, and Red Inn Orange Delight.

A footnote on Provincetown and the Red Inn: During the summer season Provincetown is filled with people and many of them have heard about the Red Inn and drop in hoping to get a table. They would be most fortunate if they could get a table, because most of the time it's necessary to reserve a few hours before dinner to avoid disappointment. Dining is a leisurely experience, even in hectic summer months, because Marci Barker, who is totally in charge of all the activities in the kitchen, simply refuses to serve "hurry-up meals." Incidentally, the new kitchen is a model for country inns anywhere.

THE RED INN, Commercial Street, Provincetown, Mass. 02657; 617-487-0050. A waterside country restaurant with a striking view of Provincetown harbor. No lodgings. Open for dinner only every day except Christmas night. Within walking distance of all Provincetown lodging accommodations and recreational activities and attractions. Ted and Marci Barker, Innkeepers.

Directions: Follow Rte. 6 to end of Cape Cod.

NAUSET HOUSE INN, East Orleans

I was looking at my Christmas card from Jack and Lucille Schwarz at the Nauset House Inn. It showed one end of the inn dining room with its red brick floors, pristine white walls, the long, family-style table and the ladder-back rocker in front of a blazing hearth.

With the exception of a large holly wreath, it was exactly as I remembered it from my trip in late September. On that particular morning the warm, late-summer sun had drawn many guests outside to the terrace to enjoy a second cup of coffee and the wine-like aroma of the apple orchard. The roses and beach plums were still in bloom and there was an occasional goldfinch or cardinal darting among the trees.

I had just come down for breakfast and Jack introduced me to people at the table from Montreal and Philadelphia.

"Have some cranberry muffins, I'll be right back with more sausage to go with the scrambled eggs," he said over his shoulder.

I found out that the people from Montreal had been at the inn for three days. They told me about their favorite beach walks and bike trails. "You'll probably want to go for a dip around 2:00 pm," they said. "It's very warm. This is the best time of year to be here."

The Nauset House Inn is about three-fourths of the way out to the end of Cape Cod within sight of Nauset Beach, which has some of the best surf in New England. The inn is small enough

for everyone to become quite friendly. Breakfast is the only meal served and all sorts of New England and Cape Cod things are offered including real maple syrup from the Schwarz's farm in Vermont. For lunch and dinner, they are happy to recommend restaurants from Chatham to Provincetown.

Jack and Lucille are knowledgeable collectors of antiques and this is reflected throughout the entire inn. All the beds, chests, secretaries, tables, clocks, highboys and such are handsome Early American pieces, and available for purchase. They also have a tiny antique shop in the orchard just behind the inn with still more choice selections.

The Cape is a particularly happy experience from late May through early June and after Labor Day. There's much more of an opportunity then to enjoy all of the beauty and history. It's also fun walking on Nauset Beach and finding it almost deserted.

Jack returned with the sausage and set the plate down with a flourish. "This morning," he said, "we'll call it Sausage Samuel, after Samuel Champlain, who landed in Nauset Harbor and named it after the Indian tribe who paddled out to the ship to greet him."

Now, that was some Christmas card, wasn't it?

NAUSET HOUSE INN, Nauset Beach Rd., East Orleans, Cape Cod, Mass. 02643; 617-255-2195. A 12-room country inn 90 mi. from Boston, 27 mi. from Hyannis. Mod. American Plan omits lunch and dinner. Breakfast served to inn guests only. Some rooms with shared bath. Open daily from March 1 to Nov. 15. No children under 10 yrs. No pets. Within walking distance of Nauset Beach. Riding and bicycles nearby. For antique lovers. Jack and Lucille Schwarz, Innkeepers.

Directions: From the Mid-Cape Hwy. (Rte. 6), take Exit 12. Follow signs for Nauset Beach. Inn is located ¼ mi. before beach on Nauset Beach Rd.

MELROSE INN, Harwichport

The Melrose Inn may be the last of its kind on the Cape. In fact, it may be one of the very last inns of its kind anywhere in New England. Gladys Smith, the owner, is now in her fifty-fifth year of keeping this sedate, mansard-roofed inn in Harwichport, and she has her definite ways of doing things.

One of her best ways is with food. I've received many complimentary letters about the Melrose food, and since a full American Plan is available, the really sumptuous servings at all meals are very popular with the guests. At breakfast there are freshly baked bread and muffins and a wide choice of eggs, pancakes, and other New England treats.

At all meals the number of main dishes is most impressive. For example, there's always a large variety of fish from the nearby waters of Nantucket Sound, plus excellent beef and other hearty offerings. Lobster is served almost continuously. Salads are made to delight the hearts of the most particular devotee, and the desserts are all homemade. The apple and peach cobbler are outstanding, and believe me, very hard to resist.

Gladys is also most particular about the table settings. They are done with great care and always include fresh flowers. She hovers about during all meals paying a great deal of attention to service.

The Melrose is an inn where a great many of the people have made annual visits for the past thirty or forty years. Some of them have been reserving the same room for almost every stay. And they have their favorite chairs in the TV room as well.

There's swimming on their own warm south shore beach which is just about a block away. And in recent years, Gladys has added a swimming pool and a terrace immediately behind the inn. Many of the guests who stay for two weeks or more eventually try all of the golf courses on the Cape. Others do a great deal of antiquing and shopping or just rest and enjoy each other's company.

Gladys is delightfully outspoken about many things, including the informal apparel of many of today's travelers. She feels that dungarees and sweatshirts are not exactly her cup of tea, and she's adamant on the subject of gentlemen wearing coats in the dining room in the evening. There are little notices in each room to advise her guests. It upsets her quite a bit when guests arrive dressed too casually.

The Melrose is a rather large (75 rooms), somewhat sedate, semi-formal village inn within a short walk of its own excellent beach. If you like Gladys, you'll love the Melrose. I have found a great many people who do. Even if you don't know Gladys, you will still love the Melrose!

MELROSE INN, Harwichport, Cape Cod, Mass. 02646; 617-432-0171. A 75-room village inn on Cape Cod's warm south shore, 12 mi. from Hyannis and 85 mi. from Boston. All plans available. Breakfast, lunch and dinner served to travelers. Open May 1 to October 15. Swimming in Nantucket Sound or heated pool, waterskiing and bicycles. Golf, sailing and fishing nearby. For ocean lovers. Gladys and Philip Smith, Innkeepers.

Directions: From the Sagamore Bridge, take the Mid-Cape Hwy. to Exit 10. Follow Rte. 124 south to Harwich. Turn left on Main St. to Banks St. Proceed about 1½ mi. south to junction of Rte. 28. The Melrose is just left of the junction.

JARED COFFIN HOUSE, Nantucket Island

Christmas on Nantucket! The idea has intrigued me for years. While I have not as yet had the experience, a good friend who spent Christmas there was kind enough to share a few impressions which I am happy to pass on:

"Sailing around Brant Point is like entering a different world—an era of bygone days! The visitor's imagination is immediately captured by the island's historic past—the trials of the early settlers, the determination of the Quakers and the courage of the whaling fleets setting sail to the far off Pacific.

"Arriving on the evening boat, we reflected on Nantucket's past Christmases as we walked the three blocks to the Jared Coffin House—a perfect blend of the traditional Island Holiday combined unobtrusively with the comforts of the 20th Century.

"Approaching the JC House, we noticed the classic Greek Revival Portico majestically draped with fresh laurel roping and on the front door hung a handsome cranberry wreath made by

Peggy Read, the Innkeeper's wife. Every window was decorated with a holly wreath and as we opened the door, our eyes traveled instantly upwards, following the della Robbia roping that enhanced the gracefully curved staircase to the third floor.

"Later that evening, after a delightful dinner of Nantucket Bay Scallops broiled in casserole with Chablis and the featured international dinner of the evening, Paella, we strolled downtown and stood on the steps of the bank, looking down Main Street towards the harbor.

"Dozens of Christmas trees lined both sides of the street and their lights were mutely reflected in the light frost which covered the cobblestones. With very few cars to mar our view, we were struck with the quiet beauty and peacefulness of the town.

"The next day, after biking around the island, we returned to the warmth of the fireside. Since it was Christmas Eve, the innkeepers were hosting an Eggnog Party prior to the traditional Christmas Eve candlelight dinner.

"We had been invited to put our gifts under the Jared Coffin House tree and, wonders of wonders, when it came time to pass out the presents, there was an extra gift for each of us as well as for each of the children staying at the inn."

The JC House is open year-round and in recent years Nantucket has become one of the most popular places for travelers with *Country Inns and Back Roads*. For my part I'm going to try to spend a few days next Christmas there, but Phil Read has already warned me that I'd better make my reservation well in advance.

JARED COFFIN HOUSE, Nantucket Island, Mass. 02554; 617-228-2400. A 41-room village inn 30 mi. at sea. European Plan. Breakfast, lunch, dinner served daily. Strongly advise verifying accommodations before planning a trip to Nantucket in any season. Swimming, fishing, boating, golf, tennis, riding, and bicycles nearby. For antique and "island" lovers. Philip and Margaret Read, Innkeepers.

Directions: Accessible by air from Boston and Hyannis, or by ferry from Woods Hole, Mass. Automobile reservations are usually needed in advance (617-426-1855). Inn is located 300 yds. from ferry dock.

HARBORSIDE INN, Edgartown, Martha's Vineyard Island

"Do you think they're sleeping?" I asked Arthur Young, innkeeper of the Harborside. There were eight or nine ducks on the dock, most of them standing, but with their heads tucked back underneath their wing feathers. They were all facing Chappaquidick Island and while we watched there was no movement for at least ten minutes. "It's almost as if they're decoys," Arthur mused.

Some other ducks were swimming among the Sailfish and Boston Whaler boats moored at the dock, and three or four of them hopped from the water to the dock and lined up with the others. Our waitress said that they looked like they were getting ready for a parade.

Harborside is a truly water-oriented resort-inn. Within a matter of minutes you can be in the water in either a rented sailboat or powerboat. The inn is built in the form of a three-sided square facing Edgartown harbor and Chappaquiddick Island. Within this sunwashed environment there is a swimming pool, gay beach umbrellas, reclining chairs for sunning and perhaps best of all, literally thousands of flowers in bloom. I saw Betty Priors, begonias, portulacas, impatiens and marigolds in profusion.

At Harborside the accommodations are in the seven sea captains' houses which form part of this hollow square. Most of the rooms face the pool, gardens and harbor.

This morning we were in for a real treat—a leisurely bike ride around the Edgartown shops and a chance to photograph some

of the beautiful Colonial homes as the September sun rose higher in the sky. Arthur suggested that because in September the afternoons can be quite warm, we could do some walking on one of the beaches or even go for a swim. Nancy Young showed the effects of a previous afternoon in the sun, with a considerable amount of additional tan.

When we enjoyed dinner last night in the Navigator Room, I noticed many varieties of Vineyard fish on the menu. I had a most delicious broiled bluefish, but the menu also offered striped bass, swordfish, lobster and stuffed quahaugs. This morning we were having breakfast in the sunshine and all the boats passing back and forth in the harbor presented a delightful sight.

With his now famous stubby forefinger, Arthur pointed out some of the more rewarding bike trips on a map of the island, and we set off in search of adventure. Each street seemed to present one beautiful Colonial or Greek Revival house after another. One house, three stories high, had a double balustrade and a figure of an Edgartown woman of the last century looking out over the harbor. Jan Lindstrom has reproduced this for us in this edition.

Harborside and Edgartown are both especially delightful in what islanders call the "off season." By the way, there are also great sales going on in the shops.

HARBORSIDE INN, Martha's Vineyard Island, Edgartown, Mass. 02539; 617-627-4321. A 100-room island resort inn. European Plan. Breakfast, lunch, dinner served daily from April 1 to November 1. No children under 6 yrs. No pets. Pool, bicycles, sailing, boating. Tennis, golf and riding nearby. For sailing and history lovers. Arthur Young, Innkeeper.

Directions: Take ferry from Woods Hole, Mass. to Vineyard Haven. Car reservations advisable. Contact inn for details in advance.

YANKEE PEDLAR, Holyoke

My waitress, who looked as though she had stepped out of the cast of "Upstairs-Downstairs" and who had a faint touch of an Irish brogue, wheeled in the five-decker dessert cart. "Now sir, would you like to try our cranberry cheesecake, some beautiful fresh strawberries, a pecan tart, or perhaps a piece of hot apple pie? Everything is homemade in our own kitchen."

I had been confronted with decisions like that all evening because the menu at the Yankee Pedlar is unusually bountiful. I narrowed the main dishes down to a choice of veal kidneys sauteed with shallots and Nantucket Sound swordfish. Other choices included Dover sole, Boston scrod, and roast duckling.

One of the reasons for this visit was to see the new lodging rooms which had been completed since my last visit. There are now a total of 36 rooms available, several in the former Carriage House. On my tour with innkeeper Bess Stathis, I noted that some of these had canopied beds and reproductions of 18th century furniture.

Bess talked about the necessity for more rooms. "You see," she said, "we have guests coming from all four directions, for this is where I-91 crosses the Massachusetts Turnpike. Our guests are staying longer because there's so much to do in our area."

Visiting the Yankee Pedlar is like looking through a kaleidoscope at the 18th and 19th centuries. For example, one of the many dining rooms has the paneling, heavy beams, old utensils and tools which date back to Colonial America. Another has the look of elegance and ornamentation of the 19th century with many varieties of framed prints from Mrs. Godey's book. There are engravings of gentlemen in high silk hats and pegged bottom trousers and drawings and paintings of some of the principal events of one hundred years ago.

This Victorian theme is also found in the Gilded Cage and Oyster Bar which are reminiscent of the rollicking days of the turn of the century. Whenever I walk in, I expect to see nothing but men wearing derbys and ladies with leg 'o mutton sleeves! The relishes and salads which are served with the hearty sandwiches look like the long forgotten "Free Lunch."

A trip to the Yankee Pedlar isn't complete without a peek into the Opera House which is a replica of an old Victorian theatre. It is used for weddings, banquets and business meetings. The ornate furnishings and decorations would provide a fitting background for some of the great entertainers of that time such as Anna Held, Fritzi Scheff, and Elenora Duse.

With this Victorian setting in mind, my dessert problem was solved. It would have to be the rich and elegant cranberry cheesecake.

YANKEE PEDLAR INN, Holyoke, Mass. 01040; 413-532-9494. A 36-room village inn, 8 mi. from Springfield. Near Old Storrowtown, a replica of a colonial Massachusetts village, and the Eastern States Exposition Grounds. European Plan. (Breakfast served to house guests only.) Lunch and dinner served daily except Christmas. Oyster Bar open from 11a.m. to 12:30a.m. daily, opens 5p.m. Sat. Golf, tennis, swimming, Alpine and xc-ski nearby. Bess Stathis, Innkeeper.

Directions: From I-91 take Exit 16. The inn is located at junction of Rtes. 202 and 5.

LORD JEFFREY INN, Amherst

"Your observation that the Lord Jeff had a 'Gatsby' look about it caused a lot of comments. As a matter of fact, I have a feeling that it may have been one of the reasons the inn was chosen for some of the location shots for a movie called *The Reincarnation of Peter Proud* which was filmed here last Fall. It starred Michael Sarazin and Jenifer O'Neil."

Harold Durgin and I were having our once-a-year chat in the main dining room of the Lord Jeff. It seemed very good to be back here among the round tables and Windsor chairs with the young waiters and waitresses—students from the assorted area colleges—bustling back and forth.

Harold was referring to the fact that in the 1974 edition of CIBR, I had remarked that while seated in the courtyard of the inn it reminded me of a movie set for *The Great Gatsby*. Oddly enough, at the time I wrote it I had not yet seen the movie.

The Lord Jeffrey Inn and the town of Amherst both have a great many "movie set" qualities. For example, the nucleus of the town is a long, wide Common around which there are shops, college buildings, fraternity houses and, of course, the inn. The snow was on the ground and there were tracks crisscrossing the Common, just as they have been for many, many years.

The town, which is the center of a five-college complex has an unusual number of Victorian houses, some with flat roofs, others with Mansard roofs, there's a great deal of gingerbread and fancy carvings.

The clientele at lunchtime reflected the town. There were a generous number of academic-looking types, sometimes distinguished from the students by the fact that they wore coats and ties, although one can't be sure in Amherst these days. The bearded youth in jeans might well be the instructor in the History or English Department. It was warm and relaxed—the perfect picture of a bustling college town inn in the early afternoon.

Speaking of movies, Harold was telling me that he was in an ABC movie called *Death Be Not Proud* which was filmed in Deerfield. "I play the chairman of the board of directors of a New England private school." I assured him that he certainly looked the part.

The food at this inn is inland New England, with emphasis on roast turkey, Indian pudding, Yankee pot roast, shrimp in beer batter and fresh-baked apple pie a la mode.

The resident manager, Don MacFadyen, showed me a few of the newly decorated second floor rooms which had little balconies opening out on to the courtyard. Nuthatches, chickadees, and cardinals, who stay for the winter, were flying back and forth among the chestnut, elm and apple trees. Down in the grape arbor a little birdhouse provided a very nice touch. The white spires of Amherst stood out against the bright blue winter sky.

Yes, Jay Gatsby, wherever you are, the Lord Jeff is again ready and waiting for the sound of your Stutz Bearcat.

LORD JEFFREY INN, On the Common, Amherst, Mass. 01002; 413-253-2576. A 46-room college town inn in Western Massachusetts. Open year-round. European Plan. Breakfast, lunch, dinner served daily to travelers. No pets. Xc-ski, bicycles nearby. Harold and Janice Durgin, Innkeepers.

Directions: Take Exit 19 from I-91. Follow Rte. 9 east to Amherst.

RED LION INN, Stockbridge

Henricus Bergmans, the intrepid innkeeper at the Red Lion Inn and I were taking a leisurely tour of the inn for the purpose of checking out some of the more recent antique acquisitions.

Now we were standing in front of a Norman Rockwell painting called "The Family Tree" and were picking out our Stockbridge neighbors whose faces Mr. Rockwell had used.

Henry stopped and said, "A few years ago Norman did a painting of Main Street in Stockbridge at Christmastime. However, that year the Red Lion was closed all winter, so the inn looks unoccupied. Why don't you tell your readers what we are like at Christmastime and during the holidays? I think many people know about the summer activities like Tanglewood and The Berkshire Playhouse, but it might be interesting to share Christmas as well."

Henry was right—because the festive Christmas spirit is every-

where at the Red Lion. The first glimpse of it includes magnificent wreaths, fresh and green, replacing the summer fuschia on the broad porch, where in summer one of the favorite pastimes is rocking and watching the passing Stockbridge scene. Lots of Christmas trees are in many places around the inn, all twinkling with old-fashioned Christmas lights.

The railings on the steps are covered with laurel right from the woods, and in the lobby there stands a large honest-to-goodness Christmas tree, old-fashioned in its simplicity, draped with red roping and a myriad of decorations. Each year the tree seems to be better than the one before.

Garlands of greens are hung throughout the hallways and side parlors. In the front parlor is a true delight—Ann Fitzpatrick's magnificent masterpiece—a candy replica of the inn. The Pink Kitty, the gift shop at the Red Lion is filled with Christmas gifts for every member of the family. The fireplace in the lobby is always sending forth a cheery greeting.

The main dining room, the Widow Bingham's Tavern and the Lion's Den are bright with holiday trimmings.

Now, let's talk about Christmas dinner. Naturally, there is a traditional roast beef with Yorkshire pudding. There's roast turkey with all the extra Red Lion touches. The desserts include pecan pie with whipped cream, apple pie with cheddar cheese, and a wonderful plum pudding with hard sauce.

Carolers are apt to wander in at various times during the holidays and everyone joins in the singing. Santa Claus has been making a jolly appearance for the past few years. He sounds vaguely like Massachusetts State Senator Jack Fitzpatrick, who with his wife Jane, are the owners of the inn ... but we can't be absolutely sure.

Christmas at the Red Lion Inn is just like "going home for the holidays!"

RED LION INN, Stockbridge, Mass. 01262; 413-298-5545. A 90-room historic village inn in the Berkshires. Adjacent to Tanglewood, Norman Rockwell's Old Corner House Museum, Berkshire Playhouse, Jacob's Pillow, Chesterwood Gallery and major ski areas. European Plan. Breakfast, lunch, dinner served to travelers daily. Open year-round. Outdoor pool on grounds. Tennis, golf, bicycles, swimming, xc-ski, Alpine ski nearby. Jack and Jane Fitzpatrick, Owners. Henricus Bergmans, Innkeeper.

Directions: From the Taconic State Pkwy. take Exit 23 (N.Y. Rte. 23) to Mass. Rte. 7. Proceed north to Stockbridge. From the Mass. Tpke. exit at Lee and follow Rte. 102 to Stockbridge.

STAGECOACH HILL, Sheffield

One evening last winter when the roads were all glazed and the snow was pelting against our windshield, we stopped off at the Stagecoach, returning from a trip to Connecticut. It was the perfect evening to visit this English inn in the Berkshires.

I opened the huge front doors and we walked up the steps to the lounge where there were 18 to 20 people seated in the romantic semi-darkness which was lighted by the glow from two fireplaces and the candles hidden in red hurricane lamps. There was soft piano music coming from one corner of the room.

Scotty Burns came in with

an armload of firewood and said, "Welcome. 'Tis not a fit night to be out!"

Scotty's accent is as thick as the crust on the steak and kidney pie which is one of the favorites at the Stagecoach. The old red brick building, part of which used to be the town poor house a hundred years ago, looks very much like it has been picked up from Sussex or Surrey and dropped at the base of a mountain here in Sheffield. We call it an English inn with a Scottish flavor.

Stagecoach Hill, as has already been suggested, is a wee bit on the intimate side. The local folks find its atmosphere most congenial, and the guests who come up from the city almost every weekend appreciate the fact that it is somewhat small and really quite cozy. For winter fun, it is near several South Berkshire ski areas and, in the summer, it is within an easy drive of Tanglewood, theatres, and other seasonal attractions.

Good food is another reason why Stagecoach has so many devoted followers. Wilbur Wheeler, Scotty's partner, is the chef and he has such creations as the Aldermen's Carpetbag, which is a sirloin steak lined with oysters, as well as several different kinds of veal dishes and steaks.

Other dishes in his repertoire are Blackbird Pie, Steak au Poivre, Frogs legs and an English trifle.

There are lodgings at the Stagecoach, however, they are rather austere. "We're fixing them up one by one," said Scotty. "But even so, we very seldom have a vacancy on the weekend."

A unique touch at this inn is the presence of two parrots. One called "Polly" is 90 years old, and the other one, named "Meatball" is only 26. Meatball is quite a talker, and when properly encouraged can even bark like a dog.

We asked Scotty what had happened to the peacocks that used to be kept in pens behind the inn. He replied that he had to get rid of them. "They began waking everybody up at 4:30 in the morning and I had to go out and calm them down. Of course, during the mating season they were particularly noisy. The only way I could get them to be quiet was to wet them down with a hose."

STAGECOACH HILL INN, Undermountain Road, Sheffield, Mass. 01257; 413-229-8585. An 8-room British inn with Scottish overtones on Rte. 41 midway between Salisbury, Conn. and Great Barrington. European Plan. Dinner served nightly and all day Sunday. Closed Christmas Eve, Christmas Day and every Wednesday. Near South Berkshire ski areas, Tanglewood, Jacob's Pillow and all summertime attractions. Scotty Burns and Wilbur Wheeler, Innkeepers.

Directions: From Mass. Tpke., take Exit 2 and follow Rte. 102 west to Stockbridge. Take Rte. 7 south to Great Barrington, then follow Rte. 41 south to inn.

Rhode Island

By 1775 Rhode Islanders had already arrogantly expressed themselves against the pressures being brought by the Crown on the colonists. In 1765 they battled British sailors because of the Stamp Act. The next year Newporters burned the long boats of the British war sloop, Liberty.

They were further agitated by the British armed schooner Gaspee in Providence harbor in 1772. The Gaspee, under an arrogant captain named Duddington, cruised Narragansett Bay seizing shipping and helping itself on shore to the farmers grain and burning their fruit trees for firewood. One night in late June his ship ran aground off Namquit while chasing a supposed smuggler. A few hours later some small boats commanded by John Brown, Captain Abraham Whipple and others put out from shore, captured the stranded vessel and burned it at the water's edge. This event has been called the first sea battle in the American Revolution. It was celebrated with firecrackers in Virginia by George Washington and his friends. Rhode Islanders, along with the other colonists, sturdily supported the seige around Boston and committed themselves nobly at the Battle of Breed's Hill.

In 1776 a joint operation by the American and French fleets at Newport met with failure because of a fierce gale which scattered the fleet.

LARCHWOOD INN, Wakefield

"Rhode Island," said Frank Browning, "was the inspiration for the first 'two weeks vacation with pay.' "

This one stumped me. Frank and I had been talking awhile about how Rhode Island, for its size, is one of the most interesting and intriguing experiences around for travelers and vacationers.

"Take fishing," he said. "There are flounder, cod, mackerel, tuna, swordfish, pollock and marlin in Rhode Island Sound, and just off Block Island, the fishing is some of the best in the world. By the way," he added, with a twinkle, "in season, we have most of those fish on the menu here at the Larchwood."

The point was well made, because earlier that evening I had enjoyed some broiled swordfish which was caught just a few miles from the Larchwood.

"As far as hunting is concerned, some of our guests have bagged partridge, quail, woodcock, and duck, although we tend to think of ourselves more as a place for swimming and fishing."

The swimming is done on southern Rhode Island beaches which are just minutes from Wakefield. People who have discovered them say that they're excellent.

The Larchwood was a well-established village inn in Wakefield for many years under Mr. and Mrs. Hugh Cameron. Frank was the chef, and a few years ago he became the owner. It is a community meeting place and while I was there I noticed that the Rotary Club met there each week and there were a generous number of businessmen from Wakefield as well as nearby Kingston and Narragansett who were enjoying a hearty lunch in the Scottish Lounge.

The Scottish theme established by the Camerons is being carried forward, and the walls of one of the dining rooms known as the Crest Room are covered with Scottish badges and tartans. Here and there I found an inscription from the works of Robert Burns.

My visit to the Larchwood also included a tour of the lodging rooms, which are quite large since the inn was originally built as a mansion in the 19th century. There are usually two beds in each room and the windows afford a view of spacious lawns and beech, larch, blue spruce and pine trees.

During spring and summer the rhododendrons, begonias, roses and forsythia are a colorful display. In fact, the Larchwood, during the first week in June, with all the Spring plants in bloom, is a sight anyone would enjoy.

I couldn't resist asking Frank what he meant by "the first two weeks vacation with pay."

"Oh, that," he said. "It happened in 1524 when the Italian sailor Verrazano was exploring the North American coast. He became so enthralled with Narragansett Bay that he lingered here for a fortnight!"

LARCHWOOD INN, 176 Main St., Wakefield, R.I. 02879; 401-783-5454. An 11-room village inn just 3 mi. from the famous southern R.I. beaches. Some rooms with shared bath. European Plan. Breakfast, lunch, dinner served every day of the year. Swimming, boating, surfing, fishing, xc-ski and bicycles nearby. Francis Browning, Innkeeper.

Directions: From Rte. 1, take Pond St. Exit and proceed ½ mi. directly to inn.

CASTLE HILL, Newport

Here's a country inn with a historical past, a remarkable present, and a most promising future.

It is literally on the edge of a peninsula where the Atlantic Ocean funnels into Narragansett Bay. It's just a few paces on the lawn to the water's edge. From the porches and all of the bedrooms, guests have an uncontested view of both pleasure craft and commercial ships that ply this historic beautiful waterway.

One hundred years ago the main house was built by Alexander Agassiz, the famous naturalist, who made it his summer home for many years until his death. From what I could see, it has remained essentially unchanged in character, and many of the original furnishings including the Oriental rugs and handcrafted oak and mahogany paneling are found everywhere. The main fireplace is a masterpiece of inlaid wood.

Since the inn was originally a mansion, the lodging rooms in both dimension and decor are truly opulent. Thornton Wilder found one in particular to his liking.

The view from the summer dining room is nothing short of spectacular, especially during the America's Cup and Bermuda Cup sailing races when the spectator fleets of pleasure craft glide past Castle Hill every morning and evening.

I found there is much at Castle Hill to intrigue the active sports enthusiast. Sailing, swimming at the Castle Hill beach, fishing from the rocks, and—because of the unusual depth of the water—some absolutely first-rate scuba diving. What's more, both indoor and outdoor tennis courts are just moments away, including grass courts.

The inn is located on the 10-mile-long Ocean Drive which has many fabulous mansions built by the "400" of Newport's gilded age. Quite a few of these are open to the public in all seasons.

The promising future of this inn is personified by its youthful innkeeper, Jens Retlev and his wife, Ellen. Besides their charming manner, Jens brings to the inn considerable culinary skill and knowledge. He is a native of Sweden and from what I tasted of his specialties, he was born with a wire whisk in one hand and a pastry brush in the other.

The menu, as might be expected, had many European dishes which seemed appropriate for the manorial dining room. Jens, himself, prepared some delicious breakfast crepes that were fantastically light.

Incidentally, it is my feeling that young children would not be happy at Castle Hill as there are really no facilities to amuse them.

There is much, much more about Castle Hill in Newport. For example: there's the real thrill of being there in a storm; walking the cliffs at sunrise to see the lighthouse; the charming 18th century candlelight tours of Newport houses at Christmas time; and the colonial and revolutionary war history of the town.

THE INN AT CASTLE HILL, Ocean Drive, Newport, R.I. 02840; 401-847-1913. A 30-room mansion-inn on the edge of Narragansett Bay. Near the Newport mansions, Touro Synagogue (1st in America), the Newport Casino and National Lawn Tennis Hall of Fame, the Old Stone Mill, the Newport Historical Society House. European Plan. Breakfast, lunch, dinner served daily to travelers from end of May to beginning of October. Lunch and dinner served daily except Mondays from October through May, at which time breakfast is served everyday to house guests. No pets. Swimming, sailing, scuba diving, walking. Bicycles and guided tours of Newport nearby. Jens and Ellen Retlev, Innkeepers.

Directions: After leaving Newport Bridge follow Bellevue Avenue which becomes Ocean Drive. Look for inn sign on left.

Connecticut

The gathering clouds which signified trouble with England posed no startlingly new threat to the hearty colonists of Connecticut. They had had conflicts before: first, with the Dutch who had claimed the area because of the discoveries of Captain Adriaen Block in 1614; then, with the Pequot Indians. The settlers squeezed out the Dutch and wiped out the Indians.

Connecticut's share in the events of 1775 is typified by Israel Putnam, an aging veteran of the French and Indian War. After Lexington and Concord he led 3000 Nutmeg men to the seige of Boston. A Colonel of the militia at Breed's Hill, he was appointed major general of the Continental Army by Washington in July, 1775. He was later in command of the Americans at the disastrous battle of Long Island.

HOMESTEAD INN, Greenwich

"Egad!" I trumpeted. "A television set in a country inn!" Cal Estes burst out laughing at my mock horror, and went on to explain: "Yes, it's hard to make some of our city guests happy if they can't fall asleep with Johnny Carson or the Late, Late Movie. You know, you can take the boy out of the city but you can't take the city out of the boy."

Cal is an example of a city boy who escaped to the country— almost. He and Vinny Morino keep things humming at the Homestead and both are city boys who enjoy the country. Here's an interesting sidelight. One of their associates, Donald Fraser, is originally from Halifax, Nova Scotia. He and I always enjoy talking about the Haligonians.

Well, the room had a television set, but it also had twin beds with candlewyck bedspreads, Boston rockers and several other country inn touches. When I drove up Field Point Road to Greenwich and turned into the small estate surrounded by copper beeches, red maples, birch, chestnuts, and those gorgeous roses, chrysanthemums and petunias, it was hard to realize that it's within an hour of New York City.

It is this adjacency to the big city that makes the Homestead very, very popular with people who like to "rough it" in the country. Consequently, the rooms are in demand at all times, and reservations for lunch and dinner are almost always necessary.

Now I wouldn't say that one really is roughing it at the Homestead. But the buildings are old, the stairways are creaky, some of the door frames are a little crooked, and now and then the pipes knock a little. When I wake up in the morning and see the circling doves land in the treetops, I think for a moment that I am in New Hampshire or Michigan.

Part of the menu is designed to meet the more sophisticated palates of the city dwellers. But in addition to quite a few main dishes that border on *haute cuisine,* there are country inn offerings such as homemade apple pie, steak and kidney pie, a special peppermint black bottom pie, and—something I've never had in any other country inn—New England turkey shortcake.

So, the Homestead has affected a convenient marriage between country and city tastes. No one can possibly mistake it for a super modern motel or hotel, and Cal, Vinnie, and the friendly staff are a far cry from your superior East Side *boite.* However, there is a definite touch of the "Big Apple."

Look at it this way, if you live in the city and you've never been to a country inn before, maybe this is a good place to have your first experience. If you like the Homestead, and I think you will, then you're ready for the "Big Adventure." It's like somebody once said, "If you like the book, you'll love the movie."

HOMESTEAD INN, 420 Field Point Rd., Greenwich, Conn. 06830; 203-869-7500. A 25-room sophisticated country inn on an old estate in the residential section of Greenwich. European Plan. Breakfast served daily. Lunch and dinner served to travelers daily except Sunday. Pool on grounds. Bruce Museum, Pryor Doll Museum, bicycles and tennis nearby. For antique lovers. Cal Estes and Vincent Morino, Innkeepers.

Directions: Exit 3 from I-95, and turn toward Railroad bridge. Turn left at Bridge and proceed two blocks to dead end. Turn left again and proceed ¼ mi. Only 3 min. from Exit 3 to inn.

SILVERMINE TAVERN, Norwalk

"Meet Miss Abigail," said Frank Whitman. "She's the only woman permitted by Connecticut law to stand within three feet of a bar."

I spoke courteously, but Miss Abigail just stood there in her crinoline and lace, looking inscrutable. The walls behind her and, in fact, in all of the dining rooms were covered with old farm implements and tools as well as American primitive paintings.

Frank and I continued our tour of the Silvermine Tavern. "The Tavern was named for the town," he asserted. "That name, in turn, came from an old as-yet-unfounded rumor about a silvermine discovered by an early settler. The old post office was here at the four corners."

We passed through two low-ceilinged sitting rooms, both brimming with antiques. There were fireplaces in each and one had an old clock with wooden works. Frank pointed out the beams from the original inn as well as the old-fashioned colonial hinges on the doorway. Some of the oil paintings of the colonial ladies and gentlemen looked rather forbidding.

I followed him up a winding staircase and found typical country inn bedrooms without televisions or telephones.

"You can imagine that we're quite popular with honeymooners," he said. "They like to wander the country roads and to feed the ducks and swans on the Mill Pond."

Subsequently I learned about other buildings located at the Silvermine Tavern crossroads. The Old Mill, which is well over 200 years old, is completely furnished with antiques. I visited the Country Store just across the street from the Tavern where the old counters and display tables have some very interesting adaptations of colonial skills and crafts. In the back room of the store a museum has antique tools and gadgets and a fine collection of Currier and Ives prints.

The Tavern at various times, has served as a country inn, a gentleman's country seat and a town meeting place. It has a very large outdoor dining area overlooking the Silvermine River and the Mill Pond with ducks and swans. Summer terrace dining among the oaks, maples, pines and poplar trees is very popular with playgoers at the Westport Playhouse and the Stratford Shake-

speare Theatre nearby. I also like the Silvermine in the winter when the many fireplaces are crackling.

Some of the New England dishes on the menu include Indian pudding, bread pudding, honeybuns, native scrod, lobster, scallops, and oysters. On Thursday nights there's a roast beef and fried chicken buffet.

When my tour of the Tavern and all the buildings at the Crossroads was over, I went back to ask Miss Abigail if she'd care to join me for dinner. I suggested the chicken pie. No reply. I pointed out that all the breads and desserts were homemade— even the ice cream. Still she remained inscrutable.

But I didn't feel too badly when Frank assured me that she hasn't spoken to anyone in years.

SILVERMINE TAVERN, Perry Ave., Norwalk, Ct. 06850; (203) 847-4558. A 14-room country inn in the residential section of Norwalk. Long Island Sound and beaches 6 mi. away. European Plan includes Continental Breakfast. Lunch and dinner served to travelers daily. Open year-round. Closed Christmas Day and Tuesdays during winter. Golf, tennis and fishing nearby. For antique lovers. Francis C. Whitman, Innkeeper.

Directions: From New York or New Haven via I-95, take Exit 15. Pick up the new Rte. 7 going north. At end of Rte. 7 (approx. 1 mi.) turn left, go to first stop light, turn right. at next stop light by Firehouse turn right onto Silvermine Avenue. Proceed down Silvermine Ave. about 1½ mi. to Tavern. From Danbury and points north, follow Rte. 7 past Caldor under Merritt Pkwy. Bridge into Norwalk. Go past MacDonalds on left and first stop light after MacDonalds turn right onto Perry Ave. Follow Perry Ave. 2 mi. to Tavern. From Merritt Pkwy. take Exit 39 or 40 and follow Rte. 7 directions above.

GRISWOLD INN, Essex

It was a cold day in January. Sam and I were shopping our way from the Square in Essex down the street to the Griswold Inn.

Once inside we exchanged a few words with Charlotte Iverson, the Reservations Manager at the main desk and started to renew our pleasant acquaintance with this old Connecticut landmark.

And old, indeed, it is. The "Gris" was opened as an inn in 1776, and has been under the ownership of only five families since then.

We got no further than the big pot-bellied stove in the Tap Room when Innkeeper Bill Winterer came zooming around the corner. He immediately insisted on showing us what he called his "nationally famous popcorn machine," as well as several new additions to the really incredible collection of marine paintings, prints, posters, brass plates, binnacles, banners, and miscellaneous bits and pieces which have been collected by keepers of the "Gris" since 1776. It is in reality a magnificent museum of both the days of sailing and steamboating.

Bill is one of the most enthusiastic people I've ever met. He first visited the inn when he was an officer candidate at the nearby New London Coast Guard Academy and, after years of honest labor, decided to start life anew as an innkeeper.

He and I talked about innkeeping, with its joys and vicissitudes, while Vicky, his wife, took Sam across the street to look at the newly constructed Griswold Square.

Sam later reported that Vicky admitted, somewhat modestly, that she had been quite involved with its design which was copied from formal colonial gardens. On that particular night in early January the Christmas tree in the Square was still lighted and still looked festive.

They rejoined us just as the menus were being given out for dinner. Immediately my eye fell upon the fried oysters, something I haven't had for years. During dinner Bill and Vicky told us about the Hunt Breakfast which is served every Sunday morning from noon to 2:30. "It's a traditional English buffet," said Bill. "In addition to eggs, ham, bacon, grits and potatoes, we have kippered herring, Maine smelts, creamed chipped beef, finnan haddie in egg sauce, fried chicken, lamb kidneys and some of our homemade 1776 sausages. By the way, they're from a recipe that's 200 years old and we have them in take-home bags."

After dinner, we looked at some of the lodging rooms which were quite cozy with their antique furnishings. Some were newly redecorated.

As we took leave reluctantly, I can still hear Bill saying, "Don't forget to tell everyone that we have some type of music here every night in the week. I mean where else can you go to a banjo and tuba concert!"

GRISWOLD INN, Main St., Essex, Conn. 06426; 203-767-1812. A 16-room inn in a waterside town, steps away from the Connecticut River, and located near the Eugene O'Neill Theatre, Goodspeed Opera House, Ivoryton Playhouse, Gillette Castle, Mystic Village and Hammonasett State Beach. Some rooms with shared baths. European Plan. Complimentary Continental breakfast served daily to inn guests. Lunch and dinner served daily to travelers. Hunt breakfast served Sundays. Closed Christmas Eve and Christmas Day. Bicycles, tennis and boating nearby. For antique lovers. Victoria and William G. Winterer and A.W. Lovell, Innkeepers.

Directions: From I-95 take Exit 69 and travel north on Rte. 9 to Exit 3, Essex. Turn right at stop light and follow West Avenue to center of town. Turn right onto Main Street and proceed down to water and inn.

KILRAVOCK INN, Litchfield

Phil Hoyt had a brochure about the town of Litchfield in his hand and the light of enthusiasm in his eye. He pointed to the map and said, "There are at least nineteen houses in the village built before 1800. Litchfield is probably New England's finest surviving example of a typical late 18th century New England town."

Kilravock as an inn is a most fitting complement to these beautiful old homes. It sits back in its own park behind a low stone wall among great sugar maples, beeches, birches, oaks, and fruit trees. The building was a private mansion for many years

and, as you can see from Jan Lindstrom's drawing, it has both Tudor and Scottish influences. The Scottish pronunciation is Kilrook.

Phil and Lis and I were seated in the living room where a small fire crackled merrily and other guests were reading and talking.

One of the things that came out in our conversation was that both transient and inn guests must reserve their luncheon tables by 11:00 a.m., and dinner by 5:00 p.m.

"We're limiting the number of people that we can serve so that we can do the best possible job," explained Phil. "Lis, of course, is still in charge in the kitchen, and instead of serving great numbers of people, we're planning to serve fewer people in a much more relaxed and enjoyable way."

Kilravock is really a unique adventure. The house is dominated by a great, beautifully carved mahogany staircase that circles upward for three stories. Many of the rooms have working fireplaces and extra large bathrooms with spacious bathtubs. One of the corner rooms has a good view of the formal gardens, the large corn field, and adjacent tennis courts and swimming pool.

The two little West Highland Terriers, which are a part of the inn, escorted me on a tour of the grounds which included a peek at the Rose Cottage which is a few paces from the main house and has a nice view of the fields and woods. The rooms are a bit more modern than those in the main inn.

When I rejoined Lis and Phil, Lis said, "Personally, I get great satisfaction out of the compliments that we've been receiving about our food. I've planned our menu to include a great many European specialties. For instance, tonight we have Shrimp

51

Provençal and Pork Tenderloin a la Marsala, on the same menu with loin lamb chops, sirloin steak and Cornish game hen. Our soups are very well-known, particularly the scallion soup and cream of mushroom. Tonight we're having West Indian squash soup."

As we walked out the door into the late autumn twilight, Phil said, "Say, let's take a short walk before dinner. I want to show you where one of our best cross country ski trails is located. Be sure to come down right after the first snow and we'll do some skiing together."

KILRAVOCK INN, Brush Hill Rd., Litchfield, Conn. 06759; 203-567-8100. A 30-room resort-inn, on 146 acres, 2 mi. west of Litchfield. European Plan. Breakfast available to inn guests year-round. Lunch and dinner served to travelers daily (by reservation only) except Tuesdays and Wednesdays and the months of November and December. Tennis, pool, xc-ski, snowshoeing, bicycles. Golf and riding nearby. Phil and Lis Hoyt, Innkeepers.

Directions: From Litchfield, go 2 mi. west on Rte. 202. Turn right on Brush Hill Rd.

BOULDERS INN, Lake Waramaug

It was an absolutely crystal clear August day without a wisp of a cloud. I wove my way among the hills on the beautiful roads of northwest Connecticut that lead to Lake Waramaug. I was on my way to see Dick and Jane Lowe at the Boulders.

Suddenly I could see the raft just off shore from the inn and people sunning themselves on the dock. I pulled in between the big stone gates and wheeled around to park under the trees.

There was a sort of midafternoon lull. Four people were having a rather relaxed doubles game on the tennis court, I could see a couple walking leisurely down the trail that leads to Pinnacle Mountain. And there was Jane Lowe standing in the doorway with a big smile. "Come on, change into your trunks," she said. "Let's go swimming."

I needed no urging and in the trice she and I were walking down the stone steps accross the lawn under the great maples, oaks, and hickory trees and between the hedges leading out to the water's edge. We sat for a while in a pair of captain's chairs and watched the activity on the lake.

"The lake has remained pretty much the same as it was when my grandfather was here," she mused. "Families would come with horses and carriages. They had large homes where they could stay for weeks on end. I wish you could be here for the Fourth of July. All the people who live on the lake light flares about 9 o'clock and it's just gorgeous to see the reflection on the water all the way around the lake."

This time I discovered that the Boulders has over a hundred kinds of birds, and Dick and Jane supply lists to their guests. I knew there were birds in those hills and on the lake, but I never had the faintest idea that there were so many varieties. The Boulders is a family inn in every sense of the word. Every year that I've been writing about them I've heard from families with children of all ages who stayed there from a weekend to two weeks and I'm delighted to say that the kids love it.

Well, they ought to. There are all kinds of boats available, including fishing boats and sailboats and there's the big barn to play in on rainy days. The barn is also used for the Monday night barbecues. There are simply acres and acres of woods and trails and in winter, tobogganing, cross-country and downhill skiing, sledding and skating keep the young folks happy.

And I musn't forget the food. There are all the dishes which we associate with the country including pumpkin and apple pie, apple sauce, custards, blueberry pudding, prime ribs with Yorkshire pudding, leg of lamb and turkey. American Plan guests can have the eating time of their lives, young and old alike.

As we came back from our swim, Jane added, "Lots of people come up just to be here in the woods and watch the sun rise and set over the lake. It's beautiful in any season."

BOULDERS INN, Lake Waramaug, New Preston, Conn. 06777; 203-868-7918. A 30-room year-round resort-inn, 1½ mi. north of New Preston, 20 mi. from Danbury. All Plans available. Breakfast, lunch and dinner served daily to travelers from late May to mid-September and some weekends through the year. European Plan during the weeks from mid-September to May and late fall and early spring weekends. Monday dinner served to house guests only. Rooms and breakfast only on Thanksgiving. Closed Christmas. Tennis, bicycles, swimming, boating, sailing, fishing, hiking, skiing, tobogganing. Golf and riding nearby. For nature lovers. Dick and Jane Lowe, Innkeepers.

Directions: From I-84, take Exit 7 and follow Rte. 7 north to Rte. 202 (formerly 25) through New Milford. Proceed 8 mi. to Rte. 45 and 1½ mi. to inn.

MOUNTAIN VIEW INN, Norfolk

It was Thanksgiving Day. Sam and I had decided to visit Karl and Joan Jokinen at the Mountain View Inn, and part of the fun was to take the back roads from Stockbridge through Monterey, New Marlborough and Southbridge and come into Norfolk through the Litchfield Hills. It's a little longer but a lot more fun. The spires of the church and the buildings from the Yale Summer School of Music stood out against the late afternoon sky, reminding us to return in the summer for the concerts.

When we walked through the front door of the Mountain View, there was Joan looking radiant as usual. Karl came out with his white chef's hat and we had a joyful reunion.

As we marvelled over the menu, trying to decide whether to order the traditional dinner, Karl came up with a brilliant thought. "Why don't you just let me make a plate for you and leave the decisions up to me!"

I agreed with the one proviso that he include duck, which I have always enjoyed at Mountain View. He disappeared into the kitchen as Joan returned to say that our table was ready. She showed us to a table near the fireplace. The room was unusually cheerful on this holiday with many happy families reunited.

The Mountain View is truly a family inn. Joan's mother and father, Helen and George Linonis, are the owners, and Joan and Karl are the keepers of the inn. Karl, as I've pointed out in previous editions, is a most experienced chef in spite of being quite young. He supervises everything that comes in and out of his kitchen. He returned and introduced his 15-year-old son, Larry. "He's my righthand man, and really an accomplished cook. He's not only on the soccer team at his high school, but he's also on the honor roll. We're very proud of him."

Now came the pièce de résistance. Karl, to our amazement, had arranged a plate that included not only slices of duck, but also goose, turkey and the real topper—country ham. There were also candied yams, green beans, mashed turnips, creamed onions, and Hubbard squash. For dessert there were four pies on the menu and I had a sampling each of mince, pecan, chocolate coconut and apple.

The Mountain View is in a picturesque corner of Connecticut with all kinds of summer and winter sports, music, art and drama within a short distance. There always seem to be a number of guests enjoying the generous-sized bedrooms and good food when I'm there. This Thanksgiving was no exception.

MOUNTAIN VIEW INN, Norfolk, Conn. 06058; 203-542-5595. A 7-room village inn, 40 mi. west of Hartford in the picturesque Litchfield Hills. European Plan. Breakfast, lunch and dinner served daily to travelers except Mondays and Christmas Day. Open year-round. Golf, tennis, hiking, swimming, mountain cilmbing, bicycles, ice fishing, Alpine and xc-ski nearby. Karl and Joan Jokinen, Innkeepers.

Directions: Norfolk is on US 44 which runs east-west. North-south roads which intersect 44 include US 7, I-91, and US 22.

WHITE HART INN, Salisbury

John Harney put his foot on the line, raised the dart, and took aim. Then he stopped, turned around and said, "Would you care to venture a mild wager?"

The dart board at the White Hart Inn has, in a relatively short time become a tradition. During the disastrous winter of '73-74 with no gas, no snow and no customers, he held various contests of darts among the local people just to relieve the monotony of winter.

The White Hart is a lot of different things. For example, it's not content with just being a very active village inn. It's also a country store jam-packed with such diverse items as wooden toys, herbs, horse collars, candy sticks, soap, candles, ice tongs, and freshly made bread.

John is always full of beans. This time he was full of tea. It's called Sarum Tea. "There are ten kinds of Sarum Tea" quoth he. "The word Sarum is the old Roman name for Salisbury."

I must say that I really wasn't prepared to buy that bit of trivia. However, he said it with a straight face, so for the moment I went along with it. He went on to explain: "Sarum Tea has been imported by Mr. Stanley Mason since 1927 and is now distributed by the White Hart."

Lodgings are typical country inn bedrooms. There is an oak or maple chest of drawers, a chair or two, and perhaps a braided rug. There are two pillows for every bed and John has generously distributed a few old books and magazines in each room.

56

For the past few years, in early December, Olive DuBois has assembled her miniature gingerbread village in one of the parlors of the inn. This is a most delectable display of houses, churches, farms and homes of a New England village at Christmastime. It is really the principal attraction of the White Hart during the holiday season. Many people make it a point to return each year to see what changes Olive has made.

Now back to the challenge. We left off where John had just thrown down the gauntlet. His guileless manner prevailed over my intuition. I failed to see that beneath that boyish grin and behind those twinkling eyes there lurked the heart of an Edward Teach.

I did the best I could with my three darts. Then he took his place at the line and just from his stance I could see that I had made my mistake. He took aim and fired the first one right into the middle of the black spot in the center. He did the same thing with the second and third.

Then he had the audacity to turn around and say to me, "Shall we do it again, double or nothing?"

WHITE HART INN, Salisbury, Conn. 06068; 203-435-2511. A 25 room village inn, 55 mi. west of Hartford. European Plan. Breakfast, lunch, dinner served to travelers daily. Alpine, xc-ski, ski-jumping, golf, swimming nearby. John Harney, Innkeeper.

Directions: Exit the Taconic Pkwy. at Millbrook, N.Y. Proceed west on U.S. 44 to Salisbury. Inn is located at Jct. of U.S. 44 and 41.

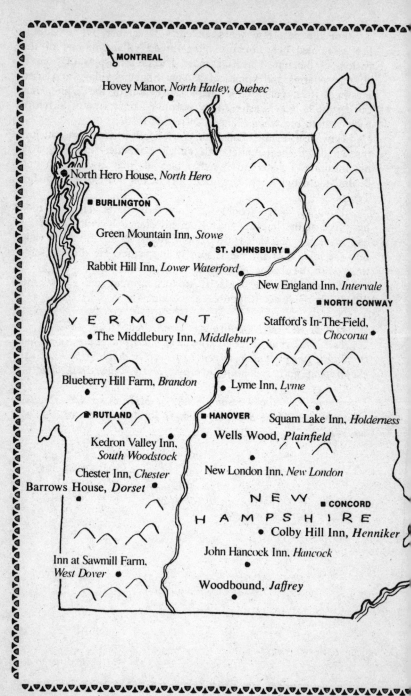

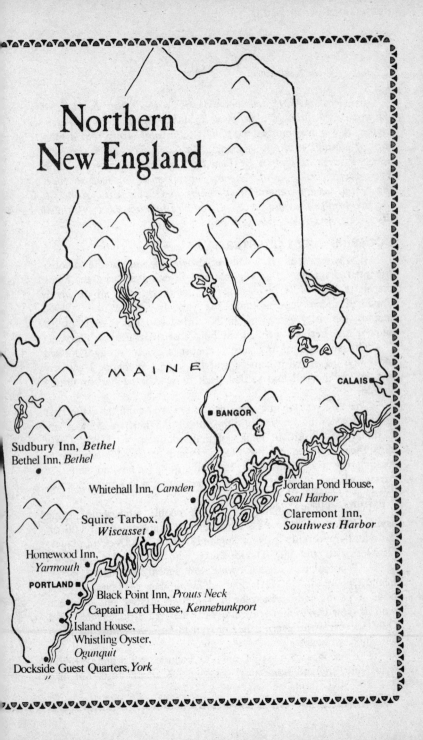

Northern New England

MAINE

CALAIS

■ BANGOR

Sudbury Inn, *Bethel*
Bethel Inn, *Bethel*

Whitehall Inn, *Camden*

Jordan Pond House,
Seal Harbor

Squire Tarbox,
Wiscasset

Claremont Inn,
Southwest Harbor

Homewood Inn,
Yarmouth

PORTLAND ■

Black Point Inn, *Prouts Neck*
Captain Lord House, *Kennebunkport*

Island House,
Whistling Oyster,
Ogunquit

Dockside Guest Quarters, *York*

Maine

In October, 1775, elements of the British fleet bombarded the town of Falmouth, almost totally destroying it. George Washington, the new commander of the Continental Army sent a message of courage to the townspeople. In November, 1775, the Kennebec River was chosen by Benedict Arnold as the route of a two-pronged invasion of Quebec. This expedition was to meet the prong, led by General Montgomery at Quebec City. Although the two armies did join forces, a frontal attack on the city proved disastrous, and the Americans retreated.

DOCKSIDE GUEST QUARTERS, York

It was dawn on York Harbor. I awakened when the October sun peeked into my east window and illuminated the trees along the shore—the white pines and firs, native spruces, all of which remained green year around. The yellows and oranges of the maples, the rusty greens of the hickories, and the scarlets of the sumacs and beeches were at the height of their autumn glory.

The sundeck of my room, almost at water's edge, looked most inviting so with camera and binoculars in hand, I put my feet up on the rail and settled back to watch the harbor drama unfold.

The tide was on the way in, the sea was calm, and the first of the lobster boats was gliding out of the harbor. Almost immediately the "resident flock" of mallard ducks, as David Lusty calls them, came quacking into view and hesitated momentarily looking for a handout. They're really quite tame and serve as perfect decoys to bring literally hundreds of migrating ducks to the nearby marsh.

I thought immediately of all the people who write to me saying, "Can you help us find a country inn located directly on the water—preferably in New England?" Well, the Dockside Guest Quarters fills the bill. David Lusty who is a native "state-of-Mainer," complete with a Down-Easter accent, purchased Harris Island, where the DGQ is located, a number of years ago. He hired a young lady whom he had met in college and fourteen months later David and Harriette were married at Dockside Guest Quarters. Over the years it has proven to be a very popular place with honeymooners.

The inn has grown not only to include the original 1880's style New England homestead called the Maine House, but also

other multi-unit cottage buildings of a contemporary design each with its own porch and a view of the ocean. Some have a casual studio feeling.

At breakfast which is continental style at the Maine House, David enthusiastically made suggestions to all of us about a foliage tour of the Maine coast. As he said, "I think this is the best time of the year to be here.

A few years ago David and Harriette added the Dockside Dining Room, now managed by Steve and Sue Roeder, serving luncheon and dinner with a great deal of emphasis on food from the waters of the nearby Atlantic. One of the non-sea offerings is a splendid roast duckling "a la Hickory Stick."

The first order of the day was a guided tour of York Harbor in the DGQ launch with the Lusty's son Paul. In his laconic way he said he did it everyday, but never got tired of it.

Pointing due east toward the open sea, he said, "Next stop—Spain."

DOCKSIDE GUEST QUARTERS, York, Maine 03909; 207-363-2868. An 18-room waterside country inn 10 mi. from Portsmouth N.H. York Village is a National Historic District. American Plan available. All lodgings include continental breakfast. Dockside Dining Room serves lunch and dinner to travelers daily except Mondays. Open from May 24 to Oct. 15. Fishing, sailing and boating on grounds. Golf, tennis, hiking, swimming and deep sea fishing nearby. For nature lovers. David and Harriette Lusty, Innkeepers.

Directions: From US 1 or I-95, take Exit 1 at York to Rte. 1A (the main street of York). Take Rte. 103 and follow signs to Harris Island Rd.

WHISTLING OYSTER, Ogunquit

It was a really cold Berkshire night in the middle of January. I was seated in front of the fireplace making some notes for the upcoming edition of *Country Inns and Back Roads* when the telephone rang. It was John Parella innkeeper of the Whistling Oyster in Ogunquit. He sounded quite excited.

"Hello," he said. "Tell me, how's your cold weather." I explained that it was about as cold as his weather in Ogunquit this time of year. "Well, I'm not in Ogunquit," he said, "I'm in Palm Beach!" "Oh," I said, "you're staying at the Brazilian Court?" (Some of our northern innkeepers find that a very delightful experience in the wintertime.)

"No," he said, "I just wanted to let you know that the Florida extension of the Whistling Oyster is now open and in full swing. We're having a wonderful time. Come on down."

Oddly enough, just a few days earlier I'd finished the account of the sunny afternoon when Sam and I visited John at the Whistling Oyster in Perkins Cove. At the time, I had taken some photographs of the harbor with all of the fishing boats and pleasure craft. The scene with the tiny drawbridge often reminds me of a Van Gogh painting.

John had gone into enthusiastic detail about some of the flowers that are planted around the inn—the begonias, geraniums, hibiscus, marigolds, lilacs, phlox and snapdragons. We had a lunch of lobster Provençale and crabmeat Snug Harbor. The harbor view from the glass-walled dining room was undisturbed.

"Well John," I asked, "where's the Palm Beach Whistling Oyster located?" "It's in the Royal Poinciana Plaza," he said, and it's going to have the same kind of food we've served at Ogunquit for years because we have the same chef. There'll be luncheon and dinner, and also an after-theatre buffet. We're right across the street from the Royal Poinciana Playhouse.

"We'll be open in Palm Beach from November to April. This means that the Whistling Oyster in Maine will close for the season in mid-October and we hope everyone will have Thanksgiving dinner with us in Palm Beach. Incidentally, the Whistling Oyster gift shop in Ogunquit will stay open through Christmas, and everything re-opens in Maine on Memorial Day."

Well, there it is. A tale of two Whistling Oysters. One on the golden sands of Palm Beach in the winter, and the other on Perkins Cove on the rocky shores of Maine in the summer.

I make haste to point out that there are no lodgings available at either of the two Whistling Oysters. In Maine John refers everybody to the Island House which is just a few steps away.

As for John's invitation to come to Palm Beach in January—I need no urging.

WHISTLING OYSTER, Perkins Cove, Ogunquit, Me. 03907; 207-646-9521. In Palm Beach: 336 Royal Poinciana Plaza, 33480; 305-832-2432. A waterfront restaurant in Perkins Cove at Ogunquit. No lodgings. Lunch and dinner served daily. Open Memorial Day weekend through mid-October. Reservations most advisable. (For accommodations: the Island House just a few steps away.) For ocean lovers. John Parella, Innkeeper.

Directions: From the south, take the York exit from I-95. Turn north on Rte. 1 to Ogunquit Square. Proceed south on Shore Rd. for about 1 mi. to Perkins Cove turnoff. In Palm Beach, Whistling Oyster is located where Coconut Row meets Royal Poinciana Way.

THE ISLAND HOUSE, Ogunquit

Sometimes letters tell the story of an inn more succinctly than I can. Here is an excerpt from such a letter from New York City:

"My wife and I have just returned from a little vacation in New England and I think we have you and your book to thank for a lot of our fun. We stayed at the Island House and dined

63

both at the Whistling Oyster in Ogunquit and the Jordan Pond House in Seal Harbor. We also stayed at the Colby Hill Inn in Henniker, New Hampshire.

"The Island House was perhaps the most spectacular for us because we arrived there directly from the city. A door at the rear of our room, which I assumed led to a closet, was tightly stuck. My wife said that she saw light through the crack so we both pulled on the knob and when the door sprang open, it revealed a small porch and the ocean itself crashing over enormous rocks. I had no idea that we would be that close to the sea.

"Paul Laurent was very nice. He seemed to be expecting us when we arrived and even remembered which street we lived on in New York. He had grown up in the same neighborhood. Anyway, the Island House, right down to the wildflowers, was everything you said it would be."

Of course, we always like to get letters like that. Incidentally, when we get complaints, which we do every once in awhile, we contact the innkeepers and also try to straighten things out with the disappointed guest.

Well, back to the Island House. It sits on the end of Perkins Cove, out on the rocks, which have a cover of honeysuckle and sumac. There are snapdragons, blue thistles, marigolds, and many

other flowers. Cormorants, gulls, mourning doves, ducks and humming birds abound in the area.

There are two points I must make about the Island House. First, children under twelve years of age would simply not be happy there. There are no facilities to entertain young people. There are also no facilities for pets. The second is, that during the height of the season which in Ogunquit is July and August, it is almost always necessary to have reservations in advance.

This means that June and September are more plausible times if you like to travel casually without advance reserving.

The Island House serves a continental breakfast to its guests. Many of them take their coffee either on the porch overlooking the cove, or stroll out to the rocks at oceanside. No other meals are served. However, the Whistling Oyster which is within a short walking distance serves both lunch and dinner.

ISLAND HOUSE, Ogunquit, Me. 03907; 207-646-8811. A 6-room oceanside inn overlooking Perkins Cove, 15 mi. from Portsmouth, N.H. Lodgings include continental breakfast, served daily except Sundays to inn guests only. (Lunch and dinner available at the Whistling Oyster nearby.) No children under 12. No pets. Open from early June to October 1. Advance reservations necessary. Golf, swimming, fishing, scenic walks, interesting shops and art galleries, all within walking distance. For ocean lovers. Paul and Marge Laurent, Innkeepers.

Directions: From Maine Tpke., exit at York or Wells. Follow US #1 to Ogunquit. Go 1 mi. on Shore Rd. to Perkins Cove. Inn is last house in Perkins Cove.

CAPTAIN LORD MANSION, Kennebunkport

Jim led the way on the climb up to the cupola. When we reached the third floor he called out, "It's just a little bit farther." Well, we made it and it was worth it. We looked down upon the host of impressive, stately homes of Kennebunkport, many built by ship's captains during the early part of the 19th century. There was the broad lawn leading down the road next to the river. We could see many boats gently swaying with the tide. It was a bird's-eye view of the neat gardens, wooden fences and hip roofs of the town.

Jim then invited us down to the parlor for a cup of afternoon tea and promised some homemade Greek pastry. Something I

find most interesting about this beautifully restored mansion is the innkeepers—Jim Throumoulos and his wife, Shirley. Because the place is so elegant and stately, I rather expected someone like Arthur Treacher to greet me at the front door. Instead I found two enthusiastic young people who have done a great deal of the restoration work themselves, and who go out of their way to be accommodating to their guests.

The three floors of the mansion had different types of rooms with most impressive antiques. Quite a few of the rooms have working fireplaces, and each one has a pleasant view of the village, the garden or the river. There are additional rooms in a fascinating old barn, which may well be a craft center soon. The house has so many antiques that Jim and Shirley are kept busy during the day giving house tours.

Breakfast is served to everyone in the big, friendly kitchen. All of the guests sit around the big table and Jim and Shirley make the introductions. On that particular morning there were warm homemade blueberry muffins and scrambled eggs. Breakfast is the only meal served, and Jim and Shirley happily recommend nearby restaurants including the Whistling Oyster for lunch and dinner.

After breakfast I browsed through a little shop which sells many things crocheted by Jim's mother, who is most helpful with needlework problems.

All in all, I found the Captain Lord a singular experience. It's a 19th century mansion being kept by two young enthusiastic innkeepers, and located in one of the most beautiful villages on the Maine coast.

As for me, later that morning I did something I had wanted to do from the first moment that I saw the inn. I took a book and sneaked back up to the cupola for a couple of quiet hours.

No one would ever find me there.

THE CAPTAIN LORD MANSION, Box 527, Kennebunkport, Me., 04046; 207-967-3141. A 10-room seacoast village inn, 3 tenths of mi. from Dock Square in Kennebunkport, off Ocean Ave. Near Rachel Carson Wildlife Refuge, Trolley Museum and Shaker community. Lodgings include breakfast. Some rooms with shared bath. Breakfast and tea served daily. No pets. Open year-round. Bicycles, xc-ski, horseback riding, sailing, deep sea fishing, golf and indoor swimming and tennis nearby. For antique lovers. Shirley and Jim Throumoulos, Innkeepers.

Directions: From Boston follow I-95 into Maine. Take Exit 3 and follow signs to Kennebunkport.

BLACK POINT INN, Prouts Neck

The sun, although still bright in the sky, was beginning to cast longer shadows beside the Black Point Inn pool. I stood for a quiet moment at the head of the flagstone walk, which leads directly to the pool, and looked out over the waters of the bay. I spotted the bobbing buoys of the lobster pots. In the distance I could see a sailboat beating 'round the point. The flags at the pool, Canadian and American, were now flapping somewhat listlessly as the breeze had not yet freshened. There were now only a few people in the pool catching a last minute dip before dressing for dinner.

Earlier that day, the lunch served at poolside could best be described as bounteous. There were several different kinds of salad and a special plate of corned beef hash, which Mary Petteys explained, "was not from the can." It was very tempting to take a little of everything and I think I succeeded nobly in accomplishing this feat. The tray with the iced tea and dessert was carried over by one of the personable waitresses, and Mary, Hank, Sam and I sat down in a corner underneath one of the blue and white umbrellas. Hank explained that there were only three days throughout the summer that lunch could not be served outside.

The Black Point remains, as always, one of the really impressive resort-inn experiences on the Maine coast. Lodging guests are accommodated only on the American Plan, although all three meals are available to travelers. We started talking about how fashions in travel have changed several times in recent years and Hank said that, according to the advance reservations for 1975, guests will be coming for longer stays. In fact, the reservation list is already almost filled and I would suggest that anyone planning a visit to the Black Point act as quickly as possible.

The inn is ideal for a vacation experience. There are several tennis courts at the Prouts Neck Club available to inn guests as well as the sandy beach and the inn pool. There are eighteen holes of good golf and if sailing or boating has an appeal, they're just up at the Point. Basically, Black Point is an adult resort-inn and I don't believe that small children would really be happy here. As Mary pointed out there is neither facilities for them, nor a children's counselor. But there are many other inns that do have this service.

The inn has its touches of elegance. For example, Hank and Mary, who have been there for many years, are most particular about the service. It's the kind of place where it feels right to put on your best looking resort clothes for dinner. And, of course, there's dancing afterward.

I turned back toward the inn to enjoy a game of backgammon with one of the guests whom I'd met during the afternoon. This was lobster night and I was looking forward to a most pleasant evening.

BLACK POINT INN, Prouts Neck, Me. 04070; 207-883-4311. A 76-room luxury resort-inn on Rte. 207, 10 mi. south of Portland. American Plan. Breakfast, lunch and dinner served to travelers. Open late-June to early-September. No children under age 12. No pets. Pool, bicycles, sailing, dancing, golf, tennis and ocean bathing all within a few steps. For sports lovers. Henry and Mary Petteys, Innkeepers.

Directions: From Maine Tpke. take Exit 7. Turn right on Rte. 1. Proceed 2.7 mi. to Rte. 207. Turn left. This is the road to Prouts Neck.

HOMEWOOD INN, Yarmouth

The postcard was from La Grange, Illinois, and it said, in part, "Using the list from *Country Inns and Back Roads*, we looked up the Homewood Inn yesterday. We were charmed by our accommodations in the White House Cottage. While a storm raged outside with wind, rain and lightning, we were snug in front of our fireplace. The food was excellent and reasonably priced. We hope to return for a longer stay sometime."

Would you believe that I get postcards every year, starting from the first of June right into winter, that say pretty much the same thing about the Homewood? I called Fred Webster on the telephone a couple of days before writing this and congratulated him on having so many enthusiastic, satisfied guests. "Well, we love that," he said, "but that means that we've got to work that much harder to see that they remain satisfied."

The old-fashioned work ethic is alive and well on the shores of Casco Bay at the Homewood Inn. It's been a family proposition for many, many years and right now Fred, Jr., his wife Colleen, his mother Doris, and assorted Webster, Jr., children have been and still are very much involved with the hard work of keeping a good country inn.

My most recent visit happened, quite by design, on a Monday night. That's the night that the Websters give all of their staff the night off, and they have Jim Lumsden, a State of Maine man of some girth and stature, come in and put on a real Maine clambake for their guests.

It was a beautiful evening, and the guests all gathered outside along the rough wooden tables, all dressed informally. We fell to work on the clams with a will.

As I was taking them apart and dipping them in the sauce, it occurred to me that no one can really go to a Maine clambake

69

and feel left out. It's the kind of experience that brings everybody together. In fact, I looked up and there, smiling at me from across the table, was another one of our innkeepers, John Gasser from the Sudbury Inn in Bethel, Maine. (And now also from the Bethel Inn in Bethel, Maine.)

"Well, if it isn't the Berkshire Traveller doing his most favorite thing," he said. "Eating!" I was delighted to see him and he was greeted like a long-lost brother by Fred Webster who was busy major-domoing everybody into the right lines for steak, chicken or lobster.

The Homewood is certainly well named. It's very home-like and looks happily settled among the woods, fields and harbor. Its informal atmosphere invites vacationers, including those with children, to enjoy a real country resort-inn experience. The accommodations are cozy cottages strung along the shores of the bay. Sooner or later everyone meets back at the central lodge in front of the tennis court for introductions, indoor games, and browsing through the antique barn.

Small wonder I get so much mail about it.

HOMEWOOD INN, Drinkwater Point, Yarmouth, Me. 04096; 207-846-3351. A 36-room waterside inn on Casco Bay north of Portland. European Plan. Breakfast, lunch, dinner served to travelers except Mondays when Continental breakfast, box lunch served and steak or lobster cookout at night (by advance reservation). Open May 30 through October 13. (Some rooms and cottages with kitchenettes available from May 10 and after October 13.) Bicycles (incl. tandems), pool, tennis, croquet court, sailing, boating, hiking, salt water swimming. Nearby: golf, riding, fishing, state parks, theatre. For nature and water lovers. Fred, Colleen and Doris Webster, Innkeepers.

Directions: From the south, take Exit 9 from Maine Tpke. (I-95) to Rte. 1-N and follow signs to inn. From the north, take Exit 11 from I-95 at Grey and follow Rte. 115 to Yarmouth. Follow signs to inn.

SQUIRE TARBOX HOUSE, Westport Island

"What's for dinner tonight?" I walked into the kitchen at the Squire Tarbox House where Mary Wright was working a pie crust.

"How does lamb chops, string beans from the garden, potatoes au gratin, onion soup, a tossed salad, and chocolate pudding with real whipped cream sound to you?"

It sounded marvelous, of course.

"Well, we're not going to have that," she said with her eyes twinkling. "We're going to have baked mackerel, mashed potatoes, Swiss chard, beets, salad and sweet potato pie."

At that precise moment, Eleanor Smith, the keeper of the Squire Tarbox House, came in the kitchen and said, "Is that sister of mine teasing you again? She knows how much you like home-cooked food." I gave Eleanor a big hug and we all sat down to talk about our favorite subject—keeping an inn.

"I knew you were coming today," she said, "so I brought you a little letter that I received just yesterday." And then she went on to read, " 'Just a note to tell you how much we enjoyed our stay at your inn. Hope to return next year. Thanks so much for the bread, the recipe, the Johnnie Jump-ups, the remedies for an upset tummy, and your great hospitality. The experience was truly unique. I especially enjoyed breakfast and the lobster stew.'"

I immediately turned to Mary and asked, "How did she get an upset tummy here?" Mary replied adroitly that she had it when she arrived.

And so the ball was tossed back and forth with good-natured conversation while the pie crusts were finished, filled with apples and peaches and popped into the oven.

We wandered out into the main portion of the inn which is as neat as a New England pin. The chairs and sofas in the main living room are all placed around a friendly fireplace which on cool evenings in summer has, what Eleanor calls, "a stick or two on the fire." No one would think of turning on a television set, for this kind of atmosphere brings out the best conversation in everyone.

71

The Squire Tarbox House is like the proverbial visit to grandmother's. It's a beautifully restored country home of the early 19th century, set in the middle of the unspoiled woods of Westport Island in Maine's Booth Bay Harbor area. I just can't begin to enumerate all of the flowers, trees and birds that flourish here.

We walked out on the sundeck which is right on the edge of the woods and Eleanor remarked, "I'm no innkeeper. I really don't know very much about inns, but I like having a great many friends."

SQUIRE TARBOX HOUSE, R.D. #2, Box 318, Wiscasset, Me. 04578; 207-882-7693. A tiny 7-room island inn on Rte. 144 in Westport, 10 mi. from Wiscasset. American Plan. 6 rooms with shared baths. Breakfast served to houseguests only. Lunch and dinner served to travelers by reservation only. Open from June 1 to October 1. No pets. Golf, tennis, pool, sailing nearby. Mrs. Eleanor H. Smith, Innkeeper,

Directions: From Maine Tpke. take Exit 9 and follow Rtes. 95 and 1 to Rte. 144, 8 mi. north of Bath. Follow Rte. 144 to Wiscasset-Westport Bridge. Inn is located 6 mi. south of bridge on Westport Island.

WHITEHALL INN, Camden

"There are at least three ways that every visitor to Camden should see the town."

Ed Dewing and I were walking the tree-lined street that leads from the Whitehall Inn to the Town Landing.

"A walk around town or at least a bike ride is the first way," he continued. "This brings you into direct contact with the old houses, streets and shops. The second way is to follow the road to the top of Mt. Battie with a bird's-eye view of the harbor, Penobscot Bay, and all the islands. The Windjammers, if they are in port, are most impressive from that height. Edna St. Vincent Millay loved to walk on Mt. Battie and I have always heard that the view of land and sea inspired a number of her poems including her best known one, 'Renascence.'

"The third way is to cruise the harbor itself at least as far out as Curtis Island and then turn around and see the entire landscape—mountains, boats, the harbor waterfall."

This year, 1975, will mark the seventy-fourth consecutive year for the Whitehall Inn, which makes its own architectural contribution to the town. It is actually an 1834 sea captain's home to which two buildings have been added. A large porch winds around three sides.

The low-ceilinged lobby is covered with Oriental rugs and the furniture is placed to encourage guests to become acquainted. One particular focal point is a glass-covered table with a truly impressive collection of shells.

In one corner of the first floor an area has been set aside as a continuing tribute to Edna St. Vincent Millay. It contains many photographs and memorabilia of the poetess, who first recited her poetry at Whitehall at the age of 16.

By this time, Ed and I had arrived at the landing and were walking out on the dock to take a harbor cruise in his boat. "You'd be surprised at how many people ask for box lunches," he said. "They go for the day on the water, or walk about the

area. Incidentally, some of our longer-staying guests join our craft classes."

The Whitehall is a family inn with Chip, Jonathan and Heidi Dewing, the younger generation, all involved in the inn chores and responsibilities. "We know that they all want to eventually do their own thing," Ed said, "but we're a good working team."

I forgot that there is just one other way to see Camden, and that is to sit rocking on the front porch of the Whitehall Inn and let it come to you.

WHITEHALL INN, Camden, Me. 04843; 207-236-3391. A 38-room village inn in a Maine seacoast town, 75 mi. from Portland. Mod. American and European Plans. Breakfast and dinner served daily to travelers. Light lunch served to houseguests in annex across from inn overlooking Penobscot Bay. Open June through October. Tennis, crafts school, shuffleboard, day sailing, harbor cruises on grounds. Golf, hiking, swimming, fishing nearby. Jean and Ed Dewing, Innkeepers.

Directions: From Maine Tpke. take Exit 9 to coastal Rte. 95. Proceed on 95 to Rte. 1 at Brunswick. Follow Rte. 1 to Rte. 90 at Warren, to Rte. 1 in Camden. Inn is located on Rte. 1, ¼ mi. north of Camden.

CLAREMONT, Southwest Harbor

I hadn't been in a hammock in years. I first noticed it as I stepped off the porch and walked down toward the Boathouse. It was strung between a birch and a pine on the broad lawn leading to the water's edge. Gingerly, I let myself down and swung my feet around. In that second I had regained all of the delicate sense of balance and agility which is necessary for a devotee of the hammock. I swung gently in the breeze and turned my head to look out over Somes Sound and the nearby mountains.

The afternoon sun was beginning to cast longer shadows at the Claremont and some of the guests who had been out boating were heading toward the inn mooring. Still in this delightful supine position I watched a young waitress who was babysitting that afternoon for some of the younger inn guests. She was teaching her young charges how to play tetherball. I waved at a new-found friend with a movie camera who was preparing to film the twenty or thirty sailboats that were now in sight on the Sound.

My eye traveled to the top of the mansard roof and rested on the weathervane which has been overseeing the Claremont for

many years. Beneath it were lodging rooms which, except for the addition of modern conveniences, have remained virtually unchanged since the turn of the century. The Claremont has always been a New England summer inn and with its gleaming coat of yellow paint and background of green forest it has its own special dignity.

Around six o'clock we would all be gathering at the Boathouse for some late afternoon refreshment, and talk of the day's activities. Guests here have an almost unending choice of ways to spend their days.

Almost everyone hikes or walks in the mountains which have spectacular views of both land and ocean. There are special cassette tape tours, bicycling, horseback riding, nature walks, trips to the Rockefeller gardens, croquet, bridge, films, music, poetry readings, summer theatre, the Bar Harbor Festival—well, it goes on and on.

There's a bulletin board on the porch which is loaded with notices of special activities in the area. It's a good place to bring children.

I must have been lost in a kind of Claremont-Mt. Desert reverie because the next thing I knew I was tumbled out of the hammock and could see a tennis sneaker impatiently tapping the lawn. "Okay. You and I were supposed to play doubles at four o'clock."

That's the one thing about lazing in a hammock that I had forgotten—one can very easily be turned over.

THE CLAREMONT HOTEL and Cottages, Southwest Harbor, Me. 04679; 207-244-5036. A 55-room rambling summer hotel on Somes Sound, Mt. Desert Island, 20 mi. east of Ellsworth. Mod. American Plan omits lunch. Some rooms with shared baths. Adjacent housekeeping cottages. Breakfast and dinner served daily to travelers. Cottages open from June 1 through October 15. Hotel and dining room open from June 23 through Labor Day. A 15-minute drive to the Claremont's picnicking and freshwater swimming area; tennis, dock and deep water moorings at the hotel. Golf, bicycles, riding, boating and sailing rentals nearby. For nature lovers. Gertrude McCue, Proprietor.

Directions: From Maine Tpke., exit at Augusta and proceed east on Rte. 3 to US #1. At Ellsworth, pick up Rte. 3 again and follow Rte. 102 on Mt. Desert Island to Southwest Harbor. Follow signs approaching and in Southwest Harbor.

JORDAN POND HOUSE, Seal Harbor

Twilight was deepening at the Jordan Pond House and I was taking the opportunity to chat once again with Charles Savage, who is a native of Mt. Desert Island and the managing director of the restaurant.

We were gazing across the Pond at two low hills that are almost twins. They're called the Bubbles. "You know there is something unique about one of those Bubbles," he said. "There is a boulder on the top of one that must have been dropped by the receding glacier about a million years ago. The nature of the rock is completely different from anything that we have around here. The only force that could have carried it here must have been the glacier as it moved down from the north."

Most everyone who comes to Maine wants to enjoy a lobster dinner and I was certainly no exception. At this point our young waitress, a college student like most of the other staff, brought in two beauties. We had already eaten our popovers and both of us were ready for the main course. The menu included steak, chicken and baked potatoes. It is one of the few places I know that have finger bowls.

The Jordan Pond House first opened in 1896 and has been operating in much the same style ever since.

Part of that style includes afternoon tea with popovers and homemade ice cream. Visitors to Mt. Desert Island actually get in line half an hour before tea time in order to be certain of getting a place at the rustic tables on the lawn overlooking the pond.

Dinner at the Jordan Pond House that evening started with

a choice of three soups, almond, cream of broccoli, or cream of cheese with sherry. This was followed by a choice of three entrees: lobster, chicken or steak. These were served with baked potatoes and delicious fresh peas. Sweetener for the iced tea consisted of sugar already melted in water. Incidentally, finger bowls are still a part of the exceptional service.

By this time the light of day had faded and our friends, the Bubbles, across the pond were but a shadow.

The waitress came for our dessert order and I happily chose strawberry ice cream.

Charles was still warmed up to the subject of some of the phenomena of Acadia National Park:

"Somes Sound, which was also formed by the glacier, divides Mt. Desert Island almost in half. It is the only fjord on the east coast."

After a long browse through the Jordan Pond Gift Shop, Charles and I said good night and walked out to get in our cars. "Isn't it fascinating," he said, "that at one time everything here was covered by a two-mile thick glacier."

JORDAN POND HOUSE, Seal Harbor, Acadia National Park, Maine 04675; 207-276-3316. A country restaurant on Park Loop Rd., 1 mi. out of Seal Harbor. No lodgings. Luncheon, afternoon tea, dinner served daily. Open June 16—Oct. 1. (Area lodging info: Acadia National Park, Bar Harbor, Me.) The Acadia Corporation, Charles Savage, Managing Director.

Directions: Exit US 1 at Ellsworth. Follow Rte. 3. Jordan Pond House is located in Acadia National Park on Park Loop Rd.

SUDBURY INN, Bethel

I clomped up the steps into the front door of the Sudbury Inn making a great show of getting the snow off my parka and ski boots and then stepped inside to the cheerful warmth. Sure enough, there was Bev Gasser waiting for me with a broom in her hand and a stern look in her eye. I knew that it was all part of the good-natured kidding I would get about bringing more snow inside than I left on the slopes.

"Where did you ski today," she said. I wrenched off my ski boots and staggered over to the fireplace. "Today I went up to Sunday River," I said. "That 3½ mile run was great and the lift lines weren't long at all. Tomorrow it's Mt. Abram."

She handed me a cup of tea and sat down on the couch. "I told you that the best ski secret in New England is that we have skiing earlier and longer here." From the number of other skiers who were drifting in, I could see that the secret of the Sudbury Inn was fast becoming unguarded.

The inn dates back to 1873 when Bethel was a busy lumbering town in western Maine. It has flourished even more as four-season vacationers have learned about the beauties of inland Maine.

The inn is homey and unpretentious. The big lobby has a rack of paperback books and current magazines and very comfortable chairs which invite plenty of reading and conversation. There is an old wind-up Victrola in one corner, a big bowl of apples on the table, and countrified touches like dried flowers on the mantlepiece and kerosene lamps.

Upstairs there are more books and magazines on a big table in the hallway in case the guest runs out of reading material. The rooms are simple. They have what I call "country inn" furniture—good and solid. On each successive trip I find that five or six more rooms have been redecorated. The towels for each guest are piled up on the bureaus in the old-fashioned way. Seven of the rooms have private baths and there are ten others with shared baths.

Almost everybody wanted to know what was going to be served for dinner that evening, so the menu was posted. It offered roast beef, lamb chops, chicken Yankee-style (this is cooked with maple corn fritters, bacon strips and cranberry sauce), scallops and rainbow trout. Desserts included Indian pudding, maple rum parfait and cheesecake. It all sounded pretty good especially to skiiers with Gargantuan appetites. One couple with two children noted that there were special children's prices—which, of course, pleased them no end.

Although I was visiting in January, the Sudbury Inn is open year-round. While I was toasting myself in front of the fireplace, I heard one guest say to another, "Hey, don't tell anyone else about this place, let's just keep it to ourselves."

THE SUDBURY INN, Box 65, Bethel, Me. 04217; 207-824-2174. A 17-room village inn on the Main Street, 70 mi. northwest of Portland, within sight of Mt. Washington. Near the Sunday River, Mt. Abram and Evergreen Valley ski areas. Some rooms with shared baths. European Plan includes full breakfast. Breakfast, lunch, dinner served to travelers. Closed Mondays. No pets. Closed Christmas Day. Bicycles available. Golf, tennis, swimming, Alpine and xc-ski nearby. Beverley Gasser, Innkeeper.

Directions: From the south, take Exit 11 at Gray from I-95. Follow Rte. 26 to Bethel.

BETHEL INN, Bethel

I saw the whole thing. From my seat on the elevated porch I saw two people, probably husband and wife, walk out of the golf pro shop and head for the first tee. He waggled the club a couple of times and then lofted the ball high in the air. It was a pretty good shot, landing about ten feet in front of the first green.

His wife then stepped up and hit one that looked like it had no trajectory and wasn't going anywhere in particular. It bounced on the fairway in front of the green, huffed and puffed up onto the green, swerved to the right and to the left, and finally, with one last gasp, dropped right into the hole!

The guy picked up his clubs and walked off the tee.

It seemed to me like everyone in sight realized that she had scored a hole-in-one. The tennis players, who were having a good game on this brisk September afternoon, stopped and applauded, as did the people practicing for the shuffleboard tournament. The gardener, standing in the midst of the roses, chrysanthemums, marigolds, and other summer flowers, ran out and presented the lady with a gorgeous chrysanthemum. Other golfers waved their clubs in salute.

That was at the Bethel Inn. It's a luxurious resort-inn where the guests are quite apt to stay anywhere from three days to three weeks because there are various types of sports and recreational activities located on the grounds or nearby.

Speaking of the gardener, flowers have always been notable here. Down the entire length of the porch there were baskets of hanging flowers, and there were even flowers decorating the little lampposts that light up the lawns of the inn.

There is a regular program of activities available each evening which includes movies and an orchestra for dancing on the weekends. On different nights there are bingo games, bridge tournaments, slide talks and people from the area who give informal talks on local mineral deposits, mountain climbing and backroading.

Each of the bedrooms and suites has been carefully furnished with harmonizing colors and patterns. They are larger than usual because the inn was built a number of years ago in more opulent times. There are always fresh flowers.

Incidentally, some of the rooms have wood burning fireplaces and turn-down service is also featured.

The Bethel Inn has a long-standing reputation for excellent food, impeccable housekeeping, and personal service. It has all of the amenities of a top-drawer summer resort. These amenities are a little more expensive than other accommodations in the Bethel area.

Oh yes, I almost forgot. The man did go back and finish out the nine holes after his wife hit the hole-in-one. There was a big bash and a formal announcement that night at dinner, including the presentation of a mock cup and scroll.

The guests at the Bethel Inn love that sort of thing.

BETHEL INN, P.O. Box 26 TB, Bethel, Me. 04217; 207-824-2175. A 65-room luxury resort-inn, 70 mi. northwest of Portland. Mod. American Plan. Breakfast, lunch, dinner served daily. Open June 1 to Oct. 26. No pets. Pool, 9-hole golf, tennis. Swimming, boating and fishing at private beach club nearby. Bicycles, hiking, climbing, rock hounding, and stream fishing. For nature lovers. John and Beverley Gasser, Innkeepers.

Directions: From the south, take Exit 11 at Gray from I-95. Follow Rte. 26 to Bethel.

New Hampshire

The first English settlement in New Hampshire was made in 1623 at Little Harbour. In 1629, John Mason got two royal grants of land there, hoping to turn it into a feudal domain with the colonists as his tenants, and possibly a baron or two for flavor. A little later the Reverend John Wheelwright appeared with some of his flock. The reverend had been tossed out of Massachusetts because the Puritan hierarchy considered him too radical. When the Massachusetts Puritans discovered that the land had some value, they dug up their original charter and proved, rather shakily, that most of New Hampshire belonged to Massachusetts.

Whereupon they took over, and New Hampshire did not get its own separate royal charter until 1679. Thereafter, throughout the French and Indian wars, the inhabitants were kept busy staying alive. They still had enough spirit left in 1772, however, to stage the "Pine Tree Riot" against the royal governor—at least the citizens of Weare did. That was because Governor Wentworth wanted to force them to save their best pine trees for masts for the British Navy.

One of my New Hampshire trips during the summer of 1975 will be to visit the Dana Place in Jackson, newly acquired by my good friends Mal and Betty Jennings, formerly of the New England Inn and the Bethel Inn. Already included in Very Special Resorts *it has year-round outdoor sports. 603-383-6822.*

SQUAM LAKES INN, Holderness

I'll never forget the first time I met Ella Connelly. It was a very hot day. We had been picking our way around the back roads and lakes of New Hampshire with a vague notion of the location of Squam Lakes Inn. As it pushed toward late afternoon, I was getting very hungry and cranky.

When I drove into Holderness, near Squam Lake, I knew I had to be on the right track, since I could see some kind of an inn or lodge on the top of a little rise in the distance. We hoped it would be the right place. It was.

Although lunch is not served at the inn, Ella could easily see that we were in dire need of sustenance, so she took us right out into the kitchen, sliced some roast beef and made some absolutely smashing sandwiches. We also had a preview of the dinner menu which had stuffed shrimp, duckling, sole and several homemade desserts.

We took our sandwiches, cookies and milk to a picnic table outside and then I learned the heartwarming story of Squam Lakes Inn and the Connelly family.

There's mother Ella and father John and then a succession of sons named Jack, Ed, Paul, Jim, Bill, and Joe. There's also a daughter Ann and I'll bet she has a great time with six brothers.

The Connellys live in Boston. A short time ago they learned that the Squam Lakes Inn was up for sale, and after numerous trips and family conferences, decided to buy it and start a new way of life.

A tour of the inn and the property was the next order of business. It is most impressive. There's a beautiful Olympic swimming pool, tennis courts and extensive lakefront property with canoes, sailboats, and rowboats.

The lodging rooms vary from the large, immaculate rooms in the main lodge to more informal rooms in housekeeping cottages scattered among the trees. Squam Lake is between the big country of the White Mountains, and the sparkling New Hampshire lakes. It's a very short drive to dozens of recreational attractions. It would certainly be a great place to spend a few days with children of any age. After all, any family with that many children, knows how to show kids a good time!

Later on that afternoon, Ed took me down to the lakefront with its sandy beach and I tried my hand at sailing on Squam Lake. It was from the lake that I got the feeling of these New Hampshire mountains. With billowy cloud formations overhead and the trees lining the water's edge, I had a feeling, at least for a few moments, of being all alone in the world.

Squam Lakes Inn was a great find. I know the Connelly family is going to have a marvelous time being country innkeepers.

SQUAM LAKES INN, Box 28, Holderness, N.H. 03245; 603-968-3348. A 15-room mountain inn, 6 mi. from Plymouth. European Plan. Breakfast and dinner served daily to travelers. Open from late June to mid-October. Tennis, swimming, boating, and fishing on the grounds. Golf, tennis and hiking nearby. John and Ella Connelly, Innkeepers.

Directions: From I-93, take Exit 24 and travel south on Rte. 3, 4½ mi. to inn.

COLBY HILL, Henniker

Bettie Gilbert and I were seated at the picture window in the dining room on a wonderfully cold snowy morning. Most of the other guests had taken to the slopes and a few were putting on their cross-country skis, preparing to glide over the meadows and into the nearby woods.

The snow on the herb garden was now piled up to the top of the gate. Beyond that we could see the old farm machinery barn with two wide open arches. Jan Lindstrom's scratchboard drawing depicts it aptly.

"My son, Dan, has caged those openings in," explained Bettie. "He is breeding Lady Amherst pheasants, Chukka partridges and Royal Palm turkeys. We're all anxiously awaiting to see the outcome of this experiment."

Speaking of birds, there were at least thirty grosbeaks fighting for the sunflower seeds on the feeder right outside the window. "I'm already on my second fifty-pound bag this season. But we all love the beautiful yellow, black and white color of the birds against the snow." There were other feeders in the birch trees which had African thistle seed for the redpolls and goldfinches.

This morning the breakfast was sourdough pancakes with maple syrup, which Betty explained, was made right here in Henniker. "Once in a while I make hot muffins or blueberry coffeecake, but almost everyone likes the pancakes."

Our conversation on this beautiful morning was frequently interrupted by Polly, the inn parrot, who seems to be at his liveliest when the day is bright and sunny. He still manages a 'hello' or 'good-bye' to many of the guests although he is over forty years old.

Bettie began to make signs that her day was about to begin. She said she was going to start the soup pot for dinner and was deciding between cream of cauliflower or cream of broccoli. They've both been favorites at the inn this year. She also makes Graham bread which I enjoy but seldom find these days.

I volunteered to sweep up the hearths and lay the fire if it would help out and she said, "Oh, yes. When those skiers come back they're going to want someplace to warm up."

Colby Hill Inn is a small Colonial house built about 1800. It's really quite modest with only eight bedrooms in all, so all of the guests have ample opportunity to get acquainted. Bettie, herself, does all of the cooking.

"Lots of people come here just to unwind," she said. "You know we're a college town and there are lectures, movies and recitals going on during the college year. There's plenty of opportunity for reading, walking, back roading and listening to music."

COLBY HILL INN, Henniker, N.H. 03242; 603-428-3281. An 8-room inn on the outskirts of a New Hampshire college town. European Plan. Some rooms with shared baths. Breakfast served to houseguests only. Dinner served to travelers Tuesday through Saturday. Closed Thanksgiving and Christmas, and a few days in mid-April and late November. No children under 6. No pets. Swimming pool on grounds. Alpine and xc-ski, tennis, golf and bicycles nearby. Elizabeth F. Gilbert, Innkeeper.

Directions: From I-89, take Exit 5 and follow Rte. 202 to Henniker. From I-91, take Exit 3 and follow Rte. 9 through Keene and Hillsborough to Henniker.

WOODBOUND INN, Jaffrey

On this visit to the Woodbound, I arrived just as the sun was a few points above the tree line silhouetting the birches, beech, hemlocks, maples and oaks and casting an orange glow on the white clapboard main building.

After parking the car I stood for a few minutes taking in the whole scene. The last of the golfers were headed toward the inn comparing score cards. At one of the tennis courts the game was at "set point." Quite a few people were sitting out on the porch and lawn quietly reading or talking during the few moments before dinner.

I walked into the low-ceilinged dining room noting the unusual number of spiked golf shoes all in a neat row by the door. Inside there were attractive paintings and photographs of the Monadnock Region of New Hampshire. The fireplace at one end had a long musket hanging over it, and the furniture looked comfortable and homey. I checked the bulletin board to see what had been going on here during the past few days. The children's program and the golf tournament were underway and later in the week there would be a royal circus show. On another evening there would be folk and square dancing with instruction. The nearby Peterborough Players, and the Marlborough Theatre Company were both in production. There were notices concerning the famous Cathedral in the Pines which is just a few paces from the inn. The summer season was in high gear.

The Woodbound is a genial, family resort-inn. Ed and Peg Brummer started it all, and their son and daughter-in-law Jed and Mary Ellen, are continuing. There is even a third generation of Brummers who are starting to do the inn chores as well. For guests who like active outdoor things this is a delight. The lake with sailboats, canoes and swimming is just through the woods. There are miles of hiking and walking trails, golf, tennis, and shuffleboard. In the wintertime the Brummers have two ski tows, a ski school, plenty of cross-country skiing, and even tobogganing.

When I remarked to Ed Brummer that everyone seemed well acquainted he reminded me that during July and August, guests are accepted only by the week. "Some have been returning here for years with their children and grandchildren," he said. The rest of the year stays of any length are welcome.

After dinner the children were playing on the slides and swings in the backyard. Their parents were chatting or practicing putting on the lawn. Another game of tennis was going in the twilight. Peg Brummer was putting out some feed for the chickens and other animals which are part of the children's program. For the most part, the guests were just relaxing at the end of another lovely day at Woodbound.

WOODBOUND INN and Cottages, Jaffrey, N.H. 03452; 603-532-8341. A 40-room resort-inn on Lake Contoocook, 2 mi. in the woods from West Rindge or Jaffrey. Within walking distance of Cathedral of the Pines. American Plan in summer and winter. Overnight European Plan available in May, June and late fall. Breakfast, lunch and dinner served daily. Open from May 23 to October 14; December 26 to March 16. Par 3 golf course, swimming, beach, sailing, water skiing, tennis, hiking, children's program, ski area, touring trails, tobogganing and skating on the grounds. For sports lovers. Ed and Peggy Brummer; Jed and Mary Ellen Brummer, Innkeepers.

Directions: From Boston, follow Rte. 2, then Rte. 119 to Rindge where there are directional signs to inn. From New York, follow I-95 to Bernardston, Mass. Proceed on Rte. 10 to Winchester, then Rte. 119 to Rindge and watch for signs to inn.

NEW LONDON INN, New London

Country inns are expressions of innkeepers' interests and enthusiasms. There is no place where this is more obvious than at the New London Inn.

Frank and Lois Conklin *are* the New London Inn. Before becoming an innkeeper, Frank spent many years at Deerfield Academy, both on the faculty and administrative staff. In his own words, he is convinced that: "It was the best type of preparation for running a country inn. I learned the value of patience, organizing and planning."

The inn naturally indicates a great deal about the Conklins. There is explicit attention given to details found in the extreme neatness and cleanliness. The lodging rooms, for example, have a spic and span glow about them. Recently, new firm mattresses have been installed in each twin-bedded room. This is unquestionably Frank's thinking.

On the other hand, Lois' influence can be seen in the warmth and consideration displayed by the waitresses and the remainder of the staff.

The fact that the Conklins share many interests is also obvious in the inn. They had fun selecting the comfortable furniture, books, lamps and decorative pieces in the living rooms. They have agreed, for instance, that there is no proper place for television or telephones in the guest rooms. "That's just not our way," says Frank.

The menu reflects Frank's preferences for a wide diversity of really well-prepared good food.

88

"I was brought up in New England and I like New England dishes like duck, scallops, roast leg of lamb, and Yankee pot roast," he said. "After all, I eat most of my meals right here—so I guess we serve what appeals to me. I happen to like beef burgundy, so it shows up frequently at the Sunday evening buffet." He paused a moment and chuckled at the thought. "Seriously," he said, "we serve what our guests enjoy. They just happen to enjoy my favorites like deep-dish apple pie."

Now put all this together in a college town, for New London is the home of Colby Women's College and you have a mix of academia and intellectual curiosity which is exactly the Conklins' cup of tea.

"We're not a college inn, but we are vitally interested in and a part of a great many of the college's activities," said Lois.

This then, is the New London Inn and it is also Frank and Lois Conklin, the innkeepers and their staff. They are warm, delightful, concerned people.

NEW LONDON INN, New London, N.H. 03257; 603-526-2791. A 24-room village inn in a college town, 35 mi. from Hanover and Concord, N.H. Near Lake Sunapee and King Ridge and Mt. Sunapee ski areas. European Plan. Breakfast, lunch and dinner served daily to travelers. Open year-round. Closed Christmas Day. Swimming, boating, climbing, hiking, bicycles, snow-shoeing, Alpine and xc-ski nearby. Lois and Frank Conklin, Innkeepers.

Directions: From I-89, take either Exit 11 or 12 and follow signs for New London. Inn is in the center of town.

JOHN HANCOCK INN, Hancock

In the fall of 1974 I wrote Pat Wells of the John Hancock Inn asking her to tell me of some of the things they were planning for Thanksgiving at this inn. Before I quote some excerpts from her letter, let me set the stage:

This inn dates back to 1789 which makes it the oldest operating inn in New Hampshire. It's not very large, in fact, it has only 10 rooms. One of these rooms has an American Primitive mural that must have been painted early in the 19th century. Hancock is a most picturesque village off the main roads in the midst of the Monadnock Region, in the southern section of the state. The innkeepers, Pat and Glynn Wells, came to Hancock three years ago from New Jersey and know that they have found a permanent home.

Here's a part of what Pat wrote me about Thanksgiving at the John Hancock.

"Our celebration is very much a family affair with all of us contributing toward making our guests' Thanksgiving as happy as possible. The hearths will be ablaze with fires to warm the body as well as the spirit. Tables and hutches, fireplace mantles and guest rooms will have reminders of harvestime and we hope to do much to convey the spirit of thankfulness for our blessings.

"Candles will light each table, as they do daily at the inn. Last year each table had a grace for Thanksgiving which was especially written for the occasion. Quite a few of our guests appreciated this and several took copies with them.

"We'll have three dinner seatings with a special menu which includes six or seven entrees such as prime rib, baked stuffed shrimp, roast duckling, Nantucket seafood, and of course, turkey with all the trimmings. There will be boards of fresh honey corn bread and crocks of bright red apples. The aromas of warm mincemeat and spicy pumpkin pies straight from the oven will fill the air.

"Our children, Andrew, 8, and Susan, 5, are really beginning to enjoy their roles in an innkeeping family. Even now they are looking forward to handing each departing guest a loaf of homemade Pumpkin bread—our way of saying 'thank you' to those who have shared this very special day with us."

I hope it doesn't sound corny for me to say that their Thanksgiving plans reflect the Wells' philosophy of innkeeping, which goes on throughout the entire year.

THE JOHN HANCOCK INN, Hancock, N.H. 03449; 603-525-3318. A 10-room village inn on Rtes. 123 and 137, 9 mi. north of Peterborough. In the middle of the Monadnock Region of southern New Hampshire. European Plan. Breakfast, lunch and dinner served daily to travelers. Closed Christmas Day and one week in spring and fall. Bicycles available on the grounds. Antiquing, swimming, hiking, Alpine and xc-ski nearby. Glynn and Pat Wells, Innkeepers.

Directions: From Keene, take either Rte. 101 east to Dublin and Rte. 137 north to Hancock or Rte. 9 north to Rte. 123 and east to Hancock. From Nashua, take 101A and 101 to Peterborough. Proceed north on Rtes. 202 and 123 to Hancock.

STAFFORD'S-IN-THE-FIELD, Chocorua

One of the 183 varieties of birds which Fred Stafford assured me had been sighted in the vicinity of Stafford's-in-the-Field, was on my window sill this early morning doing his version of a tribute to the sun. I opened one eye with mayhem in my heart, but as soon as I realized that it was the dawn of another beautiful day here in the New Hampshire mountains, I forgave him, and strode to the window of my third floor bedroom.

The little square window looking to the north revealed some clouds billowing over the mountains. Tops of the sugar and red maples had not yet turned, although there were some hints of the glorious color to come. My bedroom had a marble-topped table, a chest of drawers reminiscent of my grandmother's day, and a little old-fashioned rocker.

I dressed hurriedly, not wanting to miss a moment of the day, and went downstairs only to find a guest already sitting in the library. He said the real reason he came here was to just get off by himself and read and think. We both agreed that this was a great place to do that.

Momo, Ramona and Fred Stafford's daughter, who would be leaving shortly for college, was already making up a batch of apple fritters to be served with maple syrup. She made a small one for me and we talked about some of the New England food served here. Some of the dishes she mentioned were spare ribs baked in maple syrup, fried bread, keepsake brownies, and Indian pudding. While she was preparing breakfast, she was also making the first steps in a recipe she called Jade Lime Torte which would be served at dinnertime.

By this time, breakfast was ready and the guests came trooping in to the dining room with its green and white checker table-cloths and old kitchen stove in one corner. The previous evening's conversations were picked up almost immediately and friendly dialogue filled the room.

Stafford's-in-the-Field is that highly-sought-after inn "at the end of the road." It's like being in a very big farmhouse. One of the surprising things about it is that with all of its informality, many of Ramona Stafford's dishes have a tinge of *haute cuisine* and sometimes Southwestern USA. There's good cross-country skiing in the winter, and the same trails are used for hiking in the other seasons.

For an extra special thrill be sure to ask the Staffords' sons, Hans and Fritz, to take you to the swimming hole in the woods.

STAFFORD'S-IN-THE-FIELD, Chocorua, N.H. 03817; 603-323-7766. An 8-room resort-inn with 5 cottages, 17 mi. south of North Conway. Mod. American Plan at inn omits lunch. European Plan in cottages. Some rooms in inn with shared baths. Meals served to guests only. No pets. Winter specialty: ski touring. Bicycles, square dancing and xc-ski on the grounds. Golf, swimming, hiking, riding, tennis and fishing nearby. For nature lovers. The Stafford Family, Innkeepers.

Directions: Follow N.H. Rte. 16 to Chocorua Village, then turn left onto Rte. 113 and travel 1 mi. west to inn. Or, from Rte. 93 take Exit 23 and travel east on Rtes. 104 and 25 to Rte. 16. Proceed north on Rte. 16 to Chocorua Village, turn left onto Rte. 113 and travel 1 mi. west to inn.

WELLS WOOD, Plainfield

I turned off Route 12A, and drove up the winding hillside road past some beautiful homes. At the old farm cart I turned into the gravel road that leads to Wells Wood. The stand of birches were shimmering in the misty summer morning. Now I saw, once again, the truly impressive studio and home of Maxfield Parrish which had been converted into a country inn by Tom and Rosalind Wells.

It was quite early in the morning and I had the place almost to myself. I walked through the long hall and down the broad steps leading to the dining room where I was once again almost bowled over by the huge fireplace. At the opposite end of the room was a great palladian window overlooking Mt. Ascutney.

Leafing through the register I noticed that people and compliments were still coming from far and near. I picked up a menu and found entrees with an international flare. It offered crab Mornay, breast of capon Cordon Bleu, chicken amandine, and Hunter's Horn Ragout. There was also an item called Jason's Royal Feast which is a center cut filet mignon served with Seafood Constantine and other kitchen surprises. The "Jason" in this case was Tom and Rosalind's young son, who at five is already becoming a gourmet. Rosalind does all of this glamorous cooking.

I was joined on my early morning quest by a huge St. Bernard named "Duncan," who reminded me of a dog at the Chester Inn. I wondered how many bites of chicken and beef had been slipped to him underneath the table by well-meaning guests.

I followed the friendly wag of his tail out onto the terrace where there were flowers blooming around the walls and a stone archway which reminded me of a Roman garden. A huge Maxfield Parrish-type Greek urn dominated the scene.

Wells Wood is a rather elegant, intimate inn. There are just a few rooms and advance reservations are almost always required.

I did have my reunion with Tom, Rosalind and Jason. We

had a few laughs remembering that on my previous visit Charles Bronson had sat in the very spot where I was sitting.

As I left Wells Wood retracing the road down the hill, a catbird followed me calling out in shrill, insistent tones, "Return, return."

WELLS WOOD, P.O. address: R.R. #2, Windsor, Vt. 05089; 603-675-5360. An ingeniously preserved, stately country inn on Rte. 12A, Plainfield, N.H. with 4 guest rooms and extensive dining in the former mansion and studio of Maxfield Parrish. Near Hopkins Center for Performing Arts and St. Gaudens Memorial. European Plan. (Cont. breakfast served to inn guests only.) Dinner served to travelers daily except Mondays. Open mid-April through mid-March. Winter and off season hours and dates may vary. Please call ahead. Lunch limited to some summer months. No pets. Antique shop located in studio. Bicycles, hiking, golf, swimming, climbing, riding, Alpine and xc-ski nearby. For nature lovers. Thomas and Rosalind Wells, Innkeepers.

Directions: From Rte. 89, take Exit 20 and proceed south on Rte. 12A, 8½ mi. to inn. Or, from I-91 take Windsor/Ascutney Exit, drive across Windsor Covered Bridge to Rte. 12A. Turn left and travel 3½ mi. to inn.

LYME INN, Lyme

Connie and Ray Bergendoff at the Lyme Inn have a great feeling for antiques. As Connie says, "We've lived with antiques most of our lives. We feel that they should not be put off in a corner and treated like something fragile. A well-built antique can be used intelligently for many, many years."

And the Lyme Inn reflects the Bergendoffs' healthy attitude towards antique furniture. The inn is furnished almost entirely with antiques and it's interesting on each visit to see what changes have been made, because all of the antiques are for sale.

For example, on my last visit I found a newly acquired spinning wheel in my room and also several other new pieces including a desk, a chest of drawers and a low table.

I'm sure many readers saw the antiques from the Lyme Inn that were on view at the New York Flower and Antique Fair in March of 1975.

At dinner that evening, Connie remarked that she wished I could be here on Sunday because most every Sunday afternoon, in cooperation with the bookstore right next to the inn, there is a sort of literary-artistic tea that brings well-known painters, authors, poets and even Pulitzer prize-winners together with the inn guests and town folk from Lyme and nearby Hanover. It's a small, informal gathering where there might be poetry read or songs sung. But whatever, there are questions and answers and a great deal of lively discussions. It's the sort of thing you might expect at a country inn.

I congratulated the Bergendoffs on their new impressive dining room which has been furnished with Shaker reproductions and decorated in antique maps of Northern New England.

"Oh, the dining room has been a great success," said Connie, "in fact, we had to enlarge the kitchen because it just seems that more and more people are coming for dinner. Bruce, our chef, has acquired a reputation for New England things such as clam chowder, Indian pudding, fresh parsnips dug from the snow and fresh seafood—swordfish, bluefish and Boston scrod. He is also quite adventurous with things like bouillabaisse, hasenpfeffer, and coq au vin."

The Lyme Inn is small and intimate. It has nine rooms with private baths and five with shared baths. I feel certain that children would not be comfortable at the Inn because there's no entertainment specifically designed for them.

It's just a short distance away from Dartmouth Skiway—an excellent ski area—and then back to the Inn for fondue and hot spirits, the winter specialties, in front of the fireplace in the

tavern. During the summer, the Lyme town pond offers excellent swimming and nearby Dartmouth College's Hopkins Center presents concerts and plays, year-round.

In many respects, the Lyme Inn is the kind of New England inn you've always hoped to find.

LYME INN, on the Common, Lyme, N.H. 03768; 603-795-2222. A 14-room village inn, 10 mi. north of Hanover on N.H. Rte. 10. European Plan year-round. Some rooms with shared baths. Breakfast and dinner served daily to travelers, except dinner on Tuesdays. Closed Christmas Eve and Christmas Day. Rooms available year-round. No children under 8. No pets. Alpine and xc-ski, fishing, hiking, canoeing, tennis and golf nearby. For antique lovers. Ray and Constance Bergendoff, Innkeepers.

Directions: From I-91, take Exit 14 and follow Rte. 113A east to Vermont Rte. 5. Proceed south 50 yards to a left turn, then travel 2 mi. to inn.

NEW ENGLAND INN, Intervale

"Isn't that fantastic!" Those were Sam's exact words as we stood on a little rise in front of the New England Inn and looked north through Pinkham Notch to the top of Mt. Washington, approximately fifteen miles in the distance. The top of the most magnificent of all New Hampshire mountains was generously covered by an early September snowfall and glistened in the brilliant sunshine of a beautiful fall day.

It was just about one weekend before the turning of the leaves and I was glad that we had chosen this "between seasons" time for a visit to the White Mountains. In doing so we avoided the fall foliage rush.

We walked down the road a short distance to take a look at the two new red clay tennis courts, completed since my last trip. The NEI is a place where, sometimes, tennis is taken very seriously. There's a regular group of seniors, both men and women, who come to play mixed doubles at various times during the summer and fall.

Across the road from the new courts is the first tee of the inn's short golf course. All around us were the trees, freshly trimmed grass and homes of this New England community. It was interesting to realize that in just a few months there might be as much as two or three feet of snow on the ground, to please both cross-country and Alpine skiers who would be at the inn.

Walking back up to the main building I noticed for the first time a small sign on the front porch which said 1809 A.D. The main house and the grounds of the inn are spread out in a campus-like manner with several individual New England cottages with their own fireplaces. The tall elms in front and on the sides of the inn were swaying in a freshening breeze, and these would be beautiful when covered with snow. However, on this particular day the sun was warming up the air and the swimming pool might see some activity a little later on in the day.

The NEI is a White Mountain resort-inn. It's very comfortable for families with children who might want to spend the days in summer and fall riding the tramway to Mt. Washington or visiting the many nearby attractions which appeal to the younger generation. The mountains are truly magnificent and there are many well-marked roads and trails leading through them. As we were standing there, a jeep drove into the parking lot and painted around the spare tire was the legend "Just Married."

I guess the New England Inn is popular with honeymooners as well as everyone else.

NEW ENGLAND INN, Intervale, N.H. 03845; 603-356-5541. A 46-room resort-inn 3 mi. from North Conway, N.H. in the spectacular White Mountain country near several ski areas and touring trails. Mod. American Plan omits lunch. Breakfast, lunch and dinner served daily to travelers. Open June 15 to Nov. 1 and Dec. 21 to April 15. Tennis, golf, swimming on grounds. Hiking, fishing, bicycles, boating, Alpine and xc-ski nearby. James W. Brown, Innkeeper.

Directions: From North Conway take Rte. 16A and proceed 3 mi. north to Intervale.

Vermont

What with the parade of explorers, Indians and entire armies using Vermont waterways during the 17th and 18th centuries, Vermont was the scene of many battles and skirmishes, including the capture of Fort Ticonderoga by Ethan Allen and Benedict Arnold in 1775. I've included many Vermont country inns in this edition. If you are driving through East Poultney stop off and say "hello" to Walter Johnson at the Eagle Tavern. *If you are lucky, there might be room for you at the inn.*

Lower Waterford, Vermont

RABBIT HILL INN, Lower Waterford

The night was clear and pleasantly brisk. The moon was a silver crescent over the Presidential Range of New Hampshire in the distance. The Pucker Street church spire was a vague silhouette in the night sky and the lights of White Village were subdued as the inhabitants prepared for another night of up-country slumber.

I was taking a solitary stroll through the village after joining in with the overflow of guests at the Friday evening Clambake at Rabbit Hill Inn. The lobsters had been brought over from the Maine coast at noon and the clam chowder got raves from almost everybody. Interesting, isn't it, that an inn in the mountains of Vermont should have such a reputation for this seaside concoction?

Ruth Carroll and I had a few moments following dinner to talk about their busy family life here on the edge of Vermont's Northern Kingdom. "Well," she explained, "Tom is 17 now and doing well at the University of Vermont. Greg is 15 and one of our mainstays here at the inn. Cindy is 13 and runs our little country store. Chuck—he's 11—is the young man who helped you with your bags."

During our visit, Ruth told me about a most interesting event that takes place at the inn one night a year. It is called the "Waterford Bleeze."

"Bleeze is actually a derivation of the word blaze and the feast of the blaze probably originated among the English, Scottish or Welsh," she explained.

"In old England after the Christmas celebration and Epiphany, it was the custom of village folk to bring their yule greens to the courtyard of the manor house. A great feast was held and later in the evening everyone gathered around the great pile of greens to sing the last of the Christmas carols. Then the greens were set ablaze.

"We do the same thing here, with a big banquet, caroling, and then we burn all the Christmas trees from that year."

My after dinner walk had now come full circle and I was once again standing at the front door of this old inn which dates well back into the 19th century. Through its windows I could see the last happy dinner guests preparing to leave, shaking hands with John and Ruth. Those of us who were remaining overnight, would all gather the next morning for one of John's great Vermont breakfasts. He would be off a little earlier tomorrow because it was his day to teach cooking at the St. Johnsbury Academy. Incidentally, he took the entire class to Paris last year.

As I turned for one last look at the landscape, it seemed entirely appropriate that the Anglo-Saxon custom of the Bleeze would find new roots at this warm country inn at Lower Waterford, Vermont.

RABBIT HILL INN, White Village, Lower Waterford, Vt. 05848; 802-748-9766. A 20-room country inn on Rte. 18, 10 mi. east of St. Johnsbury, Vt. Marvelous panoramic view of the Presidential Range of the White Mountains. European Plan. Breakfast and dinner served to travelers daily except Tuesdays during the winter months. Dining room closed Christmas Eve and Christmas Day. Xc-ski on the grounds. Tennis, swimming, riding nearby. For mountain scenery lovers. John and Ruth Carroll, Innkeepers.

Directions: From eastern Mass., follow I-93 to Littleton, N.H., then Rte. 18 west, 8 mi. to inn. From western Mass., follow I-91 to Rygate, Vt., then Rte. 5 north to McIndoes Falls. Cross river to Monroe, N.H., then travel north on Rte. 135 to Rte. 18. Turn left on Rte. 18, 1 mi. to inn.

KEDRON VALLEY INN, South Woodstock

The name of the book was "Ride Your Pony Right" by Frederick Devereux, Jr. It was a beginner's manual on horsemanship. I looked at it a few minutes and then asked Paul Kendall, "Isn't that your son Chip?" He smiled and said, "I saw you looking at that book. Yes, you're right, he is the horseman in all of those photographs. He's come a long way since the year he was thrown from the horse, hasn't he?"

Indeed he has, but everything at the Kedron Valley Inn has

come a long way since my first visit back in the mid-sixties. At that time Paul and Barbara Kendall, native Vermonters, had just taken over this old crossroads hostelry. They had two sons, Chip and Dane, who were at that beautifully precocious age. Now the sons and the inn have matured into young adulthood.

There has been an inn at this bend of the Kedron Brook dating back well into the last century. At one time the portion of it which was used as a dance hall was supported by large rubber balls! Evidently the country folk of that day really believed in whooping it up. The chances are that some of the dancing was done by Paul's grandmother and grandfather and probably his great grandfather, and great, great grandfather, since there have been Kendalls living in this valley for seven generations.

The Kedron Valley Inn has moved with the times. A few years ago Paul, realizing that some people appreciate more conventional accommodations, added a log house with more modern lodgings. Later a pond was created in back of the inn for swimming and fishing in the summer and ice skating in the winter.

Now additional emphasis is placed on horseback riding. This particular valley is the heart of Vermont riding country, and the nearby Green Mountain Horse Association has regularly scheduled trail rides and competition every summer. Paul fell in love with horses a few years ago and now everyone in the family rides. Furthermore there is a new horsebarn at the inn, with 26 horses available for guests to enjoy trail rides. People of similar trail riding ability are grouped together. I found it exhilarating to visit the horsebarn and see and touch those magnificent animals.

Now put all these ingredients together with the beauty of

Vermont mountains, the congeniality of young Vermont inn-keepers, Vermont food such as griddle cakes with maple syrup, corn muffins, country sausage, New England boiled dinners, maple syrup cured ham, local brook trout, Indian pudding, home-made pies, strawberry shortcake, and maple chiffon pie which is made by Paul's mother, and you've got the world's longest sentence.

Seriously, what you have at Kedron Valley is a most unusual New England country inn.

KEDRON VALLEY INN, Rte. 106, South Woodstock, Vt. 05071; 802-457-1473. A 34-room rustic resort-inn, 5 mi. south of Woodstock. Near Killington, and Mt. Ascutney ski areas. All Plans available. Breakfast, lunch and dinner served daily from May to Nov. Closed Sundays from Nov. to May. Closed Christmas and month of April. Swimming, riding, hiking, xc-ski on the grounds. Tennis, golf and bicycles nearby. Paul and Barbara Kendall, Innkeepers.

Directions: Take Exit 1 from I-89 and follow Rte. 4 to Woodstock. Proceed south on Rte. 106 for 5½ mi. Or, take Exit 8 from I-91 and follow Rte. 131 for 4 mi. Proceed north on Rte. 106 for 9 mi.

MIDDLEBURY INN, Middlebury

It was a dazzling bright day after a sizable all night snowstorm. All the principal roads leading to Middlebury were clear but the sideroads were still untouched. As I came up Route 7 from the south, the sign for the Middlebury Snowbowl, which has some of the best skiing in the East, both downhill and cross-country, beckoned to me. Approaching the town I could see the old weathered red bricks of the Middlebury Inn and when I pulled up in front some of the fresh snow was being shoveled off the terrace. The village green and town square looked sparkling bright and bustling at high noon.

In the rather large main lobby there was comfortable homey furniture that invited resting, reading and talking. The jigsaw puzzle on the big trestle table was a humdinger—two Chinese theatrical figures. I'm sure it would take many hours to get it together. In one corner there was a handsome collection of photographs of Middlebury and vicinity showing Vermont in all its beauty throughout the year. There was also a cribbage game awaiting two players and a kibitzer.

The Middlebury Inn is irrevocably connected with the college which, in addition to providing a stimulating academic atmosphere, also supplies a great deal of spectator sports and creative arts attractions for both townfolk and visitors alike. The town shops, including the Middlebury Book Store and the Frog Hollow Craft Center are most interesting.

Lodgings at the inn are quite varied. Those in the main building of the inn are rather unassuming and have tubs instead of showers. There is cable TV and innkeeper Dave Beach sees to it that there is an ample supply of books for those of us who may find ourselves in need of midnight reading. A few years ago some modern units were added in an annex next to the inn.

The Vermont influence on the inn menu is undeniable with roast native turkey and ham, popovers, apple pie and tasty cheese from Cabot, Vermont. One of the real treats is a maple syrup sundae.

As soon as the warm weather arrives, tables are set up on the terrace on the sunny side of the inn and it's great fun to enjoy luncheon or dinner and watch the panorama of the town pass by.

There's much to attract the traveler in this part of Vermont. The historic sites and the museums plus the beautiful scenery and back roads of the Green Mountains delight many people in all seasons.

As innkeeper Dave Beach says, "There's one thing about us—we're pure Vermont."

MIDDLEBURY INN, Middlebury, Vt. 05753; 802-388-4961. A 75-room college town inn midway between Burlington and Rutland in the Champlain Valley. Near Lake Dunmore, Lake Champlain, historic Fort Ticonderoga, the Morgan Horse Farm and Shelburne Museum. European Plan. Breakfast, lunch and dinner served daily to travelers. Open year-round. Golf, tennis, swimming, bicycles, Alpine and xc-ski nearby. David and Jean Beach, Innkeepers.

Directions: Middlebury is accessible by major highways from all directions. The inn is located at junction of Rtes. 7 and 125.

BLUEBERRY HILL, Goshen

Tony Clark and I were doing a quick run of one of the intermediate cross-country ski trails at Blueberry Hill. We stopped to enjoy the wondrous white stillness of the deep woods and he philosophized a bit. "A lot of places are called ski touring centers, but we feel a ski touring center should be so-named because it devotes itself entirely to cross-country skiing, keeps a fully equipped shop, and supplies instruction. In our case we have complete maps of all of our trails and we make sure that everyone signs in and out. We don't allow anyone to ski alone on the trails.

"We try to encourage people to look up and around in the woods when they ski and not just at their ski tips," he continued. "They don't have to be too concerned about the markers on the trails, but we do advise them to be observant at the points where trails intersect."

Blueberry Hill sits on top of a mountain right next to the Green Mountain National Forest. It is essentially an inn centering around the enthusiasm for cross-country skiing. Even when there is no snow, Blueberry Hill is marvelous in the upland Vermont springtime, and, of course, millions of words have been written about Vermont Fall foliage. The inn is open for both of those seasons and closed only in July and August.

Guests at Blueberry Hill feel like members of Tony and Martha's family, which includes two cross-country skiing sons. It is a good place to take children, providing they are prepared to be cross-country skiers. There are really no facilities for baby-sitting very young children.

Naturally in such a homey, informal atmosphere, everyone sort of wanders in and out of the big kitchen at will for cups of coffee and tea, particularly at the end of the day. Dinner is served at a big table where guests enjoy the family-style meal together. Lunch is not served. However, there is always a big pot of soup gurgling in the warming hut.

Dinner is something special at this inn. Martha Clark is like Audrey Patterson at the Chester Inn, a true gourmet cook. That evening we were treated to a dinner of Beef Bourguignon, spinach souffle, cheese soup and apple pie. All the breads, cakes and pies are baked in the cozy kitchen.

Lodgings are diversified. In the Main House, the rooms are done in a Vermont farmhouse style with old-fashioned beds and furniture. In the sections added recently to accommodate the additional numbers of cross-country ski enthusiasts, the rooms have barnsiding and bunk beds and are decorated with gay calico prints.

Anyone who likes Vermont mountains, warm hospitality which is basically informal, and particularly cross-country skiing, will certainly appreciate Blueberry Hill.

BLUEBERRY HILL FARM, Goshen, Vt. 05733; 802-247-6735. An 8-room mountain inn passionately devoted to cross-country skiing, 8 mi. from Brandon. Mod. American Plan omits lunch. Some rooms with shared bath. Meals not served to travelers. Open from September to April. Closed Christmas. Swimming, fishing and xc-ski on the grounds. Indoor tennis, Alpine ski and bicycles nearby. For nature and xc-ski lovers. Tony and Martha Clark, Innkeepers.

Directions: At Brandon, travel east on Rte. 73 through Forrestdale. Then follow signs to Blueberry Hill.

GREEN MOUNTAIN INN, Stowe

I love country inns because each one is unique, literally "one of a kind." Naturally, because I see so many, I see some similarities, but never have I ever failed to feel that wonderful quality of singularity. So it is with the Green Mountain Inn and its innkeeper, Parker Perry.

Parker Perry is a man born out of his time. I can see him at the prow of a ship headed from Scandinavia to Greenland. I can picture him writing plays for the court of Louis XIV. I can also hear him on the floor of Commons, denouncing the Prime Minister. There's a bit of Savonarola in him, a generous dash of Stein Erickson, and just a pinch of Robert Benchley.

Recently I enjoyed a long luncheon with him at the inn, and without realizing it, I left my tape recorder on, and later discovered some of Parker Perry's own gems of wisdom. All of them deal with his philosophy of innkeeping at the Green Mountain Inn.

"Where can you find fresh apple pie everyday all through the year? I said fresh because at the GMI we use only fresh apples. No canned apples, no frozen apples, no apple slush from a tub—just fresh apples. And our crust never comes out of a package. It's handmade by a 21-year-old girl who got the recipe from her grandmother. The girl is our pastry cook. Who says kids aren't cooking? There's a piece of Cabot Vermont Cheddar cheese served with it at lunch and dinner, and at breakfast too, if you wish.

"At the inn we have no deep-fat fryer. We feel that the deep-fat fryer is the curse of American cooking. But we do have homemade doughnuts at every breakfast, lunch and dinner. We just heat an iron kettle of fat and make doughnuts, probably like Mrs. Paul Revere did. Our New England food is better without a deep-fat fryer.

"It's a rare restaurant whose trash does not include one single open soup can," he said, gaining momentum. "We make all our own soups. You can't find our Vermont Cheddar Cheese soup or our yellow split pea soup made with Harrington hambones in a can."

That's the GMI. It has comfortable rooms which never need air-conditioning (according to the innkeeper), it has beautiful flower arrangements by the innkeeper's gracious wife, Dottie Perry. It has mountains, skiing, shopping, antiquing, back roading, and, perhaps most significant of all, it has Parker Perry.

GREEN MOUNTAIN INN, Main St., Stowe, Vt. 05672; 802-253-7301. A 61-room village inn on Rte. 100, 36 mi. from Burlington, 6 mi. from Mt. Mansfield, Vermont's highest peak. Mod. American Plan omits lunch. Breakfast, lunch, dinner served to travelers daily. Open Dec. 15 to April 15 and May 28 to Oct. 27. Golf, tennis, riding, hiking, bicycles, Alpine and xc-skiing nearby. For nature lovers. Parker and Dorothy Perry, Innkeepers.

Directions: From I-89, take Exit 10, and proceed on Rte. 100 to Stowe.

INN AT SAWMILL FARM, West Dover

I had driven the back roads from Chester to West Dover and now approached Sawmill Farm from the north. The Mt. Snow ski area was on my right and in just a few months the green slopes would be covered with snow and skiers. West Dover was next.

I drove all the way through the village, enjoying the colonial houses and old country church. Then I turned over the bridge into the inn parking lot. The late summer flowers such as Indian paintbrush, gentian, and roses were still in the garden. I went up the staircase in the rustic foyer, through the handsome living room and out into the terrace and pool area. Two people were sunning themselves in the September sun. They called out to me to join them for what turned out to be a very enjoyable chat. They told me that they had come to Sawmill as a result of reading about it in "a little book about country inns," and that it was just the kind of place they were hoping to find.

"We've been here for five days because it's so wonderfully peaceful. The food is superb and our room is so attractive. It has a stairway to a loft.

"We've been driving in the mountains, going to the Marlboro Concerts, and doing some antiquing. But we love to spend a great deal of our time here at the pool."

Right on cue, innkeepers Rod and Ione Williams appeared. They had just returned from a short trip, and I was glad to have the chance to catch up on the activity at the inn.

"Well, the pond which we started a couple of years ago has filled up exactly the way we had hoped," Rod remarked. "It's surprising how many of our guests love to simply sit at the edge and look at the hills.

"My son, Brill, has replaced Ione as the chef and we continually get compliments on our meals. Rack of lamb, fillet of sole, roast duck and tenderloin of beef are very popular. Incidentally, Brill has introduced the idea of serving apples stuffed with chestnuts, maple syrup and cheese, and also smoked Vermont ham on asparagus. We have several original Vermont dishes.

"Ione still makes a lot of the desserts but, as she says, 'Brill is first cook now.' Of course our daughter, Bobbie Dee, is very much involved in everything we're doing."

The Inn at Sawmill Farm is a very well-balanced mix of all of the elements which comprise a most enjoyable country inn experience. "Our prices are a little higher than other accommodations in the Mt. Snow area," Rod said, "but we really offer a great deal."

My friend at the pool summed up the situation rather well, I think, when he said, "When we come back, we're bringing our neighbors, because this is the kind of place you want to share with your friends."

INN AT SAWMILL FARM, Box 8, West Dover, Vt. 05356; 802-464-8131. A 15-room country resort-inn on Rte. 100, 22 mi. from Bennington and Brattleboro. Within sight of Mt. Snow ski area. Mod. American Plan omits lunch. Breakfast and dinner served to travelers daily except Wednesdays. Closed Thanksgiving. No children under 8. No pets. Swimming and trout fishing on grounds. Golf, tennis, bicycles, riding, snowshoeing, Alpine and xc-ski nearby. Rodney and Ione Williams, Innkeepers.

Directions: From I-91, take Exit 2 and travel on Vt. Rte. 9 west to Vt. Rte. 100. Proceed north 5 mi. to inn. Or, take US 7 north to Bennington, then Rte. 9 east to Vt. Rte. 100 and proceed north 5 mi. to inn.

THE BARROWS HOUSE, Dorset

Marilyn Schubert and I were seated next to the new swimming pool behind the Barrows House. It was a hazy afternoon at the end of summer, filled with the pungency of ripe apples from the nearby orchard. Some errant honeybees occasionally buzzed by in quest of the last drops of nectar from the late-blooming cosmos, phlox, asters and nasturtiums.

We were talking about the past year at the Barrows House. "I think this was the year that Charlie and I really came of age as innkeepers. We were ready for the big snows of winter with cross-country skiing equipment, but the big snows never came. Then gasoline became scarce, and there were some pretty quiet nights here in Dorset. But I will say this for Charlie, he never lost his good humor. In the face of an economic sag, he persisted, and we put in the swimming pool."

The pool looked beautiful to me with the gaily colored umbrellas, and the snack bar and changing room at poolside which were modeled after a country barn. Charlie announced that two tennis courts will be installed this spring. All around me were evidences of hard work and real dedication.

The Schuberts came up here from New Jersey to run a historic country inn, and now they are a part of a sturdy stock of emerging new, young innkeepers.

"Oh yes," Marilyn said, "we have to do everything, although I don't know how we would get along without our marvelous cook. Charlie, of course, is a wonder. I never knew that he could fix things. He's turned out to be a good builder and planner, too."

Yes, the setting and the scenery for a country inn are here. But I expect there is something else here as well. It is the same

kind of spirit that years ago sent people out of the comfortable eastern seaboard homes into the unknown perils of Kentucky and the Rocky Mountains. The perils and challenges are still here— as well as the rewards.

One of the rewards stands in the flower gardens at the Barrows House. It is a lovely little fountain which was a gift from one of the many appreciative guests.

BARROWS HOUSE, Dorset. Vt. 05251; 802-867-4455. A 24-room village inn on Rte. 30, 6 mi. from Manchester, Vt. Mod. American Plan, omits lunch. Breakfast, lunch and dinner served daily to travelers. Tennis courts, pool, bicycles, xc-ski facilities, including rental equipment and instruction, on grounds. Swimming, trout fishing, golf, tennis, paddle tennis, and Alpine ski nearby. Charles and Marilyn Schubert, Innkeepers.

Directions: From Rte. 7, proceed north on Rte. 30 at Manchester to Dorset.

CHESTER INN, Chester

"Ichabod Onion!" I exclaimed. "Come on, Jim, I know you're putting me on."

Jim Patterson laughed and said, "No, I'm serious. I couldn't believe it myself at first but I saw his name on a list of Chester's early settlers. There was also a Jabez Sergeant."

We were sitting under a brightly colored umbrella next to the swimming pool behind the Chester Inn. It was a pleasant, sunny day in midsummer. We were all having generous portions of the buffet luncheon and took turns holding Jim and Audrey

Patterson's new baby. I was surprised at how quickly I got back into the old ways once again. It was a warm, happy experience being in this Vermont village setting with good friends.

I had already noted that the trim on the inn had been changed from blue to white and the lobby had been completely redecorated in a beige tone. The mirrors, which cover one entire wall of the lobby, were all back in place, and when I asked Jim how he took them down, he replied, "Carefully, very carefully."

I was glad that I had arrived at midday because it was a good opportunity to talk with Audrey. Starting at 3:30 on most afternoons, she is very busy with preparations for dinner, and later on does most of the cooking. She dons an apron and creates interesting dinner entrees such as: Caneton aux Peches, which she explained was half a tender, plump duckling flamed in brandy at the table.

"We top it with fruit and a pungent peach sauce. I think it's a more interesting complement for duckling than the usual orange sauce."

Veal dishes are very big at the Chester including Veal Estragon which Audrey slices very thinly and then sautees in olive oil blending them with shallots, wine and fresh taragon. The veal is raised by local farmers and all the calves are milk fed.

This village inn is a busy place in all seasons. In winter it is convenient to five major ski areas, and there's ample opportunity for cross-country skiing. In warmer weather, guests use it for home base while exploring Vermont's back roads and antique shops. There's golf nearby, as well.

"I think our guests like the idea of coming to a Vermont village that is unspoiled," Jim said. "Here in Chester the folks

sit out on the front porch on a summer's evening. Then they might walk down to the store for a quart of chocolate ice cream."

I wondered what flavor Ichabod Onion would have preferred.

CHESTER INN, Chester, Vt. 05143; 802-875-2444. A 30-room village inn on Rte. 11, 8 mi. from Springfield, Vt. Convenient to several Vt. ski areas. Lodgings include breakfast. Lunch and dinner served to travelers daily except Mondays. Closed from late October to late November and mid-April to mid-May. No children under 5 in dining room. No pets. Pool, tennis and bicycles on grounds. Golf, riding, Alpine and xc-ski nearby. For antique lovers. Jim and Audrey Patterson, Innkeepers.

Directions: From I-91 take Exit 6. Travel west on Rte. 103 to Rte. 11.

NORTH HERO HOUSE, North Hero Island, Lake Champlain

"The Champlain Islands certainly have seen more than their share of American history," declared Caroline Sorg. "In 1609 Samuel de Champlain discovered this lake and landed at Isle la Motte which is just to the northwest of us. In 1704 the captives from the massacre of Deerfield were marched northward on the ice of Lake Champlain to Montreal. In 1759 Rogers' Rangers passed through on their famous expedition into Canada. In 1775 Ethan Allen, accompanied by Benedict Arnold, captured Fort Ticonderoga. This was the first victorious battle of the revolution.

"The Champlain Islands were later deeded to the Allens (Ethan and Ira) for their part in carving out Vermont's place in history."

North Hero House is the summertime endeavor of Dr. Roger Sorg, his wife Caroline, and their two lovely children, David and Lynn. Together they run this "island country inn" for 12 weeks each summer.

Vacation activities at or near the inn include boating, water skiing, sailing, snorkeling, fishing, tennis, bicycling, golf and horseback riding. It's a great location for back roading, antiquing, and relaxing for young and old.

Something new has been added or restored each year. An excerpt from a letter I received from Roger a few weeks before we went to press illustrates my point. "The Cove House on the water's edge has been completely restored for additional guests. Since 1800 it has been a private home, a tearoom, and has even had a cobbler's shop in the basement.

"This winter we are restoring the old ice house and turning it into a game room for our guests. This will provide additional pleasure for evenings and rainy days.

"We've put sliding glass doors at the west side of the dining room. They will look out upon a small flower garden. The effect will almost be that of outdoor dining.

"I'm sorry to tell you that the old elm tree which towered over the lake in front of the inn finally weakened and is gone. However, now we have in its place a magnificent view of the opposite shore and the Green Mountains beyond."

Roger, Caroline, David and Lynn have urged that I "come early and stay longer this summer," and I want to assure them that nothing will give me greater pleasure!

NORTH HERO HOUSE, North Hero, Vt. 05474; 802-372-8237. A 22-room New England resort-inn on North Hero Island in Lake Champlain, 35 mi. north of Burlington and 65 mi. south of Montreal. Mod. American Plan. Lunch by arrangement only. Breakfast and dinner served daily to travelers. Open from late-June to Labor Day. No pets. Swimming, fishing, boating, water skiing, bicycles and tennis on the grounds. Roger and Caroline Sorg, Innkeepers.

Directions: Travel north from Burlington on I-89, take Exit 17 (Champlain Islands) and drive north on Island Rte. 2 to North Hero. From N.Y. Thruway (87 north), take Exit 39 at Plattsburg and follow signs "Ferry to Vermont." Upon leaving ferry, turn left to Rte. 2, then left again to North Hero. Inn is 15 min. from ferry dock on Rte. 2.

Maritime Canada

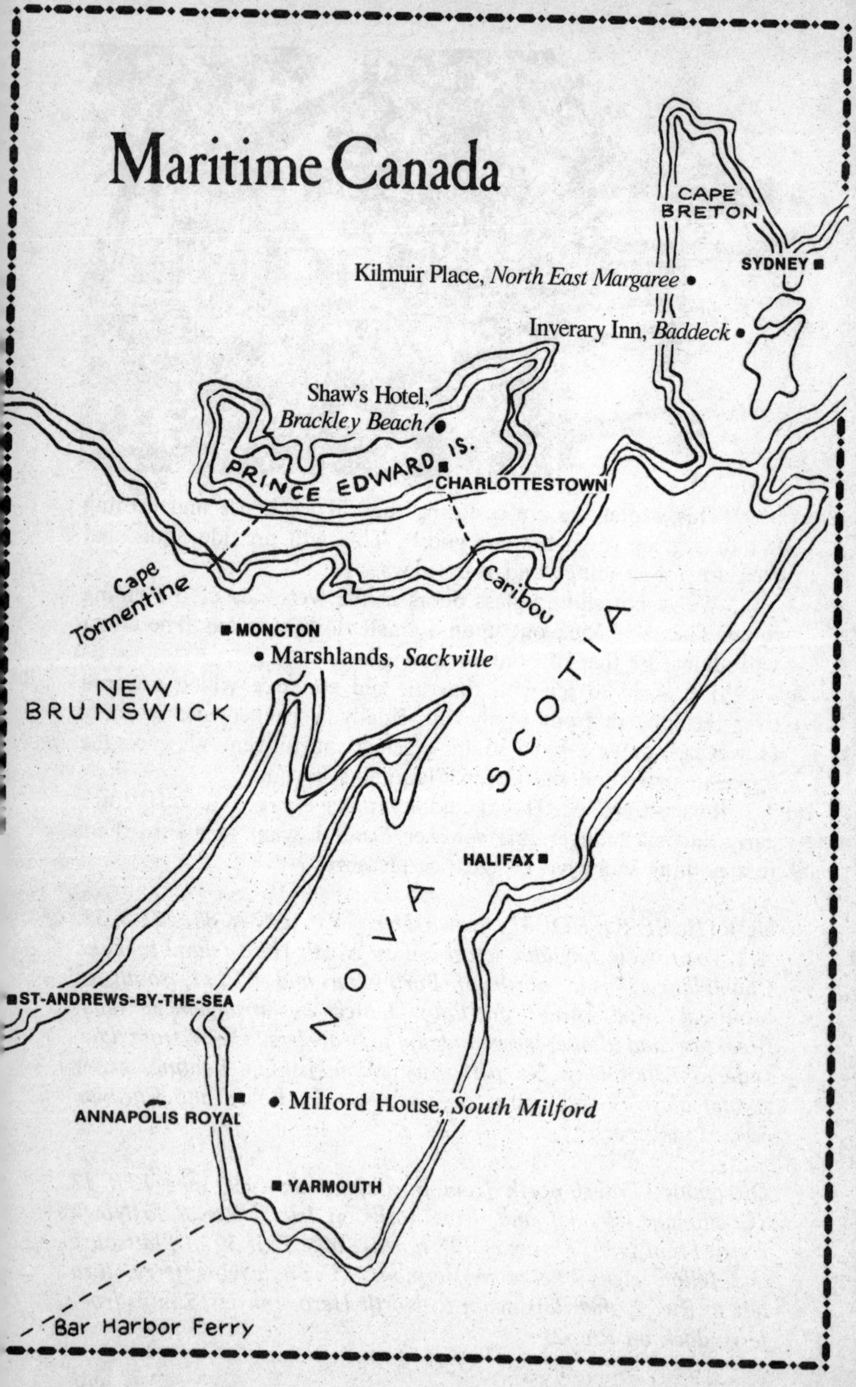

CAPE BRETON

SYDNEY

Kilmuir Place, *North East Margaree* ●

Inverary Inn, *Baddeck* ●

Shaw's Hotel, *Brackley Beach* ●

PRINCE EDWARD IS.

CHARLOTTESTOWN

Cape Tormentine

Caribou

■ MONCTON

● Marshlands, *Sackville*

NEW BRUNSWICK

NOVA SCOTIA

HALIFAX ■

■ ST-ANDREWS-BY-THE-SEA

● Milford House, *South Milford*

ANNAPOLIS ROYAL ■

■ YARMOUTH

Bar Harbor Ferry

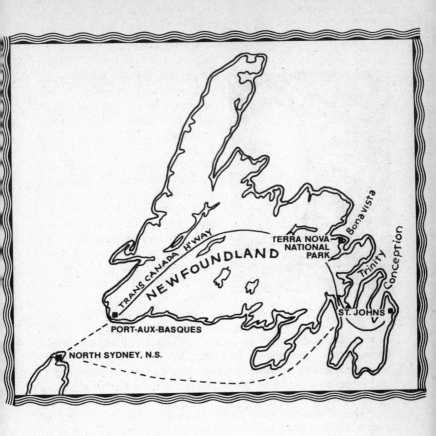

Canada's Maritime provinces provide adventuresome and rewarding travel. It can be as luxurious or conservative as you please. For years I've visited country inns in Nova Scotia and New Brunswick. In this edition, I'm happy to share my experiences during the summer of 1974 during a brief first-time visit to a country inn on Prince Edward Island. I've also included considerable detail about a three-day expedition to Newfoundland.

If you are a U.S. Citizen or a permanent resident you do not need a passport to visit Canada or a visa, but you can avoid possible delays by bringing something to establish your identity such as a birth, baptismal or voter's certificate.

NEWFOUNDLAND

THERE she was, white, beautiful and glistening in the afternoon sun. There was a magnificent serenity about her. She reminded me of a queen whose reign had been tempestuous, beset by enemies both within and without, but who had finally arrived at that period in her life where the storms were in the past. She could spend her remaining days in a sunlit placid bay, perhaps not monarch of all she surveyed, but at least an object of admiration, awe and respect.

She was an iceberg.

She was my first iceberg, and I will never forget her. I was to see literally thousands in the next two days but they would not be important. This was my first one. She didn't seem cold, lifeless or menacing. Her smooth sides and crenelated towers beckoned to me; however, I preferred this enchantment to be further enhanced by distance.

This infatuation was taking place between the villages of Hearts Content and Hearts Delight on the southern shores of Trinity Bay on the Avalon Peninsula of Newfoundland. It was 3 o'clock in the afternoon (1:30 in Boston) and I had been in this beautiful and sometimes remarkable Canadian province for about four hours.

I had come to Newfoundland (the correct pronunciation is New *Found* Land) in search of country inns and new and unusual experiences. In the short time I was there, I found very few country inns, but I did have many new and unusual experiences.

Newfoundland is an island with a population estimated at 525,000 and a capital city of more than 100,000. It has literally thousands of square miles of wilderness area without any roads, and some fishing ports that can only be reached by boat or by difficult dirt roads. I found incredible beauty in the coves and bays of the ruggedly indented coastline. I also found miles and miles of barrens with a kind of muskeg, a spongy vegetation about six or eight inches high with thousands of small ponds and lakes.

I had rented a car at the St. John's airport hoping to travel willy-nilly and "happen upon" a country inn, precisely at dinner and find a spic and span, quiet room awaiting me. Would it really happen?

The main road in Newfoundland, is the 535-mile extension of the Trans-Canada Highway (TCH) which runs from Port-Aux-Basques on the southwest corner in a semi-circle through several sizable towns to St. John's on the southeast corner. It is fully paved (don't laugh) throughout. However, the "outports" and remote locations inland are served by dirt roads.

My first real stop was Harbor Grace, a very pleasant town with a surprising amount of history and an excellent historical society. It is about halfway out to the end of the Avalon peninsula, about two and a half hours from St. John's. Harbor Grace is well-known as the origin of several important early trans-Atlantic airplane flights. There is a monument and plaque to the Pioneer Trans-Atlantic Fliers at the west end of the airport.

After looking around the village and visiting the Chamber of Commerce, I decided to cut over to the northern side of the peninsula, and here I arrived at the village of Hearts Delight, which was small, quiet and picturesque.

I wandered around taking photographs (by all means take a camera to N.F.) and chatted with some men in fishermen's caps and sweaters who were tossing fish up on the dock. I learned that this village was where the first Atlantic cable was laid in 1866. There was a little church that clung to the edge of the cliff over the water. It had its own little overgrown graveyard. Several sheep were grazing between the road and the bay.

Although I could have lingered here indefinitely, I decided to get as far as I could that first night, certain that I would find those idyllic lodgings at the precisely the right moment. I was following the course of the road, playing hide-and-seek among the bays and inlets, when I came upon my iceberg.

Fascinating though she was, I finally bade goodbye to my chilly friend, and continued on to Hearts Content, another fishing village. To my immense surprise, there the bay was filled with 948 icebergs! It looked like the Spanish Armada at Cadiz. There were floating white castles, small skyscrapers, super dreadnoughts, graceful yachts, silos, Victorian mansions, Moorish mosques, Frank Lloyd Wright houses, Spanish haciendas, 3-stack destroyers, aircraft carriers—every imaginable shape, and some beyond imagination.

I was to see many more icebergs, and while they have an

awesome type of cold beauty, they were nonetheless totally out of season and were preventing the fishermen of this section of Newfoundland from getting out into the Atlantic. In conversation with the local people I learned that overnight they might all disappear, carried by wind and tide to still another bay!

Again, I forced myself to continue the journey, and drove back to the TCH. I was ready for dinner. There was one problem—this was Dominion Day Weekend, and when I arrived at Clarenville, I could not find restaurant or lodgings. I needed a meal, a bath and a good night's sleep.

I decided to leave Trans-Canada and drive out on the Bonavista peninsula, feeling it might be less crowded. I called ahead to a guest house who reported a vacancy. I sighed with relief, and then because they were not serving dinner, went to a grocery store and purchased my first meal at Newfoundland—a quart of ice cream.

In the dark of night in an unfamiliar land, I found my lodgings, a two-story cinder-block building with a restaurant on one side of the first floor, and a sort of barroom-cum-billiard parlor on the other. Upstairs were thirteen rooms all of which shared one bath. These were austere to say the least. I was to see quite a few accommodations similar to this on the roads in Newfoundland.

Up early the next morning, I continued on to the sizable town of Port Union. The streets were very narrow, the tides were in and there were a few small merchant ships unloading. There's very little pretension here, and the further you get away from St. John's the more basic everything becomes.

I continued out to the town of Bonavista where there was only one overnight accommodation, the Oh Happy Sight Motel.

(Continued on page 280)

NEWFOUNDLAND TRAVEL SUGGESTIONS

How To Get There

By air: *Use Air-Canada and Eastern Provincial Airways. Connections can be made from all major centers in United States and Canada.*

By surface routes: *Two ferries serve Newfoundland. Both leave from North Sydney, Nova Scotia. One goes to Port-aux-Basques, N.F., on the southwest corner. The other goes to Argentia on the southeast corner, 80 miles from St. John's. To reach North Sydney from the US and Canada, the traveler can take the land route through New England, New Brunswick, and proceed to Cape Breton and North Sydney, or take a ferry from Bar Harbor or Portland, Maine, to Yarmouth, Nova Scotia, and then go to Cape Breton. It is possible to plan an auto trip from Missouri, Michigan, North Carolina and Toronto and stay each night at inns mentioned in this volume.*

Transportation After You Get There

Rental cars are available but reserve in advance. A four-wheel vehicle with sleeping facilities will take the guess-work out of the accommodations problem and enables the traveler to go anywhere. There is also bus service from both ferries but schedules should be obtained. (See "What To Bring Along.") Busses are in wide use.

Accommodations

There is a wide range, however, the number is relatively small. They range from luxury hotels to plain and simple guest houses with as few as two rooms. With careful planning the traveler should be able to use conventional accommodations. However, this method does not allow for much improvisation in the schedule. There are many campsites available in the province including 46 excellent provincial parks and two national parks.

What To Bring Along

Driver's license, proof of liability insurance coverage, naturalization certificate or proof of US citizenship (at border), map, two booklets: "Where To Stay In Newfoundland and Labrador," and "Newfoundland and Labrador Transportation and Roads." For these write: Newfoundland Department of Tourism, Confederacy Building, St. John's, Newfoundland.

A SAMPLING OF NEWFOUNDLAND ACCOMMODATIONS

I personally saw these:

WHITE SAILS INN, (A country inn), Eastport, Route 310. 5 rooms and 5 housekeeping cabins, meals provided for guests. Open from June 15—September 30. 709-677-3400. Reservations needed.

TERRA NOVA PARK BUNGALOWS, Terra Nova Park, Route 1, 24 housekeeping units each with a private shower. Restaurant. Open from May 1—October 31. 709-533-2213 (Off Season) 709-533-2298 (Season)

PROMINENT SPUR INN, Port Union, Route 230. 7 rooms with private washroom, sharing 2 public baths. Open all year. Restaurant. 709-469-2257.

ANCHOR INN, Port Union, Route 230. 8 rooms, all with wash basins, sharing 2 public baths. Restaurant. Open all year. 709-469-2591.

OH HAPPY SIGHT MOTEL, Bonavista, Route 230. 15 rooms all with private baths. Open all year. Restaurant. 709-468-7811.

TRINITY CABINS, Trinity, Route 230. 10 housekeeping cabins. Open from May 15—October 15. 709-464-3657 (Season) 709-464-3720 (Off-Season).

(continued on page 282)

120

Nova Scotia

"A WEE BIT O' HISTORY"

Nova Scotia (New Scotland) is the land of Longfellow's Evangeline, the land of the Acadians. These French people settled there in 1605 and founded Port Royal (now Annapolis Royal in southern Nova Scotia).

In 1621, Sir William Alexander was granted the peninsula and adjoining islands by the English Crown and trouble followed. In 1710 the British captured Port Royal. In 1713 France gave up all claim to the peninsula but not to Cape Breton island. In 1745, American soldiers and British ships besieged and captured the citadel of Louisburg, and in 1755, the British loaded the Acadians aboard ships and took them off to the French colony of Louisiana.

In 1758, British land and sea forces under General Jeffrey Amherst had to recapture Louisburg all over again. This time by the terms of the Treaty of Paris, France ceded Cape Breton island to England

Under the circumstances, it was not likely that in 1775 the Nova Scotians cared much either way what was going on with those Americans down to the south of them. Following the Revolutionary War, many Americans loyal to the King were deported to Canada. Some going to Halifax, Nova Scotia, and others to St. Andrews, New Brunswick, among other places.

INVERARY INN, Baddeck

It was about two minutes to eight on a sunny June morning. I was sitting in the parlor of the Inverary Inn as the sun streamed across Lake Bras d'Or and lighted up the delicate pieces of glassware in the windows. There were delicious aromas coming from the kitchen. In a few moments a Scottish breakfast of applesauce, oatmeal porridge with cream, mharagh and home fries, bannoch, and Scottish oatcakes would be brought in by the waitresses from the village.

Inverary is indeed a Scottish inn in Cape Breton, Nova Scotia.

In fact, the strong Scottish influence was one of the points of discussion the previous evening with some rather well-traveled

121

guests. They compared it favorably with English, Welsh and Irish inns that they had visited.

I hasten to add that although there is a strong Scottish feeling here at the Inverary, the food is not all Scottish. For example, the dining room, besides being famous for bannochs and oatcakes, is also well-known for many different ways to cook Nova Scotia Salmon, which has probably been caught the same day.

Isobel MacAulay, the keeper of this little gem, came through the parlor, opened the dining room doors and announced in her fetching Scottish brogue that breakfast was ready and she wished us all a good meal and a good day.

After making sure that everything was running along smoothly, she was able to join me for a cup of coffee. "Oh, we have been getting many visitors from *Country Inns and Back Roads*," she said. "Quite a few of them are Canadians too," she added. "They've come across Canada from Vancouver and the western provinces. They all want to see that Cape Breton bedwarmer that you mentioned in your last edition."

The dining room was filling up now with people getting an early start either to "do" the Cabot Trail, or perhaps go to North Sydney to take the ferry to Newfoundland. Some also would be regretfully starting their journey home. There was a flurry when everyone was comparing notes and making suggestions as to ferry schedules and things not to miss. As you can imagine, we were quite a lively group.

And lively is one of the good words to describe the Inverary. It is interesting to see the faces of newly-arriving guests light up as they step on the porch and into the parlor. In many cases, it's been a long ride, possibly from the Marshlands Inn in New Brunswick, but I can tell that they feel they have come to the right spot.

The Inverary just might be the most famous country inn in Nova Scotia.

INVERARY INN, Box 190, Baddeck, Cape Breton, N.S. 902-295-2674. A 40-room village inn on the Cabot Trail, 52 mi. from Sydney, N.S. On the shores of Lake Bras d'Or. European Plan. Some rooms with shared bath. Breakfast and dinner served to travelers daily. Open from May 15 to November 1. Bicycles and children's playground on the grounds. Boating and small golf course nearby. For nature lovers. Isobel MacAulay, Innkeeper.

Directions: Follow Trans-Canada Hwy. to Canso Causeway to Baddeck.

KILMUIR PLACE, Northeast Margaree

"I've never used a mix in my life, and never will." Isabel Taylor stood with her hands on her hips, tossed her head back and her eyes flashed. "After all, my mother and father started this place over 50 years ago and our guests love the old-fashioned ways. I can tell the difference when something is made from a mix, and I'm sure everybody else can too."

"Indeed they do. And I'm a guest that has been coming for 40 straight years."

This time the speaker was a lady from Philadelphia who walked into Isabel and Ross' cozy kitchen as if on cue.

"In those days it took some persistence and motivation to come out to the Margaree," she said settling down into one of the comfortable upholstered chairs in one corner of the kitchen. "Now you can get here from Sydney in about an hour and a half and from Halifax in about three and a half hours. In the old days the roads weren't paved and sometimes Ross had to get a team to pull us out of the mud."

Ross asked her if she would like to have another piece of his chocolate cake, reminding her that he had been up at the crack of dawn that morning making it. She demurred, saying that she couldn't possibly eat another bite.

While we were chatting, Isabel deftly carved a generous slice of roast beef and poured pan gravy over a big helping of mashed potatoes on my plate. She topped it off with some cauliflower.

"Here you are," she said, "if you don't mind eating in the kitchen." Well, I've never eaten anywhere but in the kitchen at the Kilmuir Place. It's the one way to find out what Ross and Isabel have been doing over the past winter.

"Well, one thing we do is feed birds all winter. They keep us company. All of the summer birds come back every year. Tell your friends to bring their binoculars and notebooks. This is really good bird country."

The Kilmuir Place became known for the fine salmon fishing on the Margaree. Ross knows all the good fishing holes in this most beautiful of rivers. Now, however, guests also come to the Kilmuir to tour the Cabot Trail and enjoy a few days of rest, reading and conversation.

I must add that this is a very tiny inn. It has only three rooms with private bath and two of them without. Don't even think of coming without a reservation.

But when you do come, be prepared to wish fervently on the day you leave that you could stay several days longer.

KILMUIR PLACE, Northeast Margaree, Cape Breton, N.S. BOE2HO; 902-248-2877. A 5-room country inn on Rte. 19, 28 mi. from Baddeck. American Plan. Some rooms with shared baths. Breakfast, lunch and dinner served to travelers by reservation. Open from June to mid-October. Salmon fishing in the Margaree River, touring the Cabot Trail and both fresh water and salt water swimming nearby. For salmon fishing lovers. Mr. and Mrs. Ross Taylor, Innkeepers.

Directions: After crossing Canso Causeway to Cape Breton, follow either Rte. 19 (coast road to Inverness) and turn right on Cabot Trail at Margaree Forks, or follow Rte. 105 and turn left on Cabot Trail at Nyanza.

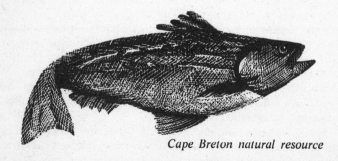

Cape Breton natural resource

REVISITING CAPE BRETON

THIS time I decided to do the Cabot Trail counter-clockwise. I left Baddeck, traveling next to the shores of Lake Bras d'Or, past the Alexander Graham Bell Museum and up the beautiful green valley leading north toward Ingonish.

I passed the Gaelic College of St. Ann's where a Gaelic Mod (a gathering) is held once a year. There are dances and craft exhibitions and it's an opportunity for people of different Scottish clans to come together.

When I crested the hills, there before me was a beautiful view of St. Ann's Bay where the pastures lead down to the ocean. It was a landscape typical of Cape Breton. On this glistening morning there were just a few whitecaps on the bay. This is the part of the Cabot Trail which closely resembles Scotland, but I was to learn that there were many other faces and aspects of this truly remarkable wild land.

I arrived at Cape Smoky where there had been a serious forest fire a number of years ago. The dead trees stood stark and lifeless. A large group of these are cut down and carted away each year and new ones are being planted to overcome the effects of this fire. Nature has also provided some second growth bushes, but the great stand of trees that was here before the fire is gone. This "burn-over" makes us acutely aware of what happens when man is careless about his ecological surroundings.

The road wound its way up Smoky and the top afforded a magnificent view of the water, sky and sun. The descent led past a ski area and curved its way around a cove into Ingonish village.

In Ingonish I stopped for a few moments to wander around the grounds of the *Keltic Lodge* and to enjoy a cup of hot chocolate at the coffee shop which overlooks Ingonish Bay. This large luxury resort operates for two and a half months each summer. It is a Provincial showplace.

From Ingonish, the Cabot Trail runs for quite a few miles next to the Atlantic Ocean at sea level. There are several turnouts where the traveler can park his car and climb among the red, black and bleached white rocks next to the sea.

There are dozens of tiny inlets and coves where the road twists, turns and switches back. Now and then a larger cove with a swimming beach comes into view.

I decided to take the one sizable side road off the Cabot Trail which leads eleven miles out to Bay St. Lawrence, a small fishing village on Cape North.

The houses and church of Bay St. Lawrence were clustered around a small, remarkably sheltered cove. There is a narrow passage from the ocean (it couldn't be more than thirty or forty yards wide), and the 25 or 30 fishing boats looked quite snug and safe against the Atlantic storms. I drove to the end of the village past the stacked lobster pots and the houses with their marvelous silver-grey weatherbeaten finish, to the point where the road actually stops at a dock on the edge of the water. I was caught up for the moment in the immense mystery of the sea beckoning me like a Lorelei to find what shores lay beyond.

It was June and still late spring here in this little community on the far reaches of Cape Breton. The flowering bushes were in bloom, the red-winged blackbirds were calling to one another and there was still a hint of chill in the air. In spite of the wild beauty of the place, which was a meeting of mountains, sea and valley, it looked like a hard life. I drove slowly back through the village, past the homes, the church and the school, pausing for just a moment on a small hill to take one last look before pressing on. It was here that I noticed the legend formed by whitewashed cobblestones on the side of the hill in front of the cemetery. It read, "Pray For Us."

Now the Trail led upward through the Cape Breton Highlands. At times it was carved out of the sides of heavily forested mountains. At the top, the Gulf of St. Lawrence seemed awesome in its blue vastness. Then the road once again twisted and turned like a roller coaster down to the water's edge. Every few feet there was a new and unique view of land and sea. Rushing streams came leaping through the mountains into the Gulf.

For the next fifteen miles the road ascended, clinging precariously to the tops of the mountains. Here and there the ocean had washed away portions of the land leaving cliff islands which have become disconnected from the main land mass. They seemed close enough to touch. The immensity of land, sea and sky contributes to a sea and landscape almost beyond description.

Now the road capriciously dropped from dizzying heights to the fishing village of Cheticamp. The predominant landmark of this small town is the church of St. Pierre. It's towering spire visible from far out in the gulf has been a heartening sight to generations of village fisherfolk.

At Cheticamp, things had changed in three years. I found a few more motels and restaurants interspersed among the older buildings and fishing shacks. The town is growing. There are at least two new supermarkets built since my last visit and in

126

some ways it appears to be like a New England fishing village not too distant from Boston or Portland. Cheticamp, however, is in quite another world.

As the road continued south, the vista continuously changed. The road runs along the seaside meadows with occasional little clusters of Cape Breton cottages which are subjected to rigorous northern winters, for they are fully exposed to the chill winds from the St. Lawrence Gulf. Here and there I saw a vegetable garden or a cow, but it is a short growing season and a long winter.

From Margaree Harbor the Trail turns inland along the beautiful Margaree River. There are actually two roads, one on each side of the river. This time I chose the one on the south side, and found a village called Belle-Cote which stretches along the north side. It looked like a fairy tale town. The lowering sun cast a golden haze over river, meadows, hills and houses. It all seemed quite unreal.

Once again I stopped off at the *Kilmuir Place* to visit Ross and Isabel Taylor and to talk of things past, present and future.

The trip on the Cabot Trail, for all intentions, had been completed. With an early start I was able to traverse it in one span of daylight hours. This, of course, is where the fallacy lies. It should be taken slowly to savor each new experience, each new vista.

Before returning to Baddeck, I stopped, as I have on each visit to Nova Scotia, for a quiet moment at a little church near Bucklaw. It has served generations of these hardy God-loving folk who find in Cape Breton a beauty and a challenge which extend beyond material things.

The province of Nova Scotia supplies extremely good maps out-lining trips that circle almost the entire island. This time I fol-lowed the Lighthouse Trail, which is Route 103 and Route 3, from Halifax and Chester, Mahone Bay, Peggy's Cove, Lunen-burg, Liverpool, and Lockeport. By the way, they're still search-ing for Captain Kidd's pirate treasure which is supposed to be buried on Oak Island. This particular section has beautiful south shore beaches and many, many lighthouses. The trip from Yar-mouth on the Bay of Fundy side through Meteghan, Littlebrook, Weymouth and Digby to Annapolis Royal has many small ship-building yards. It is a delightful experience, and one that I shall always remember.

MILFORD HOUSE, South Milford

Once again it was Wendy Miller who was my guide at the Milford House. This time, on a pleasant September afternoon, I found myself in a canoe with Wendy at the bow and her friend Macy Lawrence in the stern. They were paddling me swiftly across the lake to see more of the rustic cottages on the Point.

All around me were the woodlands of southern Nova Scotia, the many varieties of spruce, pine, balsam, hemlock, maples, birches, oaks, poplars, and ashes. Within the forest, on the banks of the lakesland in the meadows, there was an endless variety of flowers. As far as birds were concerned, this part of the world is a "birders" paradise. When I asked Wendy about this she said, "We have lists of birds as well as flowers and trees for anyone who wants them."

To me it is tremendously fascinating that there actually is a country inn in the midst of this great natural paradise. Further-more, it is owned and managed by considerate people who are tremendously involved with the preservation of the environment and the ecology.

The Milford House is a flashback to the early days of the 20th century when people from Canada and the U.S. came and stayed for months at a time. It is an old-fashioned place with turn-of-the-century rugs, furniture and decor. The parlors and living rooms have a "country elegance."

The country food served in the big dining room reminded me of my visits to my aunt and uncle's farm in New York State. There are homemade breads and pastries, fresh berries and vege-tables, and fresh fish (they will cook yours if you catch them).

We arrived at the cabins and Wendy was anxious for me to see how they had been redecorated. They're all very neat and furnished cabin-style and are within a few steps of the lake.

These cabins are spread out along a series of lakes within a short walk of the main inn. Each has a dock, a fireplace and all the conveniences including electricity and maid service.

We walked back through the woods, checking the cabins and I asked her about whether children would have a good time here.

"Oh yes. More and more people are bringing children and staying for a longer time. I'm pretty involved in keeping them amused and happy. It's not hard because there's so much to do. I teach them how to paddle, and we take them to the Kemjimku-jik National Park. One thing about those city kids is that they really eat. I think that being in the woods gives them a big appetite."

I enjoy my visits with Wendy and her mother and father at the Milford House. Like all of the other departing guests, I have a lump in my throat when I drive away and they're all standing on the porch waving good-bye.

MILFORD HOUSE, R.R. #4, South Milford, Nova Scotia, BOS IAO; 902-532-2617. A rustic resort-inn with 24 cabins on 600 acres of woodlands and lakes, 90 mi. from Yarmouth, N.S. Near Kemjimkujik National Park. Mod. American Plan. Breakfast, lunch and dinner served to travelers daily. Open from June 20 to September 10. Tennis, fishing, croquet, canoeing, bird-watching, and swimming on the grounds. Riding, deep-sea fishing and golf nearby. Warren and Margaret Miller, Innkeepers.

Directions: From Yarmouth, follow Rte. 1 to traffic lights in Annapolis Royal. Turn right and continue on to Rte. 8, 15 mi. to inn.

PRINCE EDWARD ISLAND

I WAS on the ferry from Caribou, Nova Scotia to Wood's Island, Prince Edward Island (PEI), and it was a delightful experience. The ferry was quite clean (not always true of ferries) and the food in the little lunchroom was wholesome and inviting. There was even a tourist office on board, and a two-way radio connection with PEI to make reservations from a wide choice of accommodations.

This particular trip was made even more interesting by a large group of French school children from the Magdalen Islands who were returning from an excursion to Nova Scotia. It came as a surprise to me to realize that they spoke no English. However, they sang French songs during most of the one and a half hour trip. I recorded some of them and then played them back so all could hear. It was really fun.

The PEI traveler needs three things: a map, a copy of a well-planned booklet entitled "Accommodations on PEI," and finally, schedules for the ferries between Cape Tormentine, New Brunswick, and Borden, PEI, and the Caribou-Woods Island ferry. This information can be obtained from Box 940, Charlottetown, PEI, CIA 7 M 5.

We docked at Wood's Island. My friends bade me a lyrical "au revoir," and I started toward Charlottetown on Route 1. My first impression was an excellent one—broad fields, clean well kept farmhouses, an abundance of cattle on the gently rolling landscape. It was the start of the growing season here in mid-June and some of the crops were just poking their heads out of the ground while others stood three or four inches high.

On the outskirts of Charlottetown a sign indicated that Route 2 was the bypass to the north side of the island. About thirty minutes later Route 2 turned into Route 6 and I came into Dalvay Beach, the first of several beaches bordering the Gulf of St. Lawrence.

These beaches stretch out for miles on the north side and all are clean and most inviting. There are "changing houses" at regular intervals. The bright sunshine and pristine sand were more than I could resist, so I took a few minutes to test the water and

it was surprisingly warm for mid-June. Later it would go as high as 70 degrees.

After an early dinner at Shaw's Hotel, I set out in search of the town of Cavendish to see the famous Green Gables Cottage.

It was a beautiful evening with plenty of lingering daylight since PEI is on Atlantic time (one hour later than Boston). The cattle were contentedly standing in the high grass and the lilacs were at the peak of their glory. This part of the island is extremely attractive. It is easy to get lost on the fascinating roads that crisscross the meadows and wind their way around the inlets and bays. After a visit at a pleasant little fishing village called Rustico, I came to the town of Cavendish. I am sure that everyone who visits PEI eventually finds their way to the typical Prince Edward Island House with three gables which has been set aside in memory of Lucy Maude Montgomery, the author of *Anne of Green Gables*. Actually Anne is a fictional character, but her story has been read by millions and this small, tidy house is a fitting memory to the author.

That evening I made several stops at tourist houses and farm vacation homes which are quite plentiful on the island. As a rule these are run by people who have big houses and have set aside rooms with a shared bath, for the benefit of summer tourists. Most include breakfast in the price of the room. I found one country inn, Shaw's Hotel, but I'm hopeful of finding others in the future.

A traveler visiting PEI during the height of the season should plan to find sleeping accommodations as near midday as possible, because locating rooms later in the day could be something of a squeeze. In July and August there is an increasing number of people who are drawn to the island because of its reputation for fine beaches, pleasant weather, and beautiful, gentle scenery.

Because of the unusual number of tourists during the summer, lobster dinners are served almost every night by various church and civic organizations.

I found Prince Edward Island delightful and so have many others. The result is that there are many more people than one might expect. I'm returning in September of 1975 for a longer visit.

**SHAW'S HOTEL, Brackley Beach,
Prince Edward Island, Canada**

I never thought that I could be this far north and find swimming water so wonderfully warm and enjoyable. The odd part about it was that only two days before I'd been in Newfoundland where the bays on the Atlantic side were chock full of icebergs. However, here in the gulf of St. Lawrence on the north side of Prince Edward Island it was so comfortable, pleasant and warm that it reminded me of Palm Beach in February.

I had arrived early in the afternoon, having taken the ferry from Caribou, Nova Scotia. I was filled with anticipation for this was my first trip to P.E.I. and Shaw's Hotel. Both more than exceeded my expectations.

I found that Shaw's was a part of an original pioneer farm, started in 1793. It became a hotel in 1860 and today it is still an operating farm with beef cattle and other farm animals. The barns are big and beautiful.

Some of the accommodations are in the main building which

is a Victorian house with a brilliant red mansard third story. There are also individual cottages which can accommodate from two to eight people each. These are spaced far enough apart on the property to ensure complete privacy. Each of them has its own fireplace.

The place has many trees and broad meadows. The view from the dining room window included a sailboat bobbing about in the bay. There was a good mix of both Canadian and American guests and we all agreed that the food, which featured fresh fish such as salmon, lobster, mackerel, and halibut, was excellent.

My arrival was timed with another one of a more auspicious nature. One of the two big sheep dogs had just given birth to a litter of six beautiful puppies. This was much to the delight of several children vacationing there.

Gordon Shaw says that he has had as many as thirty or forty children at one time in the height of the season. "There's always plenty of elbow room," he says. "We don't have any trouble keeping the parents of all these children amused either. Besides the beach there are riding horses nearby which is fun, especially along the beach and on the bridle paths. We have the sailboat on the bay and golf and tennis nearby.

"We're located in the sticks, at the end of the road—the best location of any resort on P.E.I. The beach is the big attraction. The water is seventy degrees and in the bay it gets even warmer. The temperature goes up to ninety here in midsummer."

Well, I could attest to that. It was mid-June and there I was in swimming and loving every minute of it!

SHAW'S HOTEL and Cottages, Brackley Point Road, Brackley Beach, Prince Edward Island, Canada COA 2HO; 902-672-2022. A 24-room country hotel within walking distance of Brackley Beach, 15 mi. from Charlottetown. American Plan. Some rooms with shared baths. 10 guest cottages. Breakfast, lunch, dinner served to travelers daily. Open from June 15 to September 15. Pets allowed in cottages only. Tennis, golf, bicycles, riding, sailing and beach nearby. For ocean-bathing lovers. Gordon Shaw, Innkeeper.

Directions: Prince Edward Island is reached either by ferry from Cape Tormentine, New Brunswick (near Moncton), or Caribou, Nova Scotia. In both cases, after arriving on P.E.I., follow Rte. 1 to Charlottetown, then Rte. 15 to Brackley Beach. P.E.I. is also reached by Eastern Provincial Airways and Canadian National Railways.

New Brunswick

I'm resolved to see a great deal more of New Brunswick in the near future. This includes another visit to St. Andrews (1974 edition) to enjoy some heavenly lobster and an overnight stay at a trim little inn called The Gables *(506-529-3337). I'll also visit the* Elm Lodge Inn *in St. Stephen (506-466-3771), just over the border from Calais, Maine. This is now owned by Pat Garbutt of the* Willow Place Inn *in Como, Quebec. Either of these would make an ideal stopover before pushing on to the* Marshlands Inn *in Sackville, New Brunswick.*

MARSHLANDS INN, Sackville, New Brunswick, Canada

We were an interesting little group. There was a gentleman from Saskatchewan who was on his way to Cape Breton to do some fishing. A lady and gentleman from Toronto were on their way home from visiting some relatives in Halifax, Nova Scotia. There was also a young honeymooning couple from Detroit who had stayed in a different Berkshire Traveller Inn for the past four nights. They would be leaving in the morning for the Inverary at Baddeck, Nova Scotia.

We were all sitting together in front of the fireplace in the living room sipping the delicious hot chocolate offered every evening at the Marshlands. Innkeeper Herb Read says, "This is for guests who simply aren't able to wait until breakfast time."

The Marshlands is literally at the crossroads. It is a perfect single day's drive from inns in both Cape Breton and Annapolis Royal. It's on the land route from the U.S. through New England to Nova Scotia, Prince Edward Island, and Newfoundland. Many of the guests stay on for an extra night or two to see the famous "tidal bore" which is visible in the nearby Bay of Fundy, or to play some golf and enjoy some hiking and swimming nearby. There is also curling.

Almost all of the letters I get from our readers who have visited here mention two things: first, the unusually extensive collection of 19th century antiques throughout the inn and guest rooms which have obviously been here from the very beginning; and second, the food.

We were talking about the food while enjoying the chocolate that evening. The gentleman from Saskatchewan had had the Atlantic salmon and couldn't say enough about it. I had thoroughly enjoyed one of my favorite dishes, curried lamb served with the Marshlands' own chutney. The young honeymooning couple had tried the fresh Miramichi salmon. His was served grilled and hers was poached with an egg sauce. Everyone agreed that the fiddlehead greens were a delicacy.

While we were exchanging travel experiences I somewhat shamefacedly admitted that before my first visit I thought that Sackville was about fifteen miles south of the polar icecap. The Canadian couple came to my rescue by admitting that they, too, had a total misconception of New Brunswick.

The hour was getting late. Someone remarked that breakfast was served starting at 7 a.m. so we could get an early start.

We all said "good night" and promised to meet for breakfast, unwilling to break the chain of friendship we had begun in the handsome inn in not-so-faraway New Brunswick.

MARSHLANDS INN, Box 1440, Sackville, New Brunswick, Canada EOA 3CO; 506-536-0170. A 10-room village inn near Tantramar Marshes and Fundy Tides. European Plan. Some rooms with shared baths. Breakfast, lunch and dinner served to travelers daily. Closed during the Christmas season. Golf, xc-ski, curling, hiking and swimming nearby. Herb and Alice Read, Innkeepers.

Directions: Follow Trans-Canada Highway to Sackville, then Rte. 6, 1 mi. to center of town.

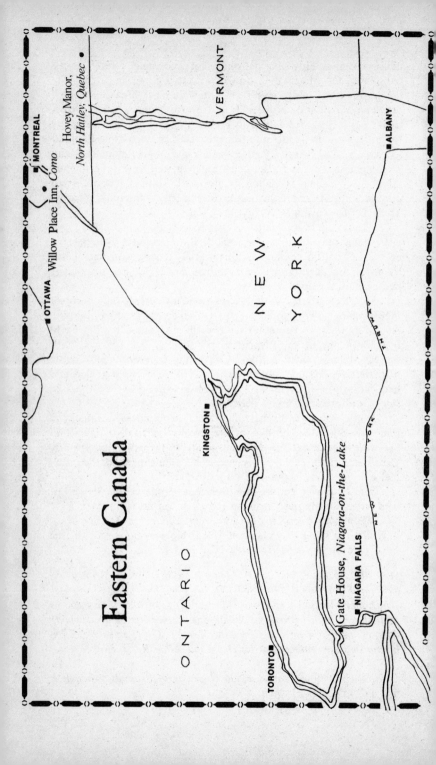

Eastern Canada

ONTARIO

TORONTO

NIAGARA FALLS

Gate House, *Niagara-on-the-Lake*

KINGSTON

OTTAWA Willow Place Inn, *Como*

MONTREAL

Hovey Manor,
North Hatley, Quebec

VERMONT

NEW
YORK

ALBANY

NEW YORK THRUWAY

Quebec

Although I dare say that most Americans are not aware of it, in 1775 General Washington conceived of a plan to invade Canada. Following Washington's instructions, General Montgomery advanced north via Lake Champlain and the Richelieu River and succeded in capturing Montreal. He then continued on to Quebec City, meeting Benedict Arnold who had led a force of Americans on another route through Maine.

In a blinding snowstorm on the last day of 1775, the Americans made an abortive attempt to storm the barricades of Quebec City and were repulsed by the brave, outnumbered defenders. Montgomery was killed and the Americans were forced to retreat. Plaques commemorating this engagement can be found in Quebec City.

In this issue I have included a newly discovered inn a few miles west of Montreal, as well as an old favorite just north of the Vermont border.

WILLOW PLACE INN, Como

"Welcome to the Willow Place Inn!" The voice had an unmistakable British accent. It belonged to a very tall, genial man in brown tweeds. "I'm Pat Garbutt. I'll tell Zena that you've arrived. Now you must come right around for a cup of tea."

The drive from Montreal had taken no more than twenty-five minutes on the Trans-Canada Highway. I left at exit 22 on Pat's advice so that I could follow the road next to the Lake of Two Mountains which is really the Ottawa River. I passed the ferry across the lake that leads to Oka and arrived at the inn.

We had a lively tea and a good chat, mostly about the trials and rewards of innkeeping. Zena Garbutt is an ebullient Scottish lass and the two of them make a very interesting team.

Pat showed me about the place, and I was very much taken with the grassy lawn behind the inn that leads down to the shore of the lake and the swimming pool. He was very enthusiastic about the Laser sailboats. There were several in sight on the lake.

I had a good dinner of steak and kidney pie that evening and noticed that there were also several French dishes on the bilingual menu. "Yes, we have a great many calls for French food. Besides, our chef is French. Incidentally, we do our own baking."

Pat blasted me in a game of darts, and after dinner we all gathered in a large room where the "locals," as Pat refers to them, were enjoying a good time. In what Pat calls "the back bar" there was another equally congenial and somewhat younger group. The whole place was really very busy and I later discovered that, like inns in England, the Willow Place is really the "home pub" for the people of the area. The Canadian visitor to the inn will be right at home in its real English pub atmosphere. The American visitor will find its genuine hospitality and congeniality most heartwarming.

The lodgings are in comfortable furnished rooms that put me at ease immediately. Zena is most particular about cleanliness.

After spending the better part of two days with Pat and Zena and exploring this quiet, beautiful area, I reluctantly departed, filled with the good English roast beef, generous helpings of French desserts, an appreciation of the Laser sailboat and a feeling of real excitement of having found another gracious country inn.

WILLOW PLACE INN, Box #70, Como, Quebec, Canada JOP 1AO; 514-458-4656. A 14-room English inn, 25 mi. from Montreal on the shores of the "Lake of Two Mountains." European Plan or Mod. American Plan which omits lunch. Some rooms with shared bath. Breakfast, lunch and dinner served to travelers daily except Mondays. (Dining room closed on Mondays, but meals are served in the bar.) Closed Christmas Day, Boxing Day (St. Stephen's Day), New Year's Day and Good Friday. Swimming, sailing, bicycles and xc-ski on the grounds. Tennis, golf and alpine ski nearby. Pat and Zena Garbutt, Innkeepers.

Directions: From Trans-Canada Highway, take Exit 17 and follow Hwy. 17 north to Como Station Road. Turn left to inn.

HOVEY MANOR, North Hatley, Quebec, Canada

"Unless someone has a new road map, it can be a little confusing here in the eastern townships. A few of the route numbers have been changed." Bob and Betty Brown and I were on the

grassy terrace in front of Hovey Manor overlooking Lake Massawippi, enjoying a midafternoon chat. Bob was showing me the small maps that he sent to each guest making an inquiry.

"Coming north from the States on the Stanstead Expressway, Rte. 55, which is an extension of Interstate 91, you should exit at North Hatley and follow Rte. 108E directly through Ste. Catherine de Katevale and past Little Lake Magog to North Hatley. Then turn right at the blinker. We're just about five miles from the expressway exit."

On my visits to Hovey Manor I've found an assortment of guests. It seems to break down about evenly among those from the States, English-speaking Canadians and French-speaking Canadians. "Oh yes, we're bi-lingual here," said Bob. "I think our menu reflects several different influences. For example, we have roast beef and steak and kidney pie, but we also have duckling a l'orange and crêpes Suzette."

The talk shifted from summertime here on the lake to the activities in winter.

"Well, as you know, we are within a short distance of six major ski areas," explained Bob. "Mt. Echo, Mt. Orford, Mt. Sutton, Bromont, Owl's Head and Jay's Peak. In fact, we can supply our guests with an interchangeable ticket which allows them to ski one or all of them."

I could well imagine how breathtakingly beautiful the lake would be when covered with snow. Bob showed me some color photographs of the terrace after a fresh snowfall. "We also have snowmobiling on the lake and lots of cross-country skiing and snowshoeing here," he said. "Some of our guests like to go ice fishing."

It was interesting to realize that this summertime scene with the sailboats, speedboats and the diving raft could change so completely with the seasons. The tennis and badminton courts would be slumbering under three feet of snow.

Betty joined in. "Say, you ought to come up during the winter. We have dancing on Saturday evening, and charcoal broiled steaks from the huge Colonial fireplace in the Taproom. That's when the atmosphere is truly international." I could well imagine the Taproom with the mellowed paneling, and rustic decorations being a lively place with redcheeked people having a good time after a day's skiing.

HOVEY MANOR, Box 60, Rtes. 10 and 55, North Hatley, Quebec, Canada, J0B2C0; 819-842-2421. A 34-room resort-inn, 85 mi. from Montreal, 35 mi. from Newport, Vt. On Lake Massawippi and near major ski areas. European Plan or Mod. American Plan which omits lunch. Breakfast, lunch and dinner served to travelers daily. Open year-round. Tennis on the grounds. Golf, Alpine and xc-ski nearby. For nature and skiing lovers. Bob and Betty Brown, Innkeepers.

Directions: From U.S., take I-91 across border to Rte. 55. From Rte. 55, exit at North Hatley and follow Rte. 108 east. Turn right at blinker, approximately 5 mi.

Ontario

Traveling in southern Ontario was made a great deal more enjoyable for me by a book entitled "Niagara—A Guide To The Niagara Frontier." It had maps and photographs. With the aid of this invaluable book I was able to tour some of the towns near the Niagara River separating the United States from Canada. These included Queenston, Niagara-on-the-Lake, St. Catharines, Chippawa and Niagara Falls, Ontario.

This is an area rich in history and cultural attractions including the famous Shaw Drama Festival at Niagara-on-the-Lake.

The main roads of this part of Canada more closely resemble the back roads of the United States. There are beautiful houses of considerable vintage everywhere, and a profusion of flowers.

In the appealing little town of Niagara-on-the-Lake, I was delighted to find the kind of country inn for which I am always searching.

THE GATE HOUSE, Niagara-on-the-Lake, Ontario, Canada

My friends, Clare and Lucy Dee Dee, of Grand Rapids, Michigan visited the Gate House last summer. Clare wrote me a short note about their stay:

"We've been driving across Canada from Port Huron to Niagara Falls for years and have seen the signs for Niagara-on-the-Lake. But it seems that we have always been in too much of a hurry. Your description of the town, the Shaw Theatre, and the Gate House convinced us that we should time our trip so that we could stay overnight. I'm certainly glad we did.

"Lucy simply couldn't get over the friendliness of Mr. and Mrs. Jamieson. Robina took us through the house, showed us all the antique beds and the collection of washbowls and pitchers. I've never seen such clean shiny floors.

"One thing that you didn't mention is the fact that Bob plays the electric organ quietly and beautifully during dinner. The Beef Stroganoff was marvelous.

"Before we left in the morning, we followed your suggestion and walked about the village. I agree with you that those names of streets really have a romantic ring. We found Byron, Melville, Simcoe and Prideaux Streets. The parkway next to the river is certainly beautiful.

"I liked the idea that there's lots of space between the houses and Lucy loved the picket fences that have been built around them. There's a wonderful feeling of tranquility and permanence."

Niagara-on-the-Lake is a most unusual little town. As Clare pointed out, it's not on the main highway so it must be sought out. But finding it is well worth the search.

The Jamiesons are most conscientious innkeepers. I know for a fact that they work very hard to get the best fresh fruit avail-

able. It may be surprising to a great many of our readers to know that this particular part of Ontario is especially famous for strawberries, raspberries, peaches, cherries, and pears, as well as all types of vegetables. Some of the produce used at the inn is grown on the nearby farm of Robina's nephew.

One of the big reasons to visit Niagara-on-the-Lake is to enjoy the performances of the Shaw Festival Theatre, presenting the plays of George Bernard Shaw and his leading contemporaries. For the '75 program, write Box 774, Niagara-on-the-Lake. Now guests at the inn can also visit the Artpark in Lewiston.

THE GATE HOUSE, 142 Queen Street, Niagara-on-the-Lake, Ontario, Canada LOS IJO; 416-468-7836. A 7-room village inn 14 mi. from Niagara Falls. Niagara-on-the-Lake is the home of the Shaw Drama Festival and the site of a significant battle in the War of 1812. European Plan includes continental breakfast. Dinner served daily to travelers. Open from April 1 to December 31. For history lovers. Bob and Robina Jamieson, Innkeepers.

Directions: From Lewiston-Queenston border, follow Niagara Pkwy. to village.

Mid Atlantic

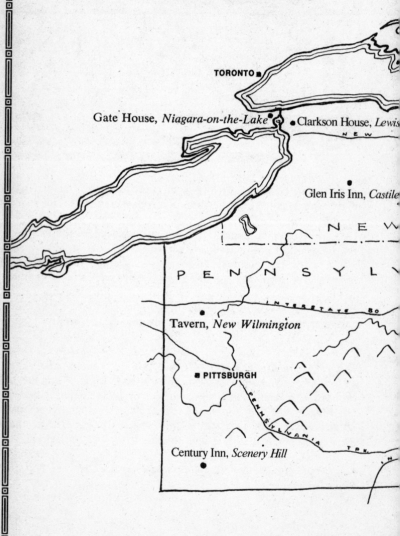

TORONTO ■

Gate House, *Niagara-on-the-Lake* ● ● Clarkson House, *Lewis*

N E W

Glen Iris Inn, *Castile*

N E W

P E N N S Y L V

INTERSTATE 80

Tavern, *New Wilmington*

■ PITTSBURGH

PENNSYLVANIA TPK.

Century Inn, *Scenery Hill*

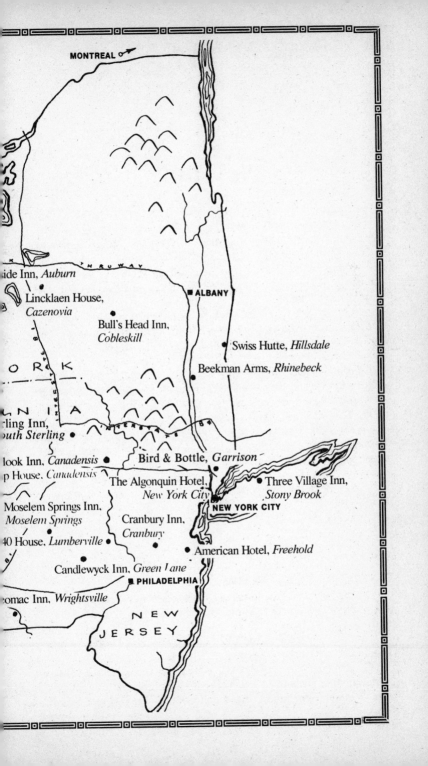

MONTREAL

side Inn, *Auburn*

Lincklaen House,
Cazenovia

Bull's Head Inn,
Cobleskill

ALBANY

Swiss Hutte, *Hillsdale*

Beekman Arms, *Rhinebeck*

ORK

NIA

rling Inn,
uth Sterling

look Inn, *Canadensis*

p House. *Canadensis*

Bird & Bottle, *Garrison*

The Algonquin Hotel,
New York City

Three Village Inn,
Stony Brook

NEW YORK CITY

Moselem Springs Inn,
Moselem Springs

Cranbury Inn,
Cranbury

40 House, *Lumberville*

American Hotel, *Freehold*

Candlewyck Inn, *Green Lane*

PHILADELPHIA

omac Inn, *Wrightsville*

NEW
JERSEY

New York

On March 1, 1775, New York's Committee of Sixty recommended the formation of a Provincial Congress. When the news of Lexington and Concord reached New York on April 23rd, there was rioting in the streets and on April 28th, the Committee of Sixty urged a more permanent revolutionary body to replace the Provincial Congress.

On May 9th Fort Ticonderoga in Lake Champlain was captured by Ethan Allen and on May 19th, Doctor Miles Cooper, the loyalist president of Kings College, was aided by Alexander Hamilton in escaping from a tar and feathering mob. On May 17th the Provincial Congress of New York assumed the functions of government and representatives from 14 counties met. July 21st was proclaimed a day of fasting and devotion following the lead of the Second Continental Congress.

New York was the scene of more Revolutionary battles and skirmishes than any other of the colonies. We shall follow the course of the war in New York State in future editions. Many of the New York State inns in this edition are located at or near the scenes of important episodes and battles of the Revolutionary War.

CLARKSON HOUSE, Lewiston

"This area," said Marilyn Clarkson, "has really arrived. After all, we've got O.J. Simpson, Ernie 'D,' the Buffalo Sabres, and now the Artpark."

My fork, spearing a succulent chunk of Maine lobster, stopped in midair and I asked, "Artpark? What is an artpark?"

I was enjoying my annual dinner at the Clarkson House restaurant in Lewiston, New York, with Bob and Marilyn Clarkson. We were surrounded by a collection of interesting memorabilia in this old building which dates back to 1815. There were cannonballs, carpet beaters, and antique kitchen utensils galore.

I had already partaken of the snack tray which included some tasty small, mild peppers, potato chips, crackers, and two different kinds of dip. There was also a delicious bean relish. The waitress had brought a huge green salad and now I was enjoying a Maine lobster. Bob explained that they're flown in everyday. They both had tried to talk me into what they call a Twin Lobster Feast. "While you are eating the first one we start cooking the second one. Then you can start all over again," said Marilyn. However I resisted, thinking ahead to the desserts.

Niagara Falls

"Well, let's get back to the Artpark," said Marilyn. "It opened in July of '74 right here in Lewiston. It's the first park in the world dedicated to all aspects of art. We have theatre, music, dance, painting, sculpture, films, crafts—just about every art form you can imagine."

Bob took up the story. "The location is one of the most dramatic in the world. The gorge of Niagara Falls supplies the background."

Marilyn handed me a program for the opening season of the theatre. The variety and range of the presentations were most impressive. The performers during 1974 included: Miles Davis, the Joffrey Ballet, Gordon Lightfoot, the Blue Oyster Cult, Weather Report, Richie Havens, Van Cliburn, the Buffalo Philharmonic, the Paul Winter Consort and Arlo Guthrie.

The City Center Acting Company performed *The Taming of the Shrew* and *Love's Labours Lost*.

I do not have space enough here to list all of the painters, sculptors, and additional artists in the shows. For the 1975 program write: Box 371, Lewiston, New York 14092.

Now my Clarkson House cherries jubilee was being brought to the table in all its flaming splendor.

"Marilyn," I said, "the Clarkson House has also really arrived."

147

THE CLARKSON HOUSE, 810 Center St., Lewiston, N.Y. 14092; 716-754-4544. A country restaurant, 7 mi. from Niagara Falls and Olde Fort Niagara. No lodgings. Dinner served daily except Mondays. Closed Christmas. For history and nature lovers. Bob and Marilyn Clarkson, Innkeepers.

Directions: From I-190, exit at Lewiston and follow Rte. 104E for 1½ mi. Turn right on Rte. 18F and travel 2 blocks west to restaurant.

GLEN IRIS INN, Castile

The post card was very simple. It was a color photograph of the Glen Iris Inn with its stately white columns and huge trees. The falls were visible in the background. On it was written, "Beautiful place, beautiful scenery, great food." There was no signature.

These were the six words that tell the story of the Glen Iris Inn.

It is located in Letchworth State Park in western New York on the 107-foot Middle Falls of the Genesee River. The wonderfully lyrical sound of the river is ever present. The nearest point to view the falls is a terrace about twenty-five steps from the front of the inn. There are several paths leading to other lookout points; however, this is really only the beginning.

Letchworth State Park is about eighteen miles long and two miles wide. It follows the course of the river in what is best described as a miniature Grand Canyon. The full length is traversed by an auto road. There are several different turn-off points with truly spectacular views of how the river has carved a path through the land on its way to the sea. There is not a single bit of commercialism to mar this enchanting experience.

The inn was the former home of William Pryor Letchworth and was built in the early 1800's. The bedrooms are very comfortably furnished and are reached by a twisting, turning staircase of dark chestnut wood that leads all the way up to the third floor. The view from each room is most pleasant. Innkeepers Corky and Peter Pizzutelli are sensitive, nature-loving people, who are deeply devoted to this beautiful inn. This feeling must run in the family, for their son, Peter, Jr., is managing another restaurant at the north end of the park, and their daughter, who has just finished her first year at Genesee College also works at the inn.

Peter is a chef with many years of experience, and the many different dishes that come out of the kitchen are always prepared under his watchful eye.

Corky's particular area of interest is the ever-growing gift shop within the inn.

"Be sure to explain to your readers," she said, "that it is practically impossible to just drop in here and expect to find lodgings. To avoid disappointment, they must reserve in advance. So many people drive a long way and come into the park only to discover that we are completely booked. Naturally we try to find other places for them because the park is so beautiful. We are happy to have them for meals, but it breaks my heart to turn them away."

Genesee River Falls at Letchworth State Park

Any visitor to the Glen Iris Inn and Letchworth State Park should certainly bring his camera. The scenery is most photogenic, and perhaps you'll be there at a time when a wedding is taking place with the falls as the background.

Isn't it interesting how much can be read between the lines of a postcard?

GLEN IRIS INN, Castile, N.Y. 14427; 716-493-2622. A 20-room country inn located at the Middle Falls of the Genesee River in Letchworth State Park. European Plan. Breakfast, lunch and dinner served to travelers daily. Open from Easter Sunday to November 2. Footpaths, tennis, swimming, and bicycles nearby. Historical sites in Park and spectacular views within walking distance. For nature lovers. Peter and Cora Pizzutelli, Innkeepers.

Directions: Inn is located off Rtes. 436, 19A and 39 in Letchworth State Park, 55 mi. from Buffalo and Rochester.

SPRINGSIDE INN, Auburn

Barbara Dove and I were seated on the front terrace of the Springside Inn on a beautiful morning in June. We were looking over the pond toward Owasco Lake, and in this park-like atmosphere it was quite natural that the conversation turned to the subject of how much effort is needed to keep these spacious grounds looking neat.

"Well, we're always working at it. Of course, the flowers like the azaleas, roses, petunias, and asters are used to decorate the tables. We've had to develop a homemade water system to water all the flowers that are hanging from the baskets. Bill bought a pressurized tank, added some plant food, and we put the nozzle in the basket and water them every morning."

The Springside Inn is traditionally a very busy place. It began with Barbara's parents, Mr. and Mrs. Steven Miller, and has been progressing continuously.

One of the developments in recent years is the Springside Dinner Theatre which plays for several weeks each summer and provides a complete evening's entertainment along with dinner. Guests remain at the dinner table for the performance.

In a short visit to the kitchen, the first thing that struck me was a real sense of organization. Everything looked extremely neat and clean. I looked at the bright red cuts of beef which were getting ready to be roasted, and I peeked inside the popover ovens which soon would be going full tilt. Popovers are very popular at the Springside.

I watched them making the homemade salad dressing and the beginnings of a large wedding cake.

Out in the main dining room a rehearsal was going on for the dinner theatre presentation of *Man of La Mancha.*

As we walked down toward the pond, Barb said, "You know these are the original streetlamps of the town of Skaneatles. Bill has refinished them all. You should see them at night."

Now we were being approached by three fat quacking ducks. Barb tossed them some leftover popovers. "Come on," she said, "let's go up on Galpin Hill behind the inn for a better look at the lake. By the way, what would you like for lunch?"

"Popovers," I quacked.

SPRINGSIDE INN, 41 West Lake Rd., Auburn, N.Y. 13021; 315-252-7247. A 7-room country inn, 1 mi. south of Auburn with a view of Owasco Lake. In the heart of the historical Finger Lakes. Lodgings include Cont. breakfast. Some rooms with shared baths. Dinner served to travelers daily except Mondays in summer and Mon.-Wed. from Jan.-March. Closed Memorial Day, July 4th, Labor Day, Christmas and New Year's Day. Boating, swimming, bicycles on grounds. Golf, riding, Alpine and xc-ski nearby. Bill and Barbara Dove, Innkeepers.

Directions: From N.Y. Thruway, take Exit 40 and follow Rte. 34 south through downtown Auburn to Rte. 38. Follow Rte. 38 south to traffic circle at Lake and take 2nd exit right at West Shore of Owasco Lake. Drive ¼ mi. to inn.

LINCKLAEN HOUSE, Cazenovia

It's now been quite a few years since my first visit to Helen Tobin and the Lincklaen House. At that time her three children, Barbara, Ann and Edward were very small. Now Ann has finished Cornell hotel school and is working for one of the large hotel chains. Barbara has her degree in nursing, but at present is helping run the inn, and Edward, at 18 is just beginning to consider his life choices.

On this particular visit Helen was, believe it or not, backpacking somewhere out in the Midwest. So Barbara and I had ample opportunity to have a good, long talk.

The patio, which now in its second full summer, is entered through big, heavy wooden doors off the little pantry. It has big flagstones and is sheltered from the outside world with a board fence and flowers cascading everywhere. We were joined for a

moment by the inn dog, Penny, who is very gentle and good with children.

Speaking of children, Barbara told me about some families who came from many different directions and had a reunion at the inn at Christmas. "You know, this is a great place for kids," she said. "They can run up and down the stairs all day long and we don't mind at all. The children have a good time and the parents can relax.

"Did mother tell you about the Grandfather's Clock? Someone left it here a few years ago because they moved to an apartment and had no room to house it. The Westminster Chimes sound every quarter hour."

When I inquired about the progress of Cazenovia College, she said that she felt that things were pretty much under control. Enrollment is increasing steadily and the community is delighted.

Barbara brought me up to date on Lorenzo, the home of Jan Lincklaen, founder of Cazenovia. Its architecture is similar to that of the Lincklaen House and is now being opened as an historical museum—perfect timing for a Bicentennial visit.

I also learned that my friend Helen is studying Spanish daily which will make her trilingual. Helen grew up in French Quebec and speaks French fluently. This is certainly an asset to foreign travelers.

The Lincklaen House is a very well-organized, friendly village inn in New York's heartland. It's a community meeting place as well as a convenient stopover for travelers and vacationers. Among the specialties are eggs Benedict, Beef Bourguignon, popovers, filet mignon with Bordelaise sauce and chocolate mousse.

This well-preserved inn was built in 1835 and still reflects the elegance of that era. The inn and the community are worth a visit.

LINCKLAEN HOUSE, Cazenovia, N.Y. 13035; 315-655-3461. A 27-room village inn, 20 mi. east of Syracuse. Near several state parks, the Erie Canal Museum and the Canal Trail. European Plan. Mod. American Plan upon request. Breakfast, lunch and dinner served to travelers daily. Open year-round. Tennis, golf, bicycles, Alpine and xc-ski nearby. Helen Tobin, Innkeeper.

Directions: From west on N.Y. Thruway, take Exit 35 and follow Rte. 92. From east on N.Y. Thruway, take Exit 34 and follow Rte. 13. From Rte. 81, travel east on Rte. 20, 18 mi. to inn.

BULL'S HEAD INN, Cobleskill

"Do you realize that one third of all the battles, skirmishes, and military engagements of the Revolutionary War were fought in New York State?" Shirley and Monty Allen and Sam and I were having dinner at their Bull's Head Inn, and Monty's Bicentennial fever was beginning to mount.

"That isn't something I made up," he said. "I read it in a publication put out by the New York State Department of Parks and Recreation.

"We're just a few miles from the Oriskany Battlefield and the Old Stone Fort," he said. "That was one of the turning points of the war."

I reminded him that I had done an extensive story on Timothy Murphy—the man who saved Schoharie—in *Country Inns and Back Roads* just a few years ago.

"Oh, yes, Timothy Murphy," he said. "Well, there's the oil painting of him right there on our wall."

We were seated in the newly-decorated dining room which has been designed in the style of a 19th century country tavern with wooden shutters that drop down over the bar. There are old-fashioned rifles, dozens of farm implements and tools hanging on the walls, and an old clock on the mantle.

The front dining room has remained the same with its handsome Indian portraits and a very good painting of a Colonial scene.

153

This country restaurant is about an hour and a half from my home in the Berkshires, so I get an opportunity to visit it two or three times a year. On each visit I'm always faced with a difficult choice among the Long Island duckling, the double lamb chops, the sliced beef tenderloin with Bordelaise sauce or the filet mignon.

Most of these are charcoal-broiled right in the dining room and the aroma is enough to drive you to distraction while you're waiting for dinner. Monty is always happy to take guests on a tour of the immaculate kitchen.

The drive to Cobleskill through the New York State countryside is most pleasant. It's fun to count the silos while driving through the Schoharie Valley and spot a few remaining windmills.

The winding road also leads right past the entrance to Howe Caverns where the temperature is always 52 degrees in its vaulted chambers. They are open year-round, and it is an adventure for the whole family. Cobleskill is also within driving distance of Cooperstown, and the Baseball Hall of Fame.

"I wonder if you realize just how important the Schoharie Valley was to General Washington's army." Monty picked up one of the pistol-handled knives and started drawing diagrams on the tablecloth. "Well here we are up here and here's where the principal armies were located and all of the grain and meat had to be transported ..." He moved my dessert to one side.

Shirley Allen looked at me and raised her eyes heavenward. "He's off again, you might as well let him go."

BULL'S HEAD INN, 2 Park Pl., Cobleskill, N.Y. 12043; 518-234-3591. A country restaurant, 5 mi. west of Howe Caverns and 30 mi. from Schenectady. Near Scotch Valley ski area. No lodgings. Lunch served Tuesday — Friday; dinner served Tuesday — Saturday and on Sunday from 1—8 P.M. Closed Christmas Day. Monty and Shirley Allen, Innkeepers.

Directions: Restaurant is 40 mi. southwest of Albany on N.Y. Rte. 7.

SWISS HUTTE, Hillsdale

It was an evening of rare magic. The sky was punctuated by countless stars. Behind our table on the terrace at the Swiss Hutte, the stately pines began to sway slightly in the light breeze. Just below us, we could hear the sounds of the brook blending with the night sounds of the woods.

We could feel the looming immensity of the Catamount ski area, just a few paces away. One tower at the top of the mountain was an amorphous silhouette in the starshine. It might be quiet now, but in six months the great flood lights would allow graceful skiers to glide from top to bottom.

Under Linda Breen's watchful eye, the waiters brought in our entrees, each simmering in a blend of herbs and wine. They were deftly transferred from the individual serving skillets to our warmed white plates. There were four of us that evening, and we decided to trade small portions in order to sample everything. The net result was that each of us enjoyed a tasty morsel of Wiener Schnitzel, Dover sole, coq au vin, and sweetbreads.

A few years ago Linda and Tom Breen bought this old farmhouse and created an Alpine theme throughout. The setting is most appropriate. Today it is a Swiss country inn with a special feeling for French food and a great deal of emphasis is placed on doing things in the Continental way. For example, there was a modest plate of thinly sliced scalloped potatoes and the coq au vin had small potatoes, mushrooms, and onions cooked with bacon bits.

Desserts have a true Swiss/French flare. Chocolate mousse, rum torte, peach melba and apricot carmel tart are just a few. These, by the way, are included in the price of the entree, and it's really difficult to narrow the choice to just one.

At the Swiss Hutte guests can enjoy tennis, swimming, hiking, skiing, cross-country skiing and many other seasonal attractions. In summer, Tanglewood, Jacob's Pillow and the Berkshire Play-

house are just a few miles away. Berkshire back roading is famous. Guests can start right from the front door, using dirt roads that lead through the forest. There are also many antique shops, art galleries and craft shops in the area.

Tom Breen came out of his busy kitchen to say "hello," and to invite us to come and try out the new inn courts.

As we were driving out on the wooded road, someone said, "It's better than being in Davos or Cervina, and so much closer!"

SWISS HUTTE, Hillsdale, N.Y. 12529; 518-325-3333. A 21-room Alpine country inn overlooking Catamount ski area, 6 mi. from Gt. Barrington, Mass. Mod. American Plan omits lunch. Breakfast, lunch and dinner served to travelers daily. Closed month of April and from Nov. 15 to Dec. 15. Pool, tennis, putting green, Alpine and xc-ski on grounds. Tom and Linda Breen, Innkeepers.

Directions: From Boston, travel on Mass. Tpke. and take Exit 2. Follow Rte. 102 to Rte. 7. Proceed on Rte. 7 to Rte. 23. From New York City, follow Taconic Pkwy. and Rte. 23. From Albany, follow N.Y. Thruway and Taconic Pkwy. Inn is 10 mi. east of Pkwy. on Rte. 23.

BEEKMAN ARMS, Rhinebeck

"The Beekman Arms," says Innkeeper Chuck LaForge, "was already old when the American Revolution began. The local militia drilled in our front yard. During the Revolution, this was known as the Bogardus Tavern and became headquarters for the patriots."

We were sitting in the Taproom—a most fitting place to be talking about events that made news 200 years ago. This low-ceilinged room has an impressive collection of mugs, pots, old glass, sabres, swords, lamps, clocks, plates, and an old brick fireplace made with Kingston brick.

"In the old days," Chuck was saying, "this was known as Traphagens Tavern. Travelers spent the night on a pile of sheep-skins and were lucky to have candles. This was a one-family stone building. Our foundation is the same stone wall. It was built as a shelter for a possible Indian attack and could withstand musket fire and incendiary arrows."

Chuck pointed out that the fireplace was still intact and its hearth two feet above the earthen floor was to make cooking less arduous.

"Mind you," he said, "this was long before the Revolution. As far as we now know, Traphagens was in existence in 1700. It was sold to Bogardus in 1769.

"In those days roast beef and venison were always on the menu. They were cooked slowly on a spit, which was revolved by a dog walking on a treadmill. They also served bear steak, pheasant, quail and turkey. There was an iron pot of soup hanging from the crane. It was added to each day so that it always contained 'some new, some old.' "

Today at the Beekman Arms the traveler still enjoys prime ribs of beef but the other items of that early menu have been

replaced by shrimp scampi, lobster thermidor and several other dishes that reflect more modern palates.

Literally thousands of visitors come here, not only to enjoy the buffet lunches and the sumptuous evening fare, but to walk about this historic town and perhaps pay a visit to Vi Suppies at the Beekman Arms Firehouse Gift and Bath Boutique.

It is most fortunate that a succession of innkeepers have been interested in preserving the best of the old, while introducing more modern methods of innkeeping. It's an excellent place to stay while visiting the many historic and natural attractions in the Hudson River Valley, such as Boscobel, Washington's headquarters in Kingston, Philipsburg Manor, the Vanderbilt mansion, Franklin D. Roosevelt's home, and West Point.

BEEKMAN ARMS, Rhinebeck, N.Y. 12572; 914-876-7077. A 13-room village inn built in 1700, 1 mi. from Penn Central Station at Rhinecliff. Short drive to F.D.R. Library and Home in Hyde Park. European Plan. Lunch and dinner served to travelers daily. Closed Christmas. Open year-round. Golf nearby. Charles LaForge, Innkeeper.

Directions: From N.Y. Thruway, take Exit 19, cross Rhinecliff Bridge and pick up Rte. 199 south to Rte. 9. Proceed south on Rte. 9 to middle of village. From Taconic Parkway, exit at Rhinebeck and follow Rte. 199 west 11 mi. to Rte. 308 into village.

BIRD AND BOTTLE, Garrison

The first thing we noticed as we got out of the car was the sound of the rushing brook. There had been heavy Rip Van Winkle thunderstorms during the previous two hours and the brook was up. In the north, the last rumbles were reverberating from the valley.

The front door of the inn flew open and there was Innkeeper Tom Noonan, looking debonair and casual in a beige cashmere sweater. "You've timed your arrival perfectly," he said. "Benedict Arnold has just left."

As we followed him through the foyer into the main part of the inn, I couldn't help but reflect that Benedict Arnold probably had been here along with several other Revolutionary War figures. After all, the fort at West Point was only a rowboat trip away.

Tom directed us to a table in one corner next to the fire-

place, and we were off on the first leg of a most enjoyable gastronomical journey.

The Bird and Bottle is "country chic." Almost everything is done with a special flair. The menu has strong Continental underscoring with the accent on French dishes.

While we watched, Tom wheeled over a cart with a chafing dish and prepared two very thin crepes, flipping them at just the precise moment. Then he filled them with lobster, crab, scallops, sea bass and shrimp.

As he cooked, he gave us a running commentary on the menu offerings. "Our specialty is roasted pheasant served with Perigeux sauce. This sauce is filled with truffles and goose liver paté. The fresh fillet of bass is sauteed in butter and served with lemon. We developed the scampi recipe ourselves—they're served in a lobster sauce and flamed in brandy."

Our entree then arrived. It was roast duck with orange sauce. Tom carved it right at the table as he does the roasted pheasant.

"We do not use frozen or canned vegetables," Tom continued. "You see, we keep changing the vegetables because we run out of one kind of fresh vegetable and go to another. We'd rather do that than have them frozen or canned."

Among their very special desserts here are cherries jubilee, crepe suzette, and banana flambé. Tom prepares a great many of these for individual tables and is quite busy all evening doing his own special thing.

The storm had passed and the moon was now visible through the great trees which surround the inn. Was I wrong or did I see a red-coated figure disappearing into the shadowy forest?

159

BIRD AND BOTTLE INN, Garrison, N.Y. 10524; 914-424-3000. A country restaurant rich in antiquity located on Rte. 9, a few miles north of Peekskill, N.Y. A short distance from Boscobel Restoration, U.S. Military Academy at West Point and Sleepy Hollow Restorations. Lunch and dinner served daily except Mondays and Tuesdays. Closed month of January. For antique lovers. Thomas and Nancy Noonan, Innkeepers.

Directions: From New York City, cross George Washington Bridge and follow Palisades Parkway north to Bear Mtn. Bridge. Cross bridge and travel on Rte. 9D north 4½ mi. to Rte. 403. Proceed on Rte. 403 to Rte. 9, then north on Rte. 9, 4 mi. to inn. From I-84, take Exit 13 and follow Rte. 9 south for 8 mi.

HOTEL ALGONQUIN, New York City

A country inn in the city! I first became intrigued with this idea when Andy Anspach, the manager of the Hotel Algonquin, wrote me a letter back in 1970. At that time he had visited several of the inns included in this book and suggested that the Algonquin had the same qualities of warm, personal hospitality. I decided to spend a few days at the Algonquin and found it such a refreshing experience that I've been staying there ever since.

Among the very nice things that have happened as a result of including it in *Country Inns and Back Roads,* is that a number of people, despairing of ever finding a good small hotel in New York, have written us letters of thanks. (I think this is one of the most rewarding aspects of writing this book every year.)

One lady wrote: "One of the reasons that I enjoy staying at the Algonquin is that the garage is located right across the street. Parking in New York is a problem and it's a great feeling just to drive into that garage and not worry about the car until I am ready to leave."

Another letter said: "One of the Algonquin's joys is the late evening supper buffet. What a pleasure to know that, after the theatre or the pro basketball or hockey game, we'll be able to swing into that warm friendly lobby and have a choice of so many different dishes. One of my favorites is Welsh rarebit. With the special salads, fluffy cakes, apple pie, ice cream, lobster Newburg, and similar goodies spread out on large tables, it's like being invited to your own birthday party."

This small hotel was made famous 50 years ago when the Algonquin Wits such as Benchley, Parker, Mencken, and others of their ilk, met there to enjoy the food and shred literary and artistic reputations.

Today you're liable to see the most interesting people in the elevator—and hear the most interesting conversations. Recently, standing in the front of an Algonquin elevator, a fragment of a conversation floated over to me. A voice of some depth and quality was saying, "And I told them I would not sign a two-picture contract."

I'm still trying to place that voice.

ALGONQUIN HOTEL, 59 W. 44th St., New York, N.Y. 10036; 212-687-4400. A quiet, conservative 200-room country inn in the heart of Manhattan. Convenient to business, theatres and shopping. European Plan. Breakfast, lunch, dinner and late supper buffet served to travelers daily except Sunday dinner. Open year-round. No pets. Very near bus, rail and air transportation. Garage directly opposite entrance, with complimentary parking for weekend visitors arriving after 3 P.M. Fri. or Sat. for minimum 2-night visit. Andrew Anspach, Innkeeper.

Directions: 44th St. is one-way from west to east; 43rd St. from east to west. Garage is accessible from either street.

THREE VILLAGE INN, Stony Brook

"George Washington's horse slept there!" Monda Roberts declared, pointing to the old Seabury place across from the Mount-Hawkins House. She and I had left the Three Village Inn (3VI) and were doing a walking-driving tour of the area.

I had seen the Suffolk Museum and carriage house, the Caroline Church, and the post office with the eagle that flaps its wings every noon. Monda had also pointed out "Hercules," the ship's figurehead that once adorned the prow of the frigate USS *Ohio,* and the Old Grist Mill which has been operating since 1699. But I was ill-prepared for this incredible bit of history.

The tour had included quite a few history lessons as Monda explained that this part of Long Island was believed to be on the side of the rebellion, but the defeat at the Battle of Long Island brought the area under British occupation for seven years. In 1777, the Americans unsuccessfully attacked a force of Tories who had taken over the Presbyterian Church at Setauket. There were also whale boat raiders from Connecticut harassing the countryside.

The "three villages" in the name of the inn come from the contiguous communities of Stony Brook, Setauket, and Old Field. They are located on the north shore of Long Island. The entire area has been considerably enhanced with the development of the Long Island campus of the State University of New York. I was delighted to learn that my good neighbor in the Berkshires, Richard Dyer-Bennett is on the faculty and stays at the 3VI several times a year. "Yes," said Monda, "we know him quite well."

The inn is an old house built by a sea captain in 1751. Today it still has the narrow clapboards and large central chimney which testify to its Colonial origin.

In addition to a few rooms at the main house there are also cottages which overlook Stony Brook Harbor and the yacht club basin.

Besides being an excellent vacation and weekend haven for the city folks, 3VI is also justifiably popular with the dining-out set on Long Island. Part of the reason is the menu, which has so many delicious offerings from nearby Long Island Sound. These include blue fish, striped bass, flounder and clam pie. The Long

Island ducklings are prepared with an orange and raisin sauce and served with rice pilaf.

Travelers to and from New England can avoid going through New York City by taking the summertime ferries from Bridgeport, Connecticut to nearby Port Jefferson, Long Island. It's best to arrive about an hour before sailing time. By the way, it's worth it.

"But how in the world did George Washington's horse happen to sleep in the Seabury place?" I asked Monda.

"Well, maybe it's only a legend. After Washington became President, he toured Long Island. It is believed that his horse was stabled there."

I looked to see if she was kidding. She wasn't.

THREE VILLAGE INN, Dock Rd., Stony Brook, L.I., N.Y. 11790; 516-751-0555. A 7-room village inn, 5 mi. from Port Jefferson, L.I. on Long Island's historic north shore. European Plan. Lunch and dinner served to travelers daily. Closed Christmas. No pets. Golf and boating nearby. For history lovers. Nelson and Monda Roberts, Innkeepers.

Directions: From Long Island Expressway, travel north on Nichols Rd. to Rte. 25A. Turn left on Rte. 25A and proceed to next light. Turn right on to Main St. and travel straight ahead to inn.

New Jersey

New Jersey was first claimed by Henry Hudson for the Dutch in 1609. Later Swedes and Quakers were permitted entry. The territory became an English colony when Peter Stuyvesant surrendered New Netherlands which included New Jersey to the English fleet. New Jersey received a separate charter from the king in 1738. On May 23, 1775, the Second Provincial Congress of New Jersey confirmed allegiance to the Continental Congress.

Revolutionary War engagements in New Jersey took place in 1776, 1777, 1778 and we will be tracing their courses in future editions.

Today, there are country inns in this book located in Freehold and Cranbury near the sites of Revolutionary War battlefields.

AMERICAN HOTEL, Freehold

This time I entered the American Hotel through the rear door and strolled down the long corridor to the main dining room and lobby, pausing frequently to admire the unusual number of old prints, paintings, and reproductions of sporting events of the 19th century, most of them having to do with horses or horse racing. The Currier and Ives collection is probably the most complete to be found anywhere.

The horse motif continues throughout the entire inn. In the main dining room there are several handsome horse paintings as well as a collection of silver reproductions of horseshoes worn by famous trotters and pacers.

The reason for the equestrian theme is the fact that Freehold has two racetracks—the Freehold Raceway and Monmouth Park.

Right now the order of the evening was dinner, and I studied the menu at the American Hotel very carefully, getting hungrier by the second. Seldom have I seen one that offered a more delectable variety of foods. For example, there were at least ten appetizers and six soups. There were twelve seafood dishes including stuffed flounder, broiled fillet of bluefish and broiled lobster tails. Two of the most continuously popular dishes are the Seafood Sampler which has stuffed flounder, crabmeat, shrimp and scallops, and the Fisherman's Platter which is a broiled lobster tail served with fried flounder, shrimp, and scallops.

Among the things that could be broiled to order were steak, lobster, ham steak, Jersey pork chops, and excellent calves liver and bacon.

However, that was just the beginning. Another section of the menu had such things as breast of chicken, veal Parmigiana, fried chicken and veal scaloppini. There was also a complete dinner which included everything from soup to nuts and offered ten different combinations.

Lodging accommodations at the American Hotel are simple and unobtrusive, but after a sumptuous Fisherman's Platter I was happy to retire early with a good book and a portfolio of information on the Battle of Monmouth supplied by the Monmouth County Historical Association Museum.

AMERICAN HOTEL, 18-28 E. Main St., Freehold, N.J. 07728; 201-462-0819. A 20-room country inn, 50 mi. from N.Y.C. in a bustling Jersey town. European Plan. Breakfast, lunch and dinner served to travelers daily except Sunday breakfast. Open year-round. Near Monmouth Battlefield, Freehold Raceway, Monmouth Park Race Track and Monmouth Museum. Richard Daesener, Innkeeper.

Directions: From N.J. Tpke. from the north, take Exit 11 and follow Rte. 9 south to Freehold traffic circle. Take 33 East to first traffic light. Turn left and follow Main St. From the south on N.J. Tpke., take Exit 8 and follow Rte. 33 East to Freehold traffic circle. Continue on 33 East to first traffic light. Turn left and follow Main St.

CRANBURY INN, Cranbury

The football sailed over the head of a small lad and bounced off the ground right into my hands. I hefted it a couple of times and then said to him, "Go on out and I'll throw you a forward pass." He looked somewhat dubious and took a few faltering steps. I let fly with a wobbly spiral which he caught—with a big grin.

It was a Sunday afternoon among the white clapboard Colonials in Cranbury, New Jersey. I had just finished a generous midday meal at the Cranbury Inn and was about to walk across the street to look at the inscriptions on some old gravestones.

I had just said good-bye to Anton Bremec and his family after a very pleasant interlude which included some most welcome news. Anton had shown me the plans for twenty lodging rooms which, hopefully, will be ready for inn guests by late 1975. This is, indeed, a happy innovation, because it means that travelers

165

between New York and Philadelphia now can enjoy a hearty country inn lunch or dinner at the country inn, and stay overnight as well.

"This was originally built as a stagecoach stop," explained Anton. "There was a tavern here during the Revolutionary War, and chances are both the redcoats and bluecoats stopped here for refreshment. There were lodgings available until recent years. Now we have renovated an entire wing and there will be twenty rooms furnished with Colonial reproductions."

Anton had enthusiastically conducted me on a tour of the inn and explained that this is one of the more pleasant aspects of being an innkeeper. "Many people who come after reading *Country Inns and Back Roads* are anxious to see our collection of firearms and the mural showing the stagecoach arriving from Bordentown. That was done about forty-seven years ago by an artist passing through Cranbury. He reproduced some of the buildings on the main street including the original school building. I guess he was very patriotic, because although the scene is supposed to be mid-19th century, he also included George Washington."

With the addition of these new lodging rooms I feel that the Cranbury Inn has come into its own. I have always enjoyed lunch and dinner there. The menu is quite extensive, consisting for the most part of dishes that are associated with New Jersey's truck farms and nearby off-shore fishing. It also has quite a noteworthy list of desserts.

As I crossed the street I noticed a handwritten sign tacked on one of the trees in front of the inn: "Lost, one gray kitten. If found, give to police or call Sally Ransom." Underneath this was an extra little note that said, "She's missed a lot."

CRANBURY INN, 21 S. Main St., Cranbury, N.J. 08512; 609-395-0609. A country restaurant on the Old King George Hwy., 6 mi. east of Princeton. Near Monmouth and Princeton Revolutionary War battlefields. No lodgings. Lunch served Tuesday through Friday. Dinner served daily except Mondays. Closed Christmas. Anton Bremec and Richard Zanyor, Innkeepers.

Directions: From the N.J. Tpke., take Exit 8A and follow Rte. 130 south 1 mi. to Cranbury.

Pennsylvania

1775 was a portentous year for the colony of Pennsylvania. On January 23rd the Provincial Convention met at Philadelphia, and on May 10th the Second Continental Congress also convened at Philadelphia. On the 15th this Congress resolved to put the 12 Colonies into one defending union (Georgia had not yet entered). On the 24th of May John Hancock was elected president of the Congress. This body continued to meet during the remainder of the year and, among other things, appointed George Washington Commander-in-Chief, approved an invasion of Canada, established an Army, Navy and Marine Corps, and rejected and offered several different proposals of conciliation. In September of that year important peace negotiations with the Indians at Pittsburgh were concluded which delayed the outbreak of the frontier war.

There are several country inns in this book within a most convenient drive of the many historic happenings, both in the eastern and western part of the state.

For further information about Bicentennial activities write the Philadelphia Visitors Bureau, 1525 John F. Kennedy Blvd., Philadelphia, Pa. 19102.

THE CENTURY INN, Scenery Hill

The letter was marked St. Louis, Missouri and had been mailed in early September 1974. It said in part:

"On my last visit to the Century Inn my young son and I were welcomed by Nancy, Mrs. Harrington's daughter. After showing us to our comfortable room she went downstairs to greet some newly arriving guests. They had driven a long way, and she very kindly offered to send them up a pot of coffee.

"After we unpacked, Mrs. Harrington herself met us as we came down the stairs and entertained us with the fascinating story of the Whiskey Rebellion Flag which is displayed in the front parlor.

"While I took photographs, my son took a walk around Scenery Hill and discovered that less than a mile north of the inn there was a fine orchard with beautiful peaches and apples.

"At dinnertime, Nancy asked us to sit in the attractive original kitchen dining room with Mrs. Harrington. We especially enjoyed the French fried asparagus and the homemade cream puff filled with ice cream and covered with butterscotch sauce—mmmm."

I think that letter gives a clue as to why we receive so many other letters from our readers who visit the Century Inn.

In the first place, although the inn is rather small, the rooms are indeed comfortable and homey. Dr. and Mrs. Gordon Harrington, who established the inn originally, have spent a great deal of time over the past twenty-five years collecting the antiques that are to be found in every room.

The Whiskey Rebellion flag in the front room dates back to 1794 and was the first test of strength that the young republic had under George Washington. Tradition says the flag was raised over a log cabin where a group of dissidents objecting to a whiskey tax were held following their arrest on the night of November 13, 1794. As Mary Harrington explained, "Men like Alexander Hamilton couldn't possibly know what whiskey meant to the back country." The inn building was constructed prior to 1794 and was a stagecoach stop on the famous National Road. History has literally passed through this inn. Andrew Jackson and Lafayette are only two of the notables who stayed overnight.

History is also represented by a handsome Chippendale highboy with a carved upside down shell. It was brought by Conestoga wagon from Carlisle, Pennsylvania by the Parkinson family in 1770.

The food at the Century Inn is about as homemade as you can get, all prepared by local cooks. It features baked green beans, turkey, chicken, carrot custard, baked corn, brandied carrots, and all kinds of homemade pies and breads.

We enjoy getting letters about readers' visits to country inns. This one was right on the mark.

CENTURY INN, Scenery Hill, Pa. 15360; 412-945-6600. A 10-room village inn on Rte. 40, 12 mi. east of Washington, 35 mi. south of Pittsburgh. American Plan. Some rooms with shared baths. Breakfast, lunch, dinner served to travelers daily. Closed December 20 to Palm Sunday, and July 4th. Golf and swimming nearby. For antique lovers. The Harrington Family, Innkeepers.

Directions:From the east, exit the Pa. Turnpike at New Stanton and turn West on I-70 to 917 (Bentlyville exit) to 40 E. From Pittsburgh and west, take 19 south to 519 South to 40 E. From Wheeling, W. Va., take I-70 east to 79 South (Waynesburg Exit). Proceed ½ mi. on 79 S. to 40 E. Take 40 E. 6 mi. to inn.

THE TAVERN, New Wilmington

I'm indebted to Mr. Joseph Eckels of New Wilmington, Pennsylvania, for setting me straight on the fact that the Old Order Amish Mennonites in the New Wilmington area do not drive black buggies as I stated in the 1974 edition, but rather buggies which are called "yellowtops," actually a mixture of brown and yellow. The blacktops are used by the Old Order in eastern Pennsylvania, Ohio and Indiana.

169

At the suggestion of Cora Durrast (the innkeeper of The Tavern), Mr. Eckels sent me some most interesting facts about these "plain" people whose ancestors first asserted their religious freedom in Switzerland during the 16th century and subsequently came to America. Their "government" is by their elders and they do not apply for either public assistance or Social Security.

The Tavern has been run by Mrs. Durrast for forty-three years. Originally I had heard about her because of the unusually tasty home-cooked food that is served there. On my first visit I learned about the Amish farms in the New Wilmington area, and the significant role they play in the community.

One of the most gratifying influences comes in the form of delicious Amish sausage which is served at The Tavern. Furthermore, Mrs. Durrast also explained that in season she gets a great many of her fresh vegetables from the Amish farms in the vicinity.

Luncheon here is a substantial meal. There are several main dishes, all of them served in generous helpings. Mrs. D. explained to me that a great many of her noontime patrons are older people and they would prefer to eat their main meal at midday. The luncheon menu includes chicken pancakes, rolled ham slices with minced chicken, baby beef liver, Tavern ham loaf, grilled smoked pork chops and fresh flounder. There's also a most unusual combination which I've never seen anywhere else: white meat of chicken and lobster tail served in a special Sherry sauce. How does that sound?

Dinners include a great many of the luncheon offerings plus about twelve other main dishes. There are always freshly made bread and rolls and homemade desserts at both meals.

The Tavern also has a small lodge across the village street with a few sleeping rooms available. One of these was occupied by my dear friends Clare and Lucy Dee Dee, of Grand Rapids, who were extremely enthusiastic about New Wilmington and Mrs. Durrast's little inn.

New Wilmington is just a few minutes from I-80, the east-west highway that traverses northern Pennsylvania. It's about 240 miles from the Poconos, where there are at least three country inns that I have found most comfortable.

During the summer of 1975, I plan to make an extended visit to New Wilmington, not only to enjoy dinner at the Tavern but to find out more about the Old Order Amish from Mr. Eckels.

THE TAVERN, Box 153, New Wilmington, Pa. 16142; 412-946-2020. A bustling country restaurant on the town square with 5 sleeping rooms in a lodge directly across the street. European Plan. Lunch and dinner served daily except Tuesdays. Closed Thanksgiving and Christmas. Sports and cultural events at Westminster College nearby. For history lovers. Mrs. Ernst Durrast, Innkeeper.

Directions: From I-80, take Exit 1-S, and follow Rte. 18 south to Rte. 208. Proceed east on 208 to town square. From I-79, follow Rte. 208 west for 14 mi. to New Wilmington.

ACCOMAC INN, Wrightsville

It was a perfect time for our first visit to this southern Pennsylvania country inn. The mid-November air was bracing, the sun had gone down behind the hills to the west, and we were on a country road leading to the banks of the Susquehanna River. When the inn, which is on a rise of land overlooking the river, came into sight with its warm, yellow lights, Sam exclaimed, "It's beautiful!"

That was the beginning of an evening of fascinating history and excellent cuisine.

From Clancy King, the maitre d', we learned that Anderson's Ferry, the original inn on this site, was built in 1775. However, in May 1935, the inn was completely destroyed by fire. The owner reconstructed it within a year using fieldstone from an old Lancaster County bridge. Except for that brief interruption the inn is now in its two hundredth year of operation.

The low-ceilinged dining room with a beautiful white-washed fireplace at one end, blazing logs, and a collection of Armetale platters on the mantle, would be a perfect setting for an Early American play or motion picture. The walls have excellent oil paintings with their own individual lights. There are square and round tables, elegant silverware, and Armetale serving plates. Each table had an Armetale candlestick and flower arrangement.

The dinner menu was most impressive. A great many of the dishes required individual attention at each table. For example, the salads were mixed with great éclat, using fresh, uncooked mushrooms. The steak Diane was made in a chafing dish while Sam and I watched completely entranced. At just the right moment, the shallots and chives were added. The great moment of the evening was when Clancy returned to prepare the dessert specialty of the inn—Bananas Foster. They are done in a chafing dish using brown sugar, vanilla ice cream, bananas and a dash of rum. A match was applied to this supreme concoction and we had flaming bananas. Sunday brunch here includes eggs Benedict, omelet Florentine, and Beef Burgundy.

As we stepped out on the terrace after dinner, I heard the sounds of a great train rumbling by on the opposite shore of the

Susquehanna. After it passed through the darkness, there was the sound of cattle lowing in a nearby field.

It was a lovely moment.

ACCOMAC INN, P.O. Box 126, Wrightsville, Pa. 17368; 717-252-1521. An elegant country restaurant on the banks of the Susquehanna River, 1½ mi. north of Wrightsville. No lodgings. Lunch served daily from mid-May to mid-September. Dinner served daily year-round from 5:00 to 11:00 Mon.—Sat. and from 3:00 to 8:00 Sun. Sunday Brunch served from 12:00 to 3:00. Closed Christmas Day. For history lovers. Ernest Wickey Helmick, Innkeeper.

Directions: From Pa. Tpke., exit at Lebanon-Lancaster and follow Rte. 70 south to Rte. 30. Proceed on Rte. 30 west and exit at Wrightsville. Turn north and travel on Cool Springs Road to Dark Hollow Road. Bear left on Dark Hollow and proceed to Accomac Road, turn right and travel to So. River Dr. Turn right to inn.

CANDLEWYCK INN, Green Lane

Dorothy Smith and I have a number of things in common. Among them is the fact that we are both great admirers of ducks. "I love ducks," she said. "I am so glad that we have them here at Candlewyck, along with the geese." The two of us were gazing at the pond right next to the inn where a great number of our feathered friends were enjoying themselves.

Dottie's affinity for ducks includes a large collection of carved, wooden ducks which are placed on the wide windowsills of the dining room. There is a woman's touch everywhere in this handsome place, including a quaint little sled, a big fireplace with a Betsy lamp on the mantle, many hooked rugs, and a sprinkling of prints of various hotels, London inns and coffeehouses. This time I discovered an old zither among the old tools and artifacts. In the evening, the inn is illuminated by at least 135 candles.

There are some unassuming lodgings at Candlewyck—nothing fancy, just comfortable for the tired traveler. It is located in the Perkiomen Valley in Green Lane, which is near Pennsburg.

I always look forward to visiting Candlewyck. Over the years I have became very well acquainted with the entire Smith family including Bob Schwind who is married to the Smith's daughter, Barbara. Bob Smith and Bob Schwind took me back to see the fine new kitchen just remodeled with tile from ceiling to floor. "The kitchen is open for the guests' inspection," explained Bob.

173

Once again the number of dishes on the menu impressed me. I mentioned this to Bob Smith and he said, "Well, certainly staying on top of the fresh meat and produce situation keeps us hopping. I still go to the market in Philadelphia to get special things. Our regular suppliers know we want only the best so they save it for us."

One of the most frequently ordered dishes is Beef Bordelaise which is tenderloin tips served in a wine sauce.

"We are in Pennsylvania Dutch country but we do not serve Pennsylvania Dutch food," explained Dorothy. "Our lunches and dinners are predominantly American and French style."

Among the hearty offerings are pork chops, roast beef, and several different types of steak. Other popular dishes are Candlewyck Sportsman a la Don which is a combination of filet mignon and lobster tails, Beef Wellington, Scallops Provincial and many other French specialties.

As I carefully ran down the menu, I noticed one interesting omission. There were no duck dishes. When I asked Dorothy about this, she replied:

"Oh, no! We just couldn't do that."

CANDLEWYCK INN, Green Lane, Pa., 18054; 215-679-2998. A 9-room country inn, 17 mi. from Allentown. European Plan. Lunch and dinner served to travelers daily except Mondays. Closed Christmas Day and New Year's Day. Bicycles on grounds. Tennis, fishing, Alpine and xc-ski nearby. Montgomery County State Park a short distance away. For history lovers. The Smith Family, Innkeepers.

Directions: From the Northeast. Extension (Rte. 9) of Pa. Tpke., exit at Lansdale and turn right after toll gate. Follow Rte. 63 north to Rte. 29. Proceed north on Rte. 29 to Green Lane.

MOSELEM SPRINGS INN, Moselem Springs

"Are you feeling 'countrified' or elegant tonight?"

There was a twinkle in Madeline Stoudt's eye as she asked this question. At first I thought it might be a bit of her Pennsylvania Dutch humor coming to the fore, but then I realized that she was expecting an answer.

"If you're feeling informal and sort of 'countrified,' then I'd suggest that you have dinner in the Golden Eagle Room. But if you're feeling a little more dignified, then I think you'll find the formal atmosphere of the Presidential Room to your liking."

This is the kind of good-natured joshing I expect from Madeline and Walter Stoudt. I'm happy to number them among the innkeepers that I've known the longest.

Madeline did make a good point, however. The Golden Eagle Room has a big fireplace, heavy wooden chairs with red leather upholstery, a pegged floor and shutters at the window. The Presidential Room has high arched windows, formal draperies and portraits of American statesmen.

A third dining room—the Blue Willow Room—strikes a happy medium between casual and formal dining with antique china displayed on the fireplace mantle and a corner cupboard with a carved cornice. There's a blue jardinière in the middle of each table and white captain's chairs.

The menu in Moselem Springs is as varied as the dining rooms. For example, there are braised short ribs of beef country style, prime ribs, stuffed boneless breast of chicken, pan-fried baby calves liver, and delicious smoked corned beef with raisin sauce.

The list of regional dishes is extensive. Among them are smokehouse beef sausage with horseradish and apple fritters, fried cheese, breaded fried mushrooms, beef and sausage pye, Dutch country scrapple, lemon butter and cinnamon crackers, and

175

delicious round loaves of homemade bread served with whipped tub butter.

I enjoyed browsing about at the Korner Kupboard which features skillfully hand-crafted gifts. The meat shop had the engaging aromas of smoked meat, cheese, molasses, ham, sausages and other delicacies.

There are two important footnotes to this historic Berks County inn. First, it is closed on Fridays and Saturdays, but is open Sundays and all other days and evenings; second, it has no lodgings.

My decision was made. "Put me in the Presidential Room," I said to Madeline. "I want to sit right next to Thomas Jefferson."

MOSELEM SPRINGS INN, R.D. #3, Box 10, Fleetwood, Pa. 19522; 215-944-8213. A historic country inn restored to 19th century opulence on U.S. 222, 13 mi. from Reading and 18 mi. from Allentown. No lodgings. Lunch and dinner served daily except Friday and Saturday. Full dinners served all day Sunday. Closed Christmas. Open year-round. Walter and Madeline Stoudt, Innkeepers.

Directions: From I-76 and Rte. 22, exit at Rte. 100 and travel south to Rte. 222. Follow Rte. 222 south to Rte. 662. Inn is located at this junction.

STERLING INN, South Sterling

The ducks at the Sterling Inn were crossing the road single file. They had just completed their constitutional from the pond next to Wallenpaupack Creek, across the putting green and shuffleboard courts, past the Lodge, and Meadowlark guest house, through the picnic area, and on to the lake. I think it's their daily ritual.

It was late May and spring in the Poconos was approaching its peak. It was a little early for the laurel but a great variety of flowering shrubs were showing delightful blooms. Robins and humming birds were building nests, and the one hundred acres of woodlands and lawns of the inn were decked out in green.

The old bell from the South Sterling elementary school was rung to announce dinner. We walked through the card room and took a moment to note that there were literally hundreds of books. Four people were finishing up a rubber of bridge and one of them waved "hello."

Carmen Arneberg showed us to a table and we immediately fell into conversation with two delightful people from Philadelphia who said that they had been married for fifty-three years and had been coming to the Sterling Inn for a long, long time. They were most enthusiastic.

"It really is hidden away in the mountains, isn't it? I don't think that you could find it if you didn't know where it was.

"Do you know why we like it here? It's because there are a lot of young people. Mr. and Mrs. Arneberg realize that people like us whose families have grown up and left home, are still very active and enjoy doing many, many things.

"Another reason is that the menu offers hearty dishes such as roast beef and roast pork and turkey—things that two people wouldn't often prepare for themselves at home. We especially like the blueberry hot cakes."

Well, these two delightful people made the meal even more enjoyable. As we parted they were planning a drive with some of their friends for the next day.

It may sound corny, but I'd say that the Sterling Inn is a place to stay young.

STERLING INN, Rte. 191, South Sterling, Pa. 18460; 717-676-3311. A 69-room secluded Pocono Mountain inn, 5 mi. from I-84 and 10 mi. from I-80. American Plan. Breakfast, lunch and dinner served to travelers daily. Open from May 1 through October 31. No pets. Swimming, putting greens and woodland walks on grounds. Golf, riding and bicycles nearby. Henry and Carmen Arneberg, Innkeepers.

Directions: From I-80, follow I-380 to Rte. 940 to Mount Pocono. At light, cross Rte. 611 and proceed on Rte. 196 north to Rte. 423. Drive north on Rte. 423 to Rte. 191 and travel ½ mi. north to inn. From I-84, follow Rte. 507 south through Greentown and Newfoundland. In Newfoundland, pick up Rte. 191 and travel 4 mi. south to inn.

OVERLOOK INN, Canadensis

We were sitting around the pool at the Overlook Inn when Stuart Pittman and Shelly de Satnick, the innkeepers, announced that they were going into town and asked if anyone needed anything. I decided to ride with them because it gave us all a chance to have a good talk.

We circled under the porte-cochere and around the driveway lined with spruce, birch and maple trees and headed out on the country road toward nearby Canadensis. Stuart was driving and said he would take the long way around so that we could see some of the Pocono scenery.

I asked them what was the best part of keeping a country inn.

"Well, it was more fun than we anticipated," said Shelly. "When we first looked at the old place we knew it would take a lot of work, and it has. But we have learned a lot and have had a good time besides."

Stuart chimed in, "We had to completely restore the interior and Shelly even got his 85-year-old aunt into the act to crochet the coverlets for the bedrooms.

"I think the two of us discovered that innkeeping involves a sixth sense of knowing when a guest is having a good time doing his own thing and when he may need a suggestion or two from one of us." Shelly nodded in agreement. "Most of them return because they like the 100-year-old farmhouse in the mountains that is filled with antiques. By the way, all the antiques in the house and in the barn are for sale."

"On weekends we have regular and square dancing." This was from Shelly, "and we can always suggest antique tours or visits to one of the several natural attractions."

"Shelly is a bridge expert," said Stuart, "and we can always arrange bridge games. Our guests like that." Shelly continued, "We try to keep it very relaxed and informal. Take lunch for instance. The guests can have it at poolside, on the porch, or wherever they happen to be. The waiter will find them."

"While we are talking about food," said Stuart, "one of the best things we have going for us is that Shelly is also our chef, and the guy can really cook. He makes all kinds of crepes and Quiche Lorraine and then comes up with Yankee pot roast or a Beef Bourguignon. The pastries and breads are also homemade."

As we approached the village, I had one final question. "With all of this bending over backwards to make the guests feel comfortable and trying to accommodate their moods, have you ever been wrong?"

"Yes," said Shelly, "we had one man from New York who was booked for a week and left after two nights. He said the whippoorwills were keeping him from sleeping. What can you do?"

THE OVERLOOK INN, Dutch Hill Road, Canadensis, Pa. 18325; 717-595-2078. A 35-room resort-inn in the Pocono Mountains. European and Mod. American Plans available. Some rooms with shared baths. Breakfast, lunch and dinner served to travelers daily. Open year-round. No pets. Swimming, volleyball, badminton, croquet, bocci, shuffleboard and archery on grounds. Golf, tennis, boating, fishing, waterskiing and Alpine ski nearby. Stuart Pittman and Shelly de Satnick, Innkeepers.

Directions: From George Washington Bridge, N.Y., follow I-80 west and take Exit 52. Proceed on Rte. 447 north to Canadensis.

PUMP HOUSE INN, Canadensis

Todd Drucquer and I were examining the blackboard which had the evening's many specialties listed. Just looking at it made my mouth water. A few of the items were: Quiche Lorraine, back fin crabmeat, country soups, shrimps in beer batter (Todd pointed out that these are served in a pungent fruit sauce), roast rack of lamb, roast tenderloin Chasseur, and striped bass vin blanc.

There was an extensive hors d'oeuvre menu, both hot and cold, and the dessert list included chocolate praline mousse, lemon cream tart, peach custard, and Swiss apple tart.

Almost everything at the Pump House is done with a Continental touch. The menu is printed almost entirely in French. The dishes are French and American and the service is quiet and elegant.

"We're Continental on the ground floor, but we're good old American country inn in our lodging rooms. Many of them have their own bath, and each are individually decorated."

There had been a few changes since my last visit. Jeff

Emmons has become the very personable resident manager, and Daniel McDole has now taken over full responsibilities in the kitchen.

Todd also pointed out that the porches had been enclosed providing a library for dining and a larger reception room.

The inn also has been painted a fresh new cream color with dark red shutters.

The Pump House has been a family affair from the start with everyone pitching in. When they were making an addition to the dining room they found a 6-ton boulder. Rather than move it they improvised and decided to make a waterfall. So now one of the dining rooms has a huge boulder with a lovely waterfall.

I'm happy to say that success attended their efforts almost immediately, and now the Pump House is one of the best known inns in the northeast. It's about equidistant from New York and Philadelphia, approximately two hours driving time. As Todd says, "You should be here on a weekend when the Giants are playing the Eagles, or the Knicks are playing the '76ers.

"Most of our guests are repeaters," he said. "They have their favorite antique shops, trout streams, or back roads. Many drive over just for dinner.

"Let's dine in the library this evening," he said. "From there we have a lovely view of the mountains."

It was good to be back at the Pump House again.

THE PUMP HOUSE INN, Canadensis, Pa. 18325; 717-595-7501. A 12-room country inn high in the Poconos, 1½ mi. north of Canadensis village and 16 mi. northeast of Stroudsburg. European Plan. Some rooms with shared baths. Sophisticated country dining. Dinner served to travelers daily. Closed Mondays in summer and Mondays and Tuesdays in winter. Closed Christmas and New Year's Day. Bicycles, golf, Alpine ski nearby. The Drucquer Family, Owners. H. Todd Drucquer, Innkeeper.

Directions: From the north, follow I-84 to Rte. 390 south. Inn is located 13 mi. south on Rte. 390. From the south, follow I-80 to Rte. 191. Travel north on Rte. 191 to Rte. 390 north. Follow signs to Canadensis. Inn is 1½ mi. north from light in Canadensis.

1740 HOUSE, Lumberville

Harry Nessler, relaxed in grey flannels and sport coat, and accompanied by his two dogs, was waiting for me at the front door of the 1740 House. "Good morning," he said, "I see you've been taking a constitutional."

I had indeed. I'd awakened about 6:00 a.m. and decided not to lose a moment of my working holiday. My room in the inn was originally an old stable and the walls were made of heavy stone. There were massive beams overhead. Through one window I could see unspoiled woods on the far side of the Delaware River and Canal and I could see the southern tip of Bull's Island. The swimming pool was visible through the other window. Each of the lodging rooms here either opens onto a terrace or has its own balcony.

I decided that this would be a good morning to take a stroll over the foot bridge from Lumberville to Bull's Island. In the growing light of the morning, the oak, walnut and sycamore trees around the inn were beginning to take shape, and I noted with approval the arrangement of plantings that Harry had made including laurel, forsythia, rhododendron, and myrtle.

After enjoying the fresh, clear quietness of the country morning, I walked back along the canal towpath. It was early November and the cardinals, grosbeaks, and doves were already busy searching out their morning meal.

That thought sent me back to the inn at a faster pace, and Harry suggested that we go right in and have breakfast.

We made our own toast from homemade bread and enjoyed delicious jams, fruit juice, croissants, pastries, cold cereal, and Pennsylvania Dutch hot hard-boiled eggs. This breakfast is included in the room tariff. Other guests came in, and one of them asked Harry about the exact place where Washington crossed the Delaware.

"It's about ten miles south of here," he said. "And Valley Forge is only about 45 minutes away." He reached into his pocket and said, "I hope you'll take a copy of this brochure. It's called 'Highways of History' and it's the best thing to take with you if you're touring Buck's County. There are well over a hundred historic sites and buildings within an easy drive. The best way is to take the three tours, one day at a time."

There are a few unique features of this country inn that reflect its "one-of-a-kind" innkeeper. For one thing, weekend reservations must include two nights. Usually these are booked well in advance. Another feature worth noting is that dinner is served between 7:00 and 8:00 p.m. in the small dining room, and it's necessary for everyone—even house guests—to have reservations.

Harry also has definite ideas about the ambiance of his inn. "It's an extension of the things I hold dear—good taste, good food, and good manners. We welcome everyone who shares these enthusiasms. I like to think of all the people who come to this inn as my house guests."

1740 HOUSE, River Rd., Lumberville, Pa. 18933; 215-297-5661. A 24-room riverside inn, 6½ mi. north of New Hope, in the heart of historic Bucks County. Lodgings include breakfast. Breakfast is served to house guests daily; dinner, except Sundays and Mondays, by reservation only. Open year-round. Pool and boating on grounds. Golf and tennis nearby. Harry Nessler, Innkeeper.

Directions: From N.Y.C., travel south on N.J. Tpke., and take Exit 10. Follow Rte. 287 north to Easton exit. Proceed west on Rte. 22 to Flemington, then Rte. 202 south over Delaware Toll Bridge. After an immediate turn onto Rte. 32 N, drive 5 mi. to inn. From Pa. Tpke., exit at Willow Grove and proceed north on Rte. 611 to Rte. 202. Follow Rte. 202 north to Rte. 32 and turn north to inn.

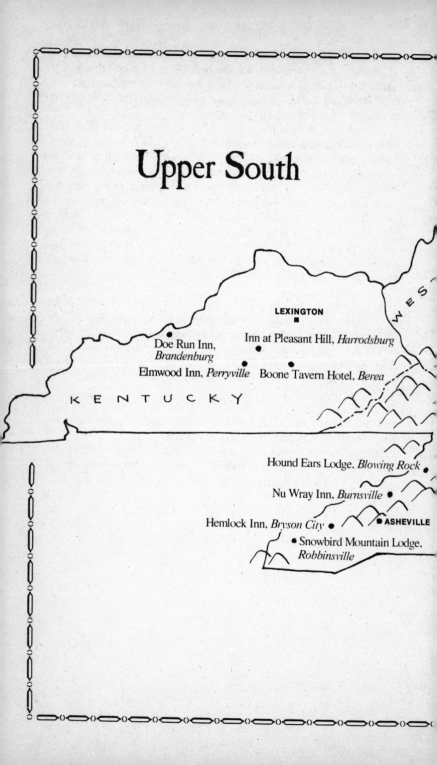

Upper South

LEXINGTON

Inn at Pleasant Hill, *Harrodsburg*

Doe Run Inn,
Brandenburg

Elmwood Inn, *Perryville*   Boone Tavern Hotel, *Berea*

K E N T U C K Y

Hound Ears Lodge, *Blowing Rock*

Nu Wray Inn, *Burnsville*

Hemlock Inn, *Bryson City*   ASHEVILLE

Snowbird Mountain Lodge,
Robbinsville

WES

• Drovers Inn, *Wellsburg*

MARYLAND

Wells Inn, *Sistersville*

• Country Inn,
Berkeley Springs

Wayside Inn,
Middletown

■ WASHINGTON

• Maryland Inn, *Annapolis*

VIRGINIA

Old Club Restaurant,
Alexandria •

• Robert Morris Inn,
Oxford

• Graves Mountain Lodge, *Syria*

■ CHARLOTTESVILLE
Hollymead Inn, *Charlottesville*

eneral Lewis Inn,
• *Lewisburg*

Alexander Withrow House,
Lexington

• Lakeview Lodge, *Roanoke*

VIRGINIA

NORTH

CAROLINA

Maryland

In 1775 the news about Lexington and Concord reached Maryland at almost the same time that the colony learned that the provisions of the New England Restraining Act applied to other colonies including themselves. These events provided the impetus for several Baltimore dissidents to seize supplies of Royal arms and ammunition. Subsequently Maryland representatives were sent to the Second Contintental Congress which convened in Philadelphia on May 10th. On July 26th the Maryland Convention met at Annapolis and voted to support the measures of the Congress and resolved to organize forty companies of Minutemen.

Maryland, the colony, and later the state, was to play an important role in the development of the country. At one time the State House in Annapolis served as the nation's Capital. The homes of three signers of the Declaration of Independence are still in Annapolis. The Treaty of Peace with England was ratified in the old Senate Chamber.

There are country inns in Annapolis itself and also on the beautiful eastern shores of Maryland.

MARYLAND INN, Annapolis

The night was filled with rain, pelting enormous drops that clouded my windshield instantly and made the lights of the Maryland Inn even more welcome than usual.

I parked my car and scampered across the brick streets, up the wooden stairway and through the big doors into the lobby of the inn feeling like a Colonial wayfarer. Peg Bednarsky was behind the main desk with her usual warm greeting.

"Well, what room would you like?" Peg asked. "We can give you a view of St. Anne's Church and the Circle, or the old town and the bay."

I chose one facing the harbor and found myself in a newly decorated room with colonial blue trim in pleasant contrast to white plaster walls.

Rain or no, it was good to be back in Annapolis because I knew that the rain would pass and hopefully tomorrow I would be able to renew my walking tour of the historic section of the

town. This time I would visit Hammond-Harwood House not far from the inn, and also take a guided tour of the U.S. Naval Academy.

Dinner that evening was in the Treaty of Paris Restaurant, named to commemorate the document officially ending the Revolutionary War. It was signed by representatives of nine states in 1784 in the Maryland State House which is just across the square.

Innkeeper Anne May joined me for a few minutes and explained that the inn is now baking not only its long-standing specialty of corn sticks, but all of the tempting items on the dessert cart, from pecan pie to almond mocha cake. I chose fillet of rockfish with its special sauce as an entree, preceded by crab bisque, for which the inn is justly famous.

Other dishes on the menu included poached fillet of flounder, scalloped shrimps and lobster in a white wine sauce, and Tournedos Rossini.

Following dinner, we went into the King of France Tavern which at various times features Charlie Byrd, Ethel Ennis, Teddy Wilson and other fine performers from the American jazz world.

This fascinating room has cleverly fashioned barrel tops as small tables for two; and the massive wood beams are original as are the brick chimney arches and rough walls of stone and brick.

Thomas Hyde built this inn in the 1770's, and since that time it has witnessed much of the history made in the town of Annapolis.

Next morning the rain had stopped and white sails were once again sparkling on Chesapeake Bay. Some of the skipjacks were on their way out to the oyster beds. Perhaps I would rent a sailboat and do a little exploring myself, savoring by sea even more of the magic of Annapolis.

MARYLAND INN, Church Circle, Annapolis, Md. 21401; 301-263-2641. A 44-room 18th century village inn in a history-laden town, 20 mi. from Baltimore and Washington, D.C. Near U.S. Naval Academy and Chesapeake Bay. European Plan. Breakfast, lunch and dinner served to travelers daily except dinner Mondays in summer and dinner Sundays in winter. Sunday brunch served year-round. Sailing and swimming nearby. Side trips to historic and scenic points of interest. Special holiday rates and tennis and sailing school arrangements. Anne Pearson May and brother Paul Pearson, Innkeepers.

Directions: From Baltimore, take Rte. 2 south to 1st directional turnoff at Washington/Annapolis. From Washington, take Rte. 50 east to exit "Annapolis Naval Academy."

ROBERT MORRIS INN, Oxford

Wendy and Ken Gibson and I were having breakfast at the Robert Morris Inn and looking at some old photographs of Oxford. Wendy had just handed me a photograph that showed the mansard-roofed inn and the Tred Avon River. There was a gas street lamp on the corner, a horse and buggy out in front of the inn, and some men with their hands in their pockets sitting on the porch.

During those days the inn was already a well-established landmark. It was built prior to 1710 and became famous as the residence of Robert Morris, Sr. It was his son, Robert Morris, Jr., who was to become known as the "financier of the Continental Army." Although the inn has been enlarged several times, some of the original construction remains including an Elizabethan staircase.

"The building was converted to an inn after the Civil War," Ken said. "However, the ferry has been operating since 1683. The ferry of which he was speaking was the famous Tred Avon Ferry believed to be the oldest, privately operated ferry service in America. It still operates today between the dock right next to the Robert Morris and the little town of Bellevue across the river.

Accommodations at this waterside inn are in themselves a very interesting story. My favorite is one that has a bed that must be reached by steps. There are others with impressive paneling and antique furniture. There are also quite a few rooms with shared baths that are somewhat austere but nevertheless comfortable. On this visit, Ken and Wendy showed me the plans for providing more rooms in the Robert Morris Lodge which is just half a block away overlooking the bay. This will also be a conference center.

I asked Ken what he thought was the most popular dish on the evening menu and he unhesitatingly replied, "The Seafood Platter with eight types of seafood, all from Chesapeake Bay waters. It includes crabmeat and shrimp, small crab Imperial, rockfish, clams, oysters—just about everything. These items are available as individual dishes also."

Wendy added that the oysters a la Gino are so distinctive that even the local oyster fishermen come in and say that they are the best oysters they've ever tasted.

Captain Bill Benson's Oxford-Bellevue ferry

ROBERT MORRIS INN, Oxford, Md. 21654; 301-226-5111. A 29-room village inn in a secluded Colonial community on the Tred Avon, 10 mi. from Easton, Md. European Plan. 4 rooms with private baths; 25 rooms with shared baths. Breakfast, lunch and dinner served to travelers daily except Mondays. Closed Christmas and New Year's Day. Open year-round. No pets. Tennis, golf, sailing, swimming and bicycles nearby. Kenneth and Wendy Gibson, Innkeepers.

Directions: From Delaware Memorial Bridge, follow Rte. 13 south to Rte. 301 and proceed south to Rte. 50, then east on Rte. 50 to Easton. From Chesapeake Bay Bridge, follow Rte. 50-301 to Rte. 50 and proceed east to Easton. From Chesapeake Bay Bridge Tunnel, follow Rte. 13 north to Rte. 50 and proceed west to Easton. From Easton, follow Rte. 333 to Oxford and inn.

Virginia

On March 20, 1775, the Virginia Provincial Convention resolved to put the colony into a "proper state of defense," and also sent delegates to the Second Continental Congress in Philadelphia. On March 23rd, Patrick Henry delivered his famous "Give me liberty, or give me death," speech in Richmond.

The British, sensing a great unrest in Virginia, seized a store of gun powder that had been hidden in Williamsburg. On August 10th Burke's speech for "Conciliation with the Colonies" was first printed in the Virginia Gazette. On November 7, 1775 Governor Dunmore of Virginia declared the colony under marshall law. He then established a base at Norfolk and began to recruit an army of men loyal to George III. This resulted in a test of strength at Great Bridge on December 11th, where the governor and the loyalists were defeated.

From Virginia came such leaders as George Washington, Thomas Jefferson, and Patrick Henry, the latter introducing in 1765 the "Virginia Resolutions" against the Stamp Act. It was at this meeting that some members of the house cried, "Treason" and to which Henry replied, "If this be treason, make the most of it."

WAYSIDE INN, Middletown

"I think the main difference, as far as our spoonbread is concerned, is that we use yellow corn meal instead of white. It gives such a different flavor. As for our Virginia ham—after it's soaked overnight we start cooking it in a big pot with water to which we add a cup of dark brown molasses. What a flavor!"

Innkeeper Bill Castro and I were seated in the Senseney Gardens at the Wayside Inn talking about southern food. The Wayside is well-known for some exceptionally fine offerings including their famous peanut soup. I always suggest that a cup of it would be sufficient; it whets the appetite for later surprises such as baked tomatoes, chicken gumbo, Mother-In-Law mustard, Slave Kitchen stew, the Virginia country ham, homemade apple pie and pecan pie.

The doors of this inn have been open to travelers and guests since 1797, offering—at various times—refuge, comfort, friendship and even respite from battle.

The battle was the Battle of Cedar Creek which took place nearby. There is a diorama at one end of the Senseney Dining Room which shows the battle, including the inn, which was then known as Wilkinson's Tavern.

As early as 1817 stagecoaches were a familiar sight on the Shenandoah Valley Pike, and the inn was selected as a relay station where fresh teams were provided.

Today, expansion and modernization have made it possible to serve the unusual number of people who seek out the Wayside at all seasons of the year.

Here is a family inn in the southern tradition that actually has a kitchen garden and serves farm fresh eggs! The bread and pastries are all made in the kitchen and the cooks, hostesses, and waitresses are all local folk with an ancestry predating the inn itself.

The Wayside is an antique-enthusiast's dream. It is jam-packed with an incredible number of chests, tables, highboys, oil paintings, and bric-a-brac. Since my first visit in 1970 I've spoken about many of them, and it is sufficient to say that on each visit I find even more.

In addition to being located just off Interstate 81, which links New England with the deep south, the community of Middletown also boasts The Wayside Theatre providing professional talent for summer musicals, comedy and drama. Belle Grove, one of the most beautifully preserved mansions in northern Virginia is just minutes away. The Battlefield Crystal Caverns which are open all year are down the pike a short distance and the Skyline Drive is close by.

Bill and I walked through the inn to the romantic Slave Kitchen where the table in front of the fireplace was set with the big pewter mugs, glimmering candles and pistol-handled knives.

"We won an award among restaurants all over the country for table-setting," he explained. "And this was the prize-winning table."

There was nothing to do but sit down and eat.

WAYSIDE INN, Middletown, Va. 22645; 703-869-1797. A 21-room country resort-inn since 1797 in the Shenandoah Valley. About 1½ hrs. from Washington, D.C. European Plan. Breakfast, lunch and dinner served daily to travelers. Open every day of the year. Professional summer stock theatre and arts center. Belle Grove, Cedar Creek Battlefield, Blue Ridge Parkway, Crystal Caverns and Shenandoah Valley historical sites nearby. For history and antique lovers. Bill Castro, Innkeeper.

Directions: Take Exit 77 off I-81 to Rte. 11. Follow signs to inn.

THE OLD CLUB, Alexandria

Innkeeper Jack Coleman was telling Roger Wunderlich and me about how to cook the famous Virginia country ham which he brings in especially from Culpeper, Virginia.

"We soak it overnight, boil for about nine hours, cool, and then put it in the oven with vinegar, brown sugar and cloves and let it glaze for about two hours."

It was a very pleasant Tuesday evening in June. Roger and I had left the American Book Sellers Association Meeting in Washington, and, following Jack's instructions, arrived at the Old Club just at the peak of a perfect northern Virginia sunset. The stone-paved courtyard looked most attractive and there was a profusion of flowering bushes around the old house with its tall southern pillars. Two large holly trees still stood guard should there be another British attack.

Roger had never eaten at the Old Club and Jack and I decided that for a "first-timer" the famous ham, black-eyed peas, and candied yams would be most suitable. "On the second visit I think the Chicken Lauralee would be a great choice," said Jack, "and, perhaps, on the third trip he might order the mountain trout."

The dark wood paneling on the walls reflecting lights from the discreet lamps on each of the tables, and the waitresses bustling in and out in their Colonial costumes gave us a feeling of being in Old Alexandria.

Of course, Old Alexandria is just a moment away from the Old Club. George Washington himself used this particular street many times and it is also said that he was a member of a club which occupied the land on which the inn now stands.

There are at least 27 historic sites and buildings in Alexandria. There is an excellent walking tour available with an explanation of such landmarks as Christ Church, Captain's Row, Gadsby's Tavern, and Carlisle House. Mt. Vernon is just a moment or two away by car.

At dessert time, Roger decided on the deep-dish apple pie with ice cream and I ordered the pecan pie, which is always served at the Old Club.

As we shook hands with Jack and moved out into what was a most pleasant spring night, Roger said, "Boy, that's one of the best places I've ever eaten."

OLD CLUB RESTAURANT, 555 So. Washington St., Alexandria. Va. 22314; 703-549-4555. Just across the river from Washington, D.C. in one of the country's best preserved Colonial cities. No lodgings. Lunch and dinner served daily except Mondays and Christmas. Convenient to Christ Church, Robert E. Lee House, Gadsby's Tavern, Old Apothecary Shop, and Potomac River. Mt. Vernon and Gunston Hall nearby. For history lovers. John Coleman, Innkeeper.

Directions: From Beltway 495, take Exit 1-North to Rte. 1A. (Mount Vernon Hwy. is Washington St. in the city.)

HOLLYMEAD INN, Charlottesville

"And here, sir, are your choice of desserts."

Right there on a gleaming silver tray just a few inches from my nose were three super-fantastic looking confections that defied description.

"This is chocolate mousse, and this is rum pie, and here's a chiffon cheesecake."

Hobson had an easier choice.

We had left Washington, D.C. a few hours earlier, after lunching at the Old Club in Alexandria. It was like old times for me to be on Route 29 through Warrenton and Culpeper. It was rolling country with many impressive, typically Virginia homes and markers from Civil War battlefields.

The directions said for us to watch for the sign for Hollymead on the east side of the road just 6 miles north of Charlottesville. And there it was.

Innkeepers Peg Bute and Marguerite Orza were both at the door to wish us welcome, and the fun of visiting a country inn for the first time began. Each of them bubbled over with information. "The floors and the beams are original," said Peg. "It

was built by Hessian soldiers taken prisoner at Saratoga during the Revolutionary War. They were housed nearby but when conditions became overcrowded they constructed the first part of the house, which we call the Hessian Room.

"The center part of the house was built around 1815 and used for a while as a private boy's school. The boys lived in two rooms on the third floor. They had their lessons in this room which we now keep as a private dining room.

There was a great deal more, including a radio program every week from the inn in which guests and well-known people visiting the nearby University of Virginia are interviewed. Peg explained that she used to be a cook at one of the fraternities and the boys from that fraternity are now waiters at Hollymead.

One of the unique features was a country butcher shop, The Hook and Cleaver, which is located in the basement where Virginia hams and beef are sold.

I was delighted with the atmosphere, cleanliness and really crisp look of Hollymead, and the food was equally exciting.

Dinner started with a relish tray that had beets, beans, creamy cucumbers, apple butter, and cranberry sauce. These were served with homemade muffins and a very good garden salad. I ordered the baked chicken with Hollymead sauce served over rice. It was so delicious, I wish I had some right now.

Peg explained that besides the steaks, seafood, and the fresh batter-fried mushrooms which are available with every meal, there are daily specials which might be Beef Wellington, trout stuffed with crabmeat, flounder stuffed with shrimp, ribeye steak, scallops in mushrooms and wine, or country stuffed pork chops.

While we were eating, a number of tweedy faculty-types from UVA popped in for dinner as well as some blue-jeaned students. "Oh yes, everyone comes here," said Marguerite.

This brings me back to where we started and I was really going to fend off the desserts with regret but the chocolate mousse was too much for me. And, like the man in the television ad I can't believe I ate the whole thing!

It didn't hurt a bit.

HOLLYMEAD INN, Rte. 8, Box 367A, Charlottesville, Va. 22901; 804-973-8488. A country restaurant a few minutes north of Charlottesville on Rte. 29. Near Monticello, Ash Lawn, University of Virginia and Skyline Drive in Blue Ridge Mts. Dinner only served Tuesdays through Saturdays. Open year-round. Closed Christmas Eve, Christmas Day and New Year's Day. For history lovers. Mrs. Peggy J. Bute and Mrs. Marguerite R. Orza, Innkeepers.

Directions: Proceed 6 mi. north of Charlottesville, Va. on Rte. 29 North.

GRAVES MOUNTAIN LODGE, Syria

I couldn't remember whether it was Wednesday or Thursday. I was rocking on the porch at Pete's House, one of the cottages at Graves Mountain Lodge, overlooking a broad valley with gorgeous fields, and the gentle rise of the Blue Ridge Mountains nearby.

The air on this early fall day had the mingling aromas of apples, peaches, pine trees, late goldenrod, and freshly cut hay. For a moment I forgot everything except the quiet and beauty that surrounded me.

A scarlet tanager darted from a wild cherry tree and perched on the rails of the rustic fence. Rachel Graves explained to me that there are many bird watchers who come to the inn armed with notebook and binoculars.

I reflected that the inn could well attract many types of enthusiasts, starting with lovers of good homestyle food. Last night and this morning would have been a banner occasion for them. Dinner consisted of fried chicken, accompanied by big platters of scalloped potatoes, string beans cooked with ham, country baked apples, hot beets, sliced homegrown tomatoes, generous helpings of tangy cole slaw, and plenty of hot home-made country biscuits. There were side dishes of apple butter and several different relishes. The meal was topped off deliciously with homemade apple pie and vanilla ice cream. There's simply no way that anyone can leave the dinner table at Graves Mountain Lodge without being totally happy.

In recent years Graves Mountain Lodge has grown from a farm guest house to a real country inn. Besides Pete's House where I was staying, there are several rustic cottages and cabins scattered over the nearby hillside. Many of these have an atmosphere of earlier times, including big fireplaces and plank floors. They also have electric heat and air-conditioning, running water, and stoves for cooking.

The newest accommodations are in the Hilltop Lodges, built among the apple trees. Each room has a spectacular view of the valley.

At the end of the day, guests gather in the Recreation Lodge which has some handsome wooden inlays of birds and outdoor scenes by W.C. Bader. These can be purchased at the gift shop, which specializes in many examples of mountain crafts.

One of the most intriguing features about this Virginia mountain inn is the fact that it is a 3,000-acre working farm with apple orchards, farm crops, cattle and hogs. I spent the morning watching farm workers and then walked down to the village apple sheds where the fruit is sent to big city markets.

There's much to do including walking and hiking on the trails in the Shenandoah National Park, swimming in the junior Olympic pool, horseback riding, and fishing.

Small wonder that I couldn't remember whether it was Wednesday or Thursday at Graves Mountain Lodge.

GRAVES MOUNTAIN LODGE, Syria, Va. 22743; 703-923-4231. A 21-room secluded resort-inn on Rte. 670, off Rte. 231, 10 mi. north of Madison, Va., 38 mi. N.W. of Charlottesville, Va. American Plan. Rustic lodgings, including 11 cottages and cabins. Breakfast, lunch, dinner served to travelers by reservation only. Closed December 1 to late March. Swimming, tennis, riding, fishing, basketball. Golf nearby. For nature lovers. Jim and Rachel Graves, Innkeepers.

Directions: Coming south from Wash., D.C., take I-66 to Gainsville. Follow Rte. 29 south to Madison, turn right onto Rte. 231 West, go 7 mi. to Banco, turn left onto Rte. 670 and follow 670 for 4½ mi. to lodge.

ALEXANDER-WITHROW HOUSE, Lexington

I first saw the Alexander-Withrow on a beautiful, sunny June afternoon and was immediately impressed with its unusual design. I was amazed to learn that such a sophisticated structure was built in 1789, just two years after the original founding of the town. It has four corner chimneys and a most elaborate brickwork, which Innkeeper Carlson Thomas said was known as "diapering." Another unusual feature is the Italianate roof.

According to an article by Royster Lyle, Jr., published in the Journal of the Roanoke Valley Historical Society, the house was described as "occupying a conspicuous place in the village, (and) was a most respected and pleasant abode. Its apartments seemed spacious and airy. The prospect of the surrounding hills and majestic mountains was beautiful and grand."

198

Today this historic house, which is now included in the National Register for Historic Places, is an exquisite guest house. Its restoration and preservation is the first chapter of an extensive and exciting development.

According to an article in Commonwealth Magazine by Robert S. Keefe, it was in the mid-60's when historic preservation began coming into its own in Lexington. In 1966 the Historic Lexington Foundation (HLF), a non-profit organization, was established. Its main purpose was to guard Lexington's architectural heritage. From the beginning, the idea gradually developed to purchase historical properties, restore the exteriors and immediately re-sell them, with perpetually binding deed restrictions regarding the appearance of the buildings.

The first property was the Alexander-Withrow House which was one of the few structures to survive a fire in 1796. It would serve as an inspiration and direction for future properties in the town.

The HLF engaged Thomas Craven of Charlottesville, a distinguished preservation architect, and the restoration work was begun.

In 1971, Carlson Thomas and his wife, Patty, bought the house, redesigned, restored and decorated the interior.

Patty and Carlson showed me through every room in the house. There are five suites, each with its own sitting room, bedroom and small refreshment center. The furnishings are beautiful antiques and reproductions. Many may even be purchased where suitable replacements are available from the Thomas' antique shop on the first floor.

There are no meals served at the AW House. However, there is an arrangement with the pastry shop next door to deliver pastries, breads, sticky buns and coffee in the morning. Guests can enjoy this right in their own suite. Patty and Carlson have many suggestions for area restaurants for lunch and dinner. They also see to it that their guests are deluged with material about Lexington including a 26-stop walking tour. Many people come for one night and stay longer because there is really so much to offer the vacationing traveler.

Lexington is also the home of both Washington and Lee University and Virginia Military Institute.

I would like to recommend to members of any historical preservation society that they visit Lexington (and stay at the Alexander-Withrow House) and learn firsthand what has been done to preserve the irreplaceable, priceless aspects of this tiny city's architectural heritage.

The AW House in Lexington proves the point that it is possible to preserve such a heritage and turn it to practical use today. I can think of no better use for the many buildings that I see in communities everywhere than to be made into country inns.

ALEXANDER-WITHROW HOUSE, 3 W. Washington St., Lexington, Va. 24450; 703-463-2044. An elegantly restored 5-suite guest house. Lodgings only. No meals served. Room service continental breakfast available. Advance reservations recommended. Open from August 15 to June 15. No pets. Lexington is the home of Virginia Military Institute and Washington and Lee University. Natural Bridge, Blue Ridge Parkway nearby. Carlson and Patty Thomas, Innkeepers.

Directions: From I-81, follow Rte. 60 west to Lexington.

LAKEVIEW LODGE, Roanoke

It was early March. I threw my golf clubs in the back of the car and headed south from New England through Pennsylvania, parts of Maryland and into Virginia. I used I-81 to bypass Harrisburg but for the most part I used roads running parallel with the highway.

After stopping at the Country Inn in Berkeley Springs, West Virginia, the Wayside Inn in Middletown, and having a most rewarding visit to the Alexander-Withrow House in Lexington, I was once again on my way to Roanoke for some early golf at Lakeview Lodge.

Route 11 again offered the best alternative to the Interstate, and I enjoyed some of the old Shenandoah Valley towns such as Woodstock, Steel's Tavern and Tom's Brook.

Once again I found myself at Lakeview. The pond was populated with ducks and the distinguished white columns of the building were a welcome sight especially with dinnertime near.

This resort-inn is a former show horse farm and the restaurant is called the Feed Box. The menu is printed on brown paper bags with a wide variety of substantial dishes to please any traveler.

The accommodations are all in small lodges (former stables) arranged in a New England common style with a heated outdoor swimming pool and a large putting green. The architectural contour is rather low so that the surrounding ring of mountains plays an important part in the general atmosphere.

The Lakeview has its own 18-hole golf course and I discovered, after playing several rounds, that there are quite a few downhill lies. It is a very sporty course and because it is possible to play quite late in the fall and early in the spring, it is very popular with golfers further north. Realizing this, Lakeview offers some very attractive three and four-day golf packages.

Golf isn't everything at this southern Virginia resort-inn. The drives on the backroads into the Blue Ridge Mountains are beautiful in every season of the year. It is a pleasant drive to Abingdon to visit the Barter Theatre, and an even shorter ride to the nearby Peaks of Otter in Bedford which afford a breathtaking view of the surrounding countryside.

I found that the Lakeview Lodge is a good place to meet spring a few weeks early.

LAKEVIEW LODGE, Roanoke, Va. 24019; 703-366-0321. A 100-room resort-inn including an 18-hole golf course on Rtes. 11 and 220, 1 mi. north of Roanoke, 1½ mi. from Exit 43 and I-81. European Plan. Breakfast, lunch and dinner served to travelers daily. Open year-round. For golf lovers. Ann Lee, Innkeeper.

Directions: From I-81, take Exit 44 and follow Rte. 11 south 1 mi. to inn.

West Virginia

The first white settler seems to have been Morgan ap Morgan, who built a log cabin in the area in 1726. The next year Germans settled at Mecklenburg (Shepherdstown). In 1768 the Iroquois Confederation ceded all claims to the land, but occasional trouble continued between settlers and native Indians. In 1771 Benjamin Franklin supported a proposal to make West Virginia into the separate colony of Vandalia, but nothing came of this.

THE COUNTRY INN, Berkeley Springs

"We just felt that although 'Park View' was a nice name, and we are a part of the village park, 'Country Inn' really expresses more directly what we are about. After all, when you say 'Country Inn,' it now has an explicit meaning." Jack and Adele Barker, Sam and I were having dinner, an experience I fervently wish I could enjoy much more frequently than time and distance permit.

Adele, eyes shining with enthusiasm, was explaining how the name came to be changed. "Well, we have changed quite a few things; for example, we have redecorated almost every room in the inn. Every bed is brand new, and we have baseboard heat in all the rooms. Would you believe that we put on one hundred and five new storm windows?"

Jack and Adele Barker were, for years, the operators of a very successful school near Washington, D.C. During many of those years they had only one dream which was to own a country inn. A few years ago, the Park View Inn in Berkeley Springs, which is a pleasant, somewhat sequestered community in the northwest panhandle of West Virginia, became available and they gave up their school and embarked on a new and exciting career.

Almost from the start, the Barkers made new friends in their new venture, and I received many letters of praise. However, they were not content to stand still, and this whole concept of changing the name of the inn and doing new exciting things was the outcome.

Jack showed me a model of a covered bridge that will become the official emblem of the Country Inn and will be built over the brook out in front. It will have cedar shingles and sport hanging baskets of petunias and boxes of bright geraniums.

As dinner progressed, I noted that each of us had something different—country ham, grits, smothered chicken, salmon soup, calf's liver, duckling with orange sauce and homemade breads.

Yes, there have been some exciting changes with my friends, Jack and Adele Barker, but underneath, it is still the same warm, truly heartfelt effort to reach out and make each guest feel very much at home.

(N.B. As if all this weren't enough, immediately next door to the Country Inn, within walking-in-your-bathrobe distance, are these amazing Roman baths where guests can "take the waters," enjoy the steam cabinet and have a massage for an extremely reasonable price. Many people visit the Country Inn for that purpose alone.)

THE COUNTRY INN, Berkeley Springs, West Va. 25411; 304-258-2210. A 34-room resort inn on Rte. 522, 34 mi. from Winchester, Va., and 100 mi. from Washington, D.C., or Baltimore, Md. Berkeley Springs Spa adjoins inn. Mod. American Plan omits lunch. Some rooms with shared baths. Breakfast, lunch, dinner served to travelers. Open every day of the year. Hunting, fishing, hiking, canoeing, antiquing, championship golf nearby. Jack and Adele Barker, Innkeepers.

Directions: Take I-70 to Hancock, Md. Six miles south on Rte. 522 to inn.

GENERAL LEWIS INN, Lewisburg

I asked Mary Hock and Larry Little whether many people had stopped at the General Lewis because of reading about it in *Country Inns and Back Roads*.

"Oh, yes. We've had dozens of people here because of the book," explained Mary. "All of them would like to have the bedroom with the canopy four-poster and fireplace."

"The thing that's most enjoyable about the Berkshire Travellers," said Larry, "is that they know exactly what to expect before they arrive. There can be misunderstandings about country inns. Some people expect to find ultra-modern places, but we're rather unpretentious with the accent on hospitality and good food. A great many of them love West Virginia country food, such as chicken, pork chops, country ham, sweet potatoes, and apple butter."

I could certainly number myself among that group because the memory of a West Virginia country dinner was still fresh in my mind.

We were seated on the spacious lawn of the inn with its oaks and maples interspersed with hemlock, dogwood and red-bud trees.

On a walk through the garden, Mary pointed out the many varieties of flowers. "There's always something in bloom," she said, "we have iris, poppies, pansies, jonquils, hyacinths, phlox, lillies, and, oh, at least a half a dozen more." I also spotted a number of cardinals and bluejays.

Mary then took me on a tour of the inn, as she does with so many of her guests. I learned that the old part of the building, where the dining room is located, was built in 1798 as a private dwelling. In 1929 it was opened as an inn by Mary and her husband, Randolph. They carefully collected all the antiques that can be found at every turn.

There seemed to be no end of utensils, spinning wheels, prints, churns, chairs, tables, oils, water colors, and literally dozens and dozens of different types of old-fashioned tools, firearms, and weapons. Mary pointed out that every room in the inn is completely furnished with antiques, and this includes the bedrooms as well. Particularly impressive was the large collection of china and the wide variety of rocking chairs scattered throughout the inn.

Later that afternoon I took another walk through the old streets of Lewisburg and once again browsed around the Old

Stone Church with its shuttered windows and ancient cemetery. It was quiet and peaceful with the confidence that comes with age. Built in 1796, it's said to be the oldest unrestored church in continuous use west of the Alleghenies. After the Civil War battle fought in Lewisburg, it was used as a hospital.

Before we retired for the night, I asked Larry if there had been any changes at the inn. He said "Oh, no. Not to speak of. We're really interested in remaining the same."

GENERAL LEWIS INN, Lewisburg, W. Va. 24901; 304-645-2600. An antique-laden 30-room village inn on Rte. 60, 90 mi. from Roanoke, Va. European Plan. (Mod. Am. Plan only during W. Va. State Fair) Breakfast and evening meal served each day, with an additional meal on Sundays at noon. Dining room closed Christmas Day. Famous golf courses nearby. For antique lovers. Laurence Little, Innkeeper.

Directions: On I-64 take Lewisburg exit. Follow Rte. 219 south to first traffic light. Turn left on Rte. 60 two blocks.

DROVERS INN, Wellsburg

Some country inns reach out and capture the imagination immediately. The Drovers Inn does that for me each time I visit. A red brick building with white trim, it sits on top of a small hill, back quite a distance from the road. As innkeeper Mary Marko and I strolled around the grounds one sunny afternoon, she explained that the maple, oak, cherry and elm trees we saw were just a sample of the 38 acres of woods behind the inn. On that particular day the wildflowers seemed to be blooming in unusual profusion and the many birds called for our attention.

The Drovers Inn is a place that one has to seek out. It is not on or near a road of any great significance. At one time it was on a direct route which led down to the Ohio River at Wellsburg, and was a stopping place for drovers as they moved their stock back and forth across the toll road from Pennsylvania and Ohio. At the inn they could obtain not only lodging and food for themselves, but fodder for their livestock which were kept in pens adjacent to the inn—hence, the name.

The inn was built by John Fowler in 1848 and for years was also a country store. In 1965 it was restored as closely as possible to its earlier bucolic identity.

The enthusiasm and motivation behind the restoration, which has been a continuing progress, belongs to Mary Marko, who has devoted much energy and time to it. It reflects her ingenuity and interests.

On the main floor are two contrasting dining rooms. One is informal, with interesting bric-a-brac, old calendars, pictures, advertisements, and posters. The tablecloths are red checkered and there are many unusual old tools and artifacts on the walls.

On the other side of the large hallway is a more formal dining room with very handsome tables, each with an individual set of matched chairs.

It is in these settings as well as in the casual rathskeller below stairs, that Mary's patrons enjoy stuffed steak stroganoff, old-fashioned ham and many other distinctive dishes.

Mary serves dinner on Wednesday, Thursday, Friday, and Saturday. Sunday dinner begins at 1:00 p.m. I hope that all of our readers will note that she does not have rooms, and with the exception of Sunday, does not serve a noonday meal.

Personally, I like to arrive at Drovers about four o'clock in the afternoon. That gives me plenty of time to walk about the grounds, visit some of the older out-buildings, and try to imagine what the Drovers Inn was like 140 years ago when it was playing its role in the development of the West.

Then I'm ready for one of Mary's great dinners.

DROVERS INN, Washington Pike, Wellsburg, West Va. 26070; 304-737-0188. A country restaurant in a historic building on Rte. W. Va. 27, 16 mi. north of Wheeling and 18 mi. from Washington, Pa. Near Meadowcroft Village, Avella, Pa. No lodgings. Dinner only served daily from Wednesday through Sunday. Closed Christmas. For history lovers. Mary Marko, Innkeeper.

Directions: From Wash., Pa. follow Pa. 844 which becomes W. Va. 27. From Wheeling, W. Va. follow Rte. 2 north to Wellsburg. Turn right on Rte. 27.

WELLS INN, Sistersville

The newspaper was the Daily Oil Review, dated January 16, 1895. The big news that day was that the Hotel Wells had opened the previous night with a reception, banquet and ball. The reporter waxed eloquent over "the most successful social event in the history of the city."

The news item went on to describe the building as "three-story, brick, situated on Charles Street within easy distance of the depot, the boat landing, and the center of town. It has two fine verandas, one on the first story and one on the second. The latter is supported by columns of the colonial period.

"The interior is a marvel of richness and good taste. In the main hallway an artistic piece of mosaic floor tiling strikes the eye, in the center of which are the words 'Hotel Wells.' "

The article speaks of the sleeping rooms "all furnished in first class style with gas and steam heat from the radiators. The house throughout is furnished with hot and cold running water."

Well, it was fun reading about the Hotel Wells which was the forerunner of today's Wells Inn.

A great deal of the description of the original hotel would certainly apply today, except that, of course, there are modern conveniences behind the Victorian furnishings.

Jack Kinkaid, the innkeeper, is very proud of the fact that the Wells Inn is right in step with the remainder of downtown Sistersville. Because of the unusually well-preserved Gothic, Greek Revival, and Romanesque buildings, Sistersville expects soon to be designated as a National Historic district. Anyone visiting Sistersville should plan to spend at least part of a day on a walking tour that would include St. Paul's Episcopal Church, the Henderson Hotel building, the Sistersville high school, and the banking buildings at the corner of Wells and Diamond Streets.

I've written in the past about the development of Sistersville as an unusual oil boom town between 1895 and 1915.

The Wells Inn today, along with most of the Sistersville downtown district, has a remarkably restored Victorian atmosphere. Incidentally, because Sistersville is on a border between north and south, the menu offers excellent examples of each

207

style of cooking. Some of them, such as roast beef with mush-rooms, French peas, turkey, chicken salad, and fresh fruit pies were served back in the early days as well.

WELLS INN, 316 Charles St., Sistersville, West Va. 26175; 304-652-3111. A restored Victorian 36-room village inn, 50 mi. south of Wheeling, 38 mi. north of Parkersburg. Sistersville is a former oil boom town of the 90's. European Plan. Breakfast, lunch, dinner served daily. Open year-round. Skiing nearby. For history and antique lovers. Jack Kinkaid, Innkeeper.

Directions: From the south, leave I-77 at Parkersburg and proceed north on Rte. 2. From the north, leave I-70 at Wheeling and travel south on Rte. 2.

North Carolina

North Carolina can boast the site of the first planned colony in America established in 1587 on Roanoke Island.

There Virginia Dare, the first white child of English parents, was born. But nobody knows what happened to her or to the other colonists. Her father went back to England for supplies, and when he came back the entire colony had vanished.

The next colonists did not disappear, but there was plenty of contention amongst them. The news of the burning of the British cruiser Gaspeé in Narragansett Bay, Rhode Island reached North Carolina to add fuel to the fires of discontent against the Royal Governor, William Tryon. An organization called the Regulators was formed, and drills under arms were carried out. Tryon moved against these insurrectionists and in a surprise attack against them at Alamance in 1771, they were crushed. The result was that a group of North Carolina colonists, unwilling to put up with the Crown's shenanigans, moved west, and in 1772, on the banks of the Watauga, adopted a constitution of their own.

HOUND EARS LODGE & CLUB, Blowing Rock

The club head moved back slowly, and at the top of the swing reversed its direction in a perfect arc, meeting the ball with that wonderfully delicious "thonk" that meant it would be out

straight and true for about 220 yards. There was a murmur among the spectators and I said to myself, "This is going to be a wonderful day."

But this couldn't be me, the King of Duffers. In fact, it wasn't. It was one of the other guests of Hound Ears off on another 18-hole tour. I would have to settle for the knowledge that if I were playing golf today, this would be one of my greater days.

Golf is the name of the game at Hound Ears. Golf in the spring, summer and fall. And in winter there's alpine and cross-country skiing. The skiing may come as something of a surprise, but this northwest corner of North Carolina is blest with cool air, both winter and summer, and the mountains provide some really first rate skiing. Hound Ears has its own ski area and is within a short distance of several others.

Now in August everything was dewy fresh, green and quite cool. I had arrived well in time for dinner on the previous evening and joined a group of four people on one of the little balconies of the dining room. We discovered that we were from all parts of the country. One man had flown in from Florida with his wife. Another gentleman from Savannah had his 16-year-old son along who was elated to find there were several teenage girls here as well. Later we were joined by people who owned one of the homes on the hillside that overlooks this secluded valley. Our conversation got around to the fact that the world was getting smaller and so many things seemed to be closing in on us. However, we all agreed that Hound Ears was one of the remaining gentle places.

It's interesting to me how many times in conversation with other guests at Hound Ears I have heard the expression: "This is my part of the world."

The day that I had planned included a trip to visit Mildred the Bear at Grandfather Mountain, a ride on the famous "Tweetsie" Railway, another trip to the Land of Oz on top of nearby Beach Mountain and perhaps an hour or two at the Hound Ears swimming pool followed by dinner and a quiet evening with my new friends.

We decided to see a performance of *Horn In West*, a drama about Daniel Boone, that evening. I had to admit that for a time at least "this was my part of the world," as well.

HOUND EARS LODGE AND CLUB, P.O. Box 277, Blowing Rock, N.C. 28605; 704-963-4321. A luxurious 30-room resort-inn on Rte. 105, 6 mi. from Boone. Near natural attractions. American Plan. Open year-round. 18-hole golf course, Alpine and xc-ski, swimming and tennis on grounds. Charlie Elliott, Jr., Innkeeper.

Directions: From Winston-Salem, follow Rte. 421 west to Boone, then travel south on Rte. 105 to inn. From Asheville, follow Rtes. 19 and 19E to Pineola, then Rte. 181 to Linville and Rte. 105 north to inn. From Bristol, Va. and I-81, follow Rte. 421 east to Vilas, (mountainous), then Rte. 321 east to Boone. In Boone, pick up Rte. 105 and head south to inn.

NU-WRAY INN, Burnsville

"Rush," I inquired, "what makes the ham here taste so different?"

Rush's dinner bell had rung a few moments earlier, and all members of the "Nu-Wray Inn Admiration Club" dutifully filed in on time to take their places at the long tables. Rush then introduced all of the newcomers and we took our places in the bentwood chairs and set about the pleasant task before us. Large platters of homemade baked beans, fried ham, hot breads, corned beef, fried chicken, green beans, corn on the cob, and many other good things were passed from hand to hand, and the room was filled with the laughing and talking of undeniably happy people.

Rush turned to answer my question. "First of all, you've got to have a genuine iron skillet, very hot. Then put in one teaspoon of grease, place the sliced ham in the pan and allow it to remain

long enough to heat thoroughly. Be certain to cook it on both sides. Then add a small amount of water which makes the gravy, pour this over the ham after it has been removed to the platter, and, by all means, be sure to serve it hot."

The fact is that while I have written extensively in previous editions about the fact that Rush rings a bell in the morning to wake everybody up, and another bell for breakfast and dinner, there's a great deal more to the Nu-Wray Inn than, perhaps, I've lead you to believe. For one thing, it's in the beautiful high country of North Carolina, and Mt. Mitchell, the highest mountain east of the Mississippi, is quite nearby. In fact, the flora and birds attract a great many visitors to Burnsville each year and quite a few of Rush's regular guests bring their binoculars, sketch pads, oils, canvases, and water colors.

The Nu-Wray dates back to 1850 when it was established by Garrett D. Ray. His daughter, Julia Ray, married William B. Wray and in time they became the owners and operators. The building was modernized, and the name was changed to the Nu-Wray Inn, spelling it with the "W." Rush is the third generation of innkeepers.

The inn is exactly what you would hope to find in a bustling village in the North Carolina highlands. It is furnished with antiques and family heirlooms. The sitting room has a welcome fireplace against the chilly highland mornings and dozens of books and magazines scattered around. It's impossible to sit there for very long without someone introducing himself and exchanging traveling adventures.

The rooms are the type I call "old-fashioned country inn." Most have private baths, but there are a few with the bath "down the hallway." They, however, do have lavatories in the room.

Every year I hear from many people who have gone out

211

of their way to stay at the Nu-Wray and experience this unique Carolina hospitality. Everyone of them says the same, that "it's really an experience."

As we finished off our dessert of apple cobbler, Rush pushed his glasses down on his nose and said, "There's one thing I forgot to tell you about cooking a Nu-Wray ham."

"What is that?" I asked expectantly.

"First you've got to catch a Nu-Wray pig!"

NU-WRAY INN, Burnsville, N.C. 28714; 704-682-2329. A 35-room village inn on town square on Rte. 19E, 38 mi. north of Asheville. A few miles from Mt. Mitchell. Mod. American Plan omits lunch and Sun. night supper. Breakfast and dinner served daily to travelers. Noon dinner served on Sundays only. Open every day of the year. Golf, swimming, hiking and skiing nearby. For nature and antique lovers. Rush T. Wray, Innkeeper. Mrs. Annie Wray Bennett, Hostess.

Directions: From Asheville, go north on Rte. 19-23 for 18 miles, then continue on 19. Five miles from Burnsville, 19 becomes 19E. From the north via Bristol or Johnson City, Tenn., take Rte. 19-23 to Unicoi. Turn left on 107 to North Carolina State Line. Take 226 and turn right on Rte. 197 at Red Hill to Burnsville.

HEMLOCK INN, Bryson City

Morning in the southern highlands. My watch said 7:30. I still had time for a brief walk in the woods before the breakfast bell would sound. A bluebird flitted past my window beckoning me to sample the forest of dew-laden flowers, bushes and trees.

Hurriedly dressing, I walked over to see if I could get something warm to drink. What aromas! Country ham frying in the pan, fresh biscuits, and apple fritters! But at that moment Ella

Jo Shell came in and picked up the thread of our conversation the night before. My thought of a morning walk died aborning.

"Since you mentioned that you needed a list of birds and flowers," she said, "I sat down and wrote out as many as I could think of. But we have so many that I don't believe we can count them all. Why, just take flowers. We have violets, May apples,

Dutchman's pipe, columbine, trillium, dogwood, lady's-slippers, little brown jug, wild geraniums, yellow fringed orchids, lillies of the valley, butterfly weeds. jack-in-the-pulpit, black-eyed Susans—" I put up my hand and cried. "Uncle!"

Ella Jo's enthusiasm was not to be daunted. "As far as birds are concerned," she went on, "we have all kinds of thrushes, thrashers, mockingbirds, warblers, wrens, cardinals, goldfinches, titmice, several different kinds of owls— the list just goes on."

The Hemlock Inn has been run by John and Ella Jo for the past few years. It is a very cozy, comfortable resort inn in one of the smaller ranges of the Great Smokies. It's a rustic place, without what John refers to as "fancy frills." In fact, I find that it's almost like visiting relatives. Breakfasts and dinners are served around Lazy Susan tables, and the bell rings at 8:30 in the morning and at 6:00 at night. People wander in and stand behind their chairs and John asks blessing. It's that kind of place.

Speaking of food, the Hemlock serves marvelous southern cooking. There's country fried steak, beef and chicken pies, coarse-ground grits, chess pie, Quaker pie, homemade cobblers and all kinds of fritters including okra. Have you ever had okra fritters?

At the Hemlock everyone gets introduced to everyone else. It's a place where you can fill your days with the woods, or driving and sight-seeing in the mountains. On the other hand, if you just care to sit and look at the scenery or read and be quiet or maybe play a little shuffleboard or ping-pong, that's okay too. There's no organized plan of recreation. John says, "It's just folks being folks."

Ella Jo, now thoroughly warmed up to her task, was telling me again about the various plants in the woods nearby. "Well, we have flame azaleas, rhododendron, boxwood, laurel, holly, all kinds of ferns ... " She was full of lists this morning.

HEMLOCK INN, Bryson City, N.C. 28713; 704-488-9820. A 25-room Smoky Mountain inn 4 mi. from Bryson City and 60 mi. from Asheville. Near Fontana Village, Cherokee and Pisgah National Forest. Mod. American Plan, omits lunch. Breakfast and dinner served to travelers by reservation only. Sunday dinner served at noontime. Open from early May to early November. No pets. Shuffleboard, skittles, horseshoes, hiking trails on grounds. Tubing and golf nearby. For nature and history lovers. Ella Jo and John Shell, Innkeepers.

Directions: located 1 mi. off Rte. 19 between Cherokee and Bryson City, N.C. Take paved road to top of mountain.

SNOWBIRD MOUNTAIN LODGE, Robbinsville

"That is a White Breasted Yellow Bill," said Ed Williams, pointing to the bird that swooped over the terrace and alighted on a nearby holly tree. I failed to notice the twinkle in his eye as he added, "They come back here every spring."

We were sitting where everyone sits at Snowbird Mountain Lodge—on the terrace which almost hangs over Lake Santeetlah, at least a thousand feet below. Gazing over the railings we could see a tiny automobile on the thin winding sliver of road climbing the adjacent mountain. Directly in front of us, almost close enough to touch, were at least fifteen majestic mountain peaks, with heights from 4,000 to 5,500 feet.

Mary, Ed's wife, joined us and the talk turned to the changing colors of leaves and flowers with each of the seasons.

"In the springtime," Mary informed me, "the trailing arbutus, all of the violets, the laurel and dogwood are indescribably beautiful. We go into midsummer with the crimson Bee Balm, cardinal flowers, Turk's cap, Carolina lillies, and of course, the rhododendron which reaches its peak bloom about the Fourth of July.

"What can we say about Fall? Can you imagine all of these trees in full color in October?"

Ed started to talk about the more than one hundred and ten birds that have been sighted at or near Snowbird, but Mary announced that lunch was ready. I noticed that there were quite a few people missing whom I had met at breakfast, and Ed explained that there were many hikers and 'back roaders' at the inn. Box lunches were provided because people preferred to be out in the great woods. The Joyce Kilmer Memorial Forest is just two miles away.

Along with the fact that the inn is located literally on the top of a mountain, there are a great many activities to enjoy in the daytime—shuffleboard, horseshoes, skittles and of course, all of the great hiking and walking trails. There's also some stream and lake fishing nearby. I'm happy to report that along with the books which are on the tables in the natural wood-paneled lodging rooms, there is a huge library that affords a lot of good vacation reading.

The glorious, nature-filled days at Snowbird result in hearty appetites. Among the tempting main dishes are fresh mountain trout Almandine, roast beef, fresh ham, and steaks. All of the baking is done in the spotless kitchen. Breakfasts also are a highlight with delicious coffee made with spring water and marvelous sausage.

That evening after dinner I was seated next to the big fireplace researching Ed's White Breasted Yellow Bill, when he came by. I buttonholed him. "I just realized that that bird wasn't a Yellow Bill at all; it was a double breasted Tarheel. A Yellow Bill has much shorter wings and flies backwards!"

SNOWBIRD MOUNTAIN LODGE, Joyce Kilmer Forest Rd., Robbinsville, N.C. 28771; 704-479-3433. A 16-room inn on top of the Great Smokies, 12 mi. from Robbinsville. American Plan. Lunch and dinner served to travelers by reservation only. No children under age 12. No pets. Open May 17 through October 27. Swimming, fishing, hiking nearby. For nature lovers. Mary and Ed Williams, Innkeepers.

Directions: Approaching from the northeast or south, take U.S. 19 and 129; from the northwest, take U.S. 129.

Kentucky

In 1763, a Royal Proclamation prohibited the English colonists from settling west of the top of the Alleghenies. This was done supposedly because of the danger of Indian warfare. Actually English merchants had gotten the proclamation through to keep the American merchants who owed them money from skipping over the mountains and getting lost from their creditors in the wilderness. In any case, Daniel Boone, who did not owe any money to the English merchants, strolled over the mountains in 1767.

A little later Richard Henderson, a land speculator from Virginia who had become a judge in North Carolina, bought most of the future state from the Cherokees for ten thousand pounds. He expected to sell it to future settlers at a tidy profit, and he would soon be asking Boone to make a road of sorts over the mountains and start a settlement or two. Meanwhile, Virginia considered that the land belonged to that colony and refused to recognize Henderson's claim. Spain also claimed it as her own by right of first discovery.

ELMWOOD INN, Perryville

The luncheon salad looked delicious. It had many varieties of fresh fruits arranged around a generous scoop of sherbet. It also had freshly made hot biscuits filled with Kentucky fried ham. Ham and hot biscuits—what a treat for a visitor from New England!

I could have ordered the southern fried chicken with cream gravy. "That's what Colonel Sanders always orders when he eats here." Innkeeper Gladys Coyle went on to explain, "He loves the chicken, hot biscuits, new small potatoes, a big salad, and a huge helping of peas. He's been here five times and says it's the best chicken he's ever eaten."

The Elmwood Inn could really only happen in Kentucky. Surrounded by a grove of maple and sweetgum trees alongside the Chaplin River in Perryville, the inn features traditional southern dishes in an atmosphere of Greek Revival elegance. The building was constructed in 1842, and became a field hospital following the Battle of Perryville, during the Civil War.

The main entrance with its twin two-story columns faces the Chaplin River. The lawns leading to the banks have sugar maples, black locusts, hemlock, pine, ash, gingko, and willows. Next to the building there is a very large and colorful bed of tulips which, I could well imagine, was breathtaking when in full bloom.

The inn has been carefully furnished in antiques, and Kentucky and Civil War memorabilia. Each of the six serving rooms has been named for some worthy individual, well-known to the region or community. For example, one is the T.C. Poynter Room, named after the founder of a school which occupied the building for many years.

After lunch, I took advantage of a few extra moments to visit some of the important features of Perryville. One is the restoration of the old Perryville historic district. It was here that I learned that Perryville was originally known as Harberson's Station and was founded by some settlers from Pennsylvania. Many of the buildings are being restored, including the Karrick-Parks House which is directly across the river from the Elmwood Inn. A footbridge is planned to connect this historic section of Perryville with the inn.

I also visited the Perryville Battlefield which is just a few miles from the town and was the scene of one of the most desperate battles of the Civil War. It is most popular with the tourists.

At the end of a pleasant afternoon of Kentucky history, I was happy to return for the evening meal at the Elmwood. Confronted by a myriad of choices including sweetbreads, fried shrimp, Florida Pompano, and other tempting dishes, I decided to try the fried chicken with cream gravy.

I think I know why Colonel Sanders keeps coming back.

ELMWOOD INN, Perryville, Ky., 40468; 606-332-2271. A country restaurant in a historically important Kentucky town on Rtes. 150 and 68, 9 miles from Harrodsburg and Danville. Near the Perryville Battlefield State Shrine. No lodgings. Lunch and dinner served daily except Mondays. Closed Christmas Eve and Christmas Day. Open year-round. For history lovers. Gladys Coyle, Innkeeper.

Directions: Exit Bluegrass Pkwy. at Bardstown and take Hwy. 150 into Perryville. From Harrodsburg take Rte. 68 to Perryville.

BOONE TAVERN HOTEL, Berea

Some people use cookbooks for bedside reading. I admit that I'm one of those people, and, believe it or not, I also enjoy reading menus.

Berea College chapel

On this particular night, I happened to be looking at the menu from the Boone Tavern hotel, which features so many of the recipes originated by Dick Hougen, the innkeeper. Dick, in fact, has already written three cookbooks, which are some of the best I've ever seen. Among other regional dishes, the menu offers Boone Tavern corn sticks, southern spoon bread, chicken flakes in bird's nests, Jefferson Davis pie, chocolate satin pie, beef cubelettes Olympia, southern fried chicken, and baked plantation ham.

All of these dishes and many more are served at this famous Berea hotel. As Dick explained to me on a recent visit, "I think there are many reasons why we've enjoyed such continuous popularity. One is our selection of outstanding regional foods. Our cooks are only too happy to innovate, and, of course, I'm always dreaming up new recipes myself."

Another reason why people come to this small central Kentucky town is to visit Berea College. It offers a liberal arts education of the highest academic standard to the promising young men and women from Appalachia. Eighty per cent of the students are from the local region and are chosen on the basis of financial need, high scholastic standing, and character. The other twenty per cent come from various locations including Europe, Asia, and Africa.

These young men and women are able to attend Berea for a most reasonable sum which includes room and board. No tuition is charged.

One of the unique features of the college curriculum is the ten-hour weekly student work program involving sixty-four different departments of the college. One of these is the Boone Tavern where ninety per cent of the staff are students. Another department is the woodworking and carpentry shop where, for example, the furniture for the hotel is made by students. The loom shop handweaving is another student industry. One of the most popular items is the game of Skittles. I've seen these games, which are made in the Berea College craft shop and sold commercially, in many other country inns.

Student-conducted tours of the campus leave the hotel twice daily and they are the best way to get the true picture of this unusual educational experience which incorporates the hotel itself.

I was delighted to learn that "Wilderness Road," by Paul Green, the drama depicting the founding of Berea College, will again be presented during the summer of 1975.

I continued reading the menu: beet relish, cinnamon apple slices, pumpkin muffins, cranberry beets, spiced sweet potatoes—the one problem was that instead of reading myself to sleep, I found myself getting very hungry and had to go downstairs for a midnight snack.

Wouldn't it be wonderful to open the refrigerator and find some Boone Tavern cherry cobbler!

BOONE TAVERN HOTEL, Berea, Kentucky 40403; 606-986-9341. A 65-room village inn in a unique college community on I-75, 40 mi. south of Lexington, Ky. European Plan. Breakfast, lunch, dinner served daily to travelers. (By sittings only.) (Dinner and Sunday noon coats for men; ladies, dresses or pant suits.) Never closed. All campus activities open to guests. Campus tours twice daily except Saturdays and Sundays. Tennis on grounds. Golf, pool and bicycles nearby. (Berea is on Central Daylight Saving Time.) Richard Hougen, Innkeeper.

Directions: Take Berea exit from I-75. One mile north to hotel.

PLEASANT HILL, Shakertown

I was strolling along the main street of Pleasant Hill, a restored Shaker Community which had its beginnings in the early 1800's. It was difficult to believe that a few short years ago this street was a blacktop road that carried autos and trucks between the clusters of red brick buildings, many in a state of disrepair. Now everything has been changed.

Trim white fences border both sides of the country dirt road. The brick and stone houses have been happily restored to their neat condition of a hundred years ago. They are now providing a real 19th century Shaker experience for the many thousands of people who visit this beautiful community every year.

I was approaching the Trustees' House, which has twin spiral staircases up to the third floor, and spotted the window of my lodging room as the sun reflected from its panes. Last night I had slept on a reproduction of a Shaker bed. There were Shaker tables and chairs and a peg-board for my clothes—even a Shaker trundle bed!

The founders of Pleasant Hill belonged to a religious group named The United Society of Believers in Christ's Second Appearing. They were actually an offshoot of the Quakers. Pleasant Hill was established in 1805 and by 1820 was a prosperous colony of 500 persons. The Shakers lived in communal dedication to their beliefs in celibacy, public confessions of sins (culminating in the frenetic, trembling dances which gave them the name of Shakers), renunciation of worldliness, and a common ownership of property.

There are now more than twenty-two Shaker buildings that have been restored and these buildings are living museums.

For example, this three-story Center Family House has been furnished with authentic Shaker furnishings as when one hundred Shakers lived there. The upper floors have various Shaker exhibits. Several restored smaller buildings are used by demonstrating craftsmen—a weaver, cooper, broom maker and cabinetmaker.

Other restored buildings include the East Family House built in 1817; the Meeting House, 1820; the Water Works, 1933; and many others.

The Trustees' House, which has some of the lodging rooms, as well as the day room, was designed to be a place where Believers could meet "the world" to transact business.

From the kitchen at the Trustees' House come such hearty country foods as ham, cornbread, fried chicken, and vegetables grown in the village garden. Many are prepared from Shaker recipes. Other Shaker goodies include a delicious lemon pie and a Kentucky chess pie. During the winter season a bountiful afternoon tea is served, including luscious nut breads and confections.

I'm happy to report that Pleasant Hill is not only an outstanding restoration, but an outstanding country inn.

INN AT PLEASANT HILL, Shakertown, Ky., P.O. address: Rte. 4 Harrodsburg, Ky. 40330; 606-734-9111. A 63 room country inn in a restored Shaker village on Rte. 68, 7 mi. northeast of Harrodsburg, 25 mi. southwest of Lexington. European Plan. Breakfast, lunch, dinner served daily to travelers. Open year-round. Suggest contacting Inn about winter schedule. Closed Christmas Eve and Christmas Day. For history lovers. Betty Morris, Innkeeper.

Directions: From Lexington take Rte. 68 south toward Harrodsburg. From Louisville, take I-64 to Lawrenceburg and Graeffenburg exit (not numbered). Follow Rte. 127 south to Harrodsburg and Rte. 68 northeast to Shakertown.

DOE RUN INN, Brandenburg

Let me share a letter with you that I received recently:

"Dear Berkshire Traveller, we would like to compliment you on your good taste in choosing the Doe Run Inn for your book. We have just spent a lovely week-long honeymoon there. We spent two nights in the honeymoon suite and the remainder in the Cardinal Room where I understand you stayed.

"Curtis and Lucille Brown are certainly most gracious hosts. The food was outstanding and the service was courteous and attentive. We wholeheartedly agree with your choice of the Doe Run Inn as a truly representative country inn.

"We hope to make a hobby of visiting your inns through the years. We are very thankful for your thoughtful book and look forward to more pleasant times such as we had at the Doe Run Inn."

There's nothing unusual in the experience of these two young people at the Doe Run Inn. I've received lots of mail indicating that Curt and Lucille Brown extend their country-style hospitality to everyone.

The Doe Run is an ideal place to spend a honeymoon or, for that matter, any kind of a holiday or vacation. It is surrounded by great numbers of trees including oak, dogwood, redbud, maple, persimmon, tulip, sycamore, black walnut, and cedars. There are dozens and dozens of different varieties of birds including the southern mockingbirds who make their homes in these trees. It's fun to go walking in the woods or fishing in Doe Run Creek.

Mention of the Cardinal Room brings back memories of many good times. I'll always remember the first time I stayed in that room. It was furnished completely in antiques, with a small wood stove at one end. The three-foot thick outer stone wall made me feel as if I were in a fort. The building was originally a water-powered woolen mill as well as a grist mill.

There are dozens of antiques generously scattered throughout the inn. Many of them have real pedigrees. One is the walnut bed in the Honeymoon room. It is over 150 years old.

As for food, imagine country ham and hot biscuits with red eye gravy or golden fried chicken, green beans, fried apples, chicken livers, and desserts like old-fashioned lemon pie. As you might well imagine, all the baking and cooking are done right in the Doe Run kitchen.

By the way, on Fridays and Sundays a tremendous smorgasbord is served. I counted over 60 different dishes.

And I'll never forget that Abraham Lincoln's father was one of the men who worked on the construction of the mill in 1816.

DOE RUN INN, Rte. 2, Brandenburg, Ky. 40108; 502-422-9982. A 17-room country inn reminiscent of the backwoods on Rte. 448, 4 mi. south of Brandenburg, 38 mi. south of Louisville. Near Fort Knox. European Plan. 5 rooms with private bath; 12 rooms with shared baths. Breakfast, lunch, and dinner served to travelers daily. Closed Christmas Eve and Christmas Day. Hiking and fishing on grounds. Swimming nearby. For history and antique lovers. Curtis and Lucille Brown, Innkeepers.

Directions: From Louisville, Ky., take U.S. 31-W south to Hwy. 1638. Take Hwy. 1638 west and turn south on Hwy. 448. Follow Doe Run signs.

Lower
South

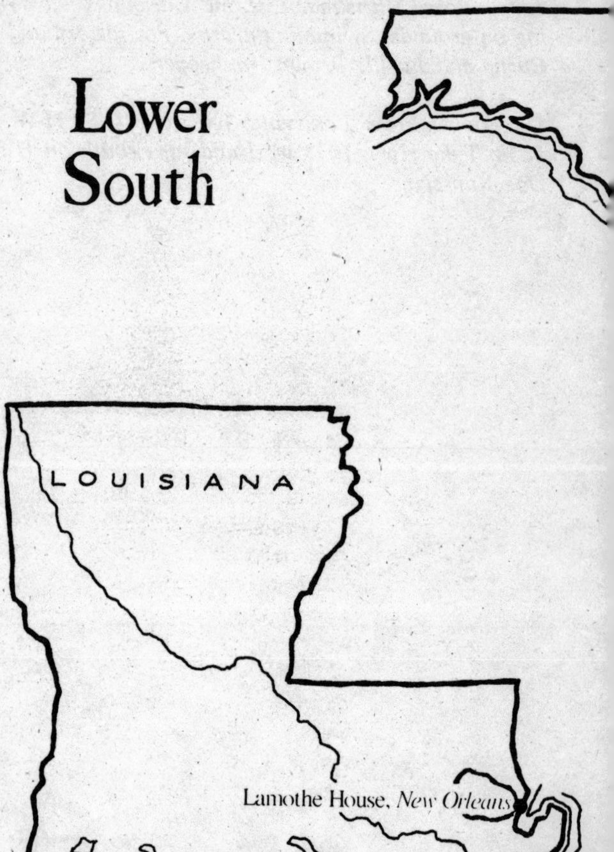

LOUISIANA

Lamothe House, *New Orleans*

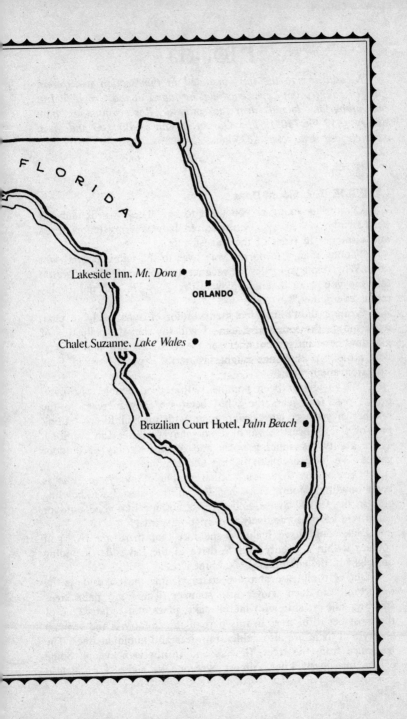

FLORIDA

Lakeside Inn, *Mt. Dora*

ORLANDO

Chalet Suzanne, *Lake Wales*

Brazilian Court Hotel, *Palm Beach*

Florida

In addition to the inns included in this section a different kind of country inn experience can be found at the Greyfield Inn on Cumberland Island (near Jacksonville). Reservations are mandatory (912-496-7503). The Gasparilla Inn in Boca Grande is a very elegant experience (813-964-2201).

LAKESIDE INN, Mount Dora

"You're as young as you want to be." These words had just been firmly spoken by a white-haired lady wearing tennis shoes and visor out in front of the Lakeside Inn.

"Young man, I'm on my way over to the tennis courts right now. Why don't you get your racquet and join me? Mr. Edgerton told me you were a tennis player. I'm 70 years old and I play tennis every day."

While I didn't find too many senior citizens ready to challenge me on the courts at 8 a.m., I will say that the collection of grandmothers and grandfathers at the Lakeside Inn had a great deal more pep than one might ordinarily expect. I asked Dick Edgerton about this.

"We've always been popular with retired people. However, in the past few years there has been a steady increase in the number of younger guests who come with their children. I think part of this is because we have so many facilities for everyone. There are two swimming pools and a wide variety of outdoor games. We have excellent fishing and boating.

"One of the diversions which people of every age like is lawn bowling. Mount Dora has the third largest lawn bowling club in the United States, and there is nothing like good outdoor activity to keep people lively and in good spirits."

Dick could have included the fact that there are five golf courses within a twenty minute drive of the Lakeside, including one right in the community of Mount Dora.

One of the pleasurable aspects of visiting the Lakeside is the opportunity to turn winter into summer. There are palm trees standing side by side with laurel, oaks, pines and cedars. One of the most beautiful trees in this part of the country is the serinam cherry and there are also golden raintrees and kumquat trees. The fragrance from the trees, flowers and shrubs is heavenly. Some of the inn guests know almost everyone by sight. This is also

where migrating and permanent birds meet and flit from tree to tree.

Dick and I agreed that there's a striking resemblance between Mount Dora and New England, and he said that a great many of the guests came from the Northeast. "We serve quite a few New England dishes," he said. "Clam chowder and Indian pudding are on the menu and you can even have cornmeal mush for breakfast." The rest of the menu at the inn reflects the tropical location and proximity to the Florida waters. The buffets are much admired.

Also admired are the pleasing shops of this tidy community. I have a pair of graceful brass candlesticks from one of them.

My new tennis friend was getting impatient. "Well, are you going to play or not?"

"Okay," I replied, "we'll play."

"Lovely," said she. "And tonight after dinner we'll get two more people and play 'Spite and Malice.' It's an old card game. You'll love it!"

LAKESIDE INN, P.O. Box 175, Mount Dora, Fla. 32757; 904-383-2151. A 110-room resort-inn on Lake Dora in central Florida, 30 mi. northwest of Orlando. American Plan. Breakfast, lunch and dinner served to travelers daily. Open from December 15 to April 15. Two swimming pools, fishing, waterskiing, putting green and shuffle board on grounds. Golf, bicycles, lawn bowling and sailing nearby. Marie and Dick Edgerton, Innkeepers.

Directions: Follow I-95 south to Daytona Beach, then Rte. 4 to Rte. 46 west to Mount Dora. Or, follow I-75 south to Wildwood, then Rte. 44 east to Rte. 441. Proceed east on Rte. 441 to Mount Dora.

BRAZILIAN COURT HOTEL, Palm Beach

I had found the other side of Palm Beach. Not the glittering social facade, but the side with more genuine people. Furthermore, I was amazed to find a Palm Beach Hotel with the simplicity and good taste that appealed to such people. It is called the Brazilian Court although most everyone refers to it as the "BC."

It was built back in the 1920's, and the Palm Beach residential area with sedate homes and beautifully landscaped gardens grew up and around it. The building is a two-story Palm Beach Mission design with two completely enclosed patios. One patio, with several varieties of palm trees, begonias and poinsettias, is a marvelous place to catch the morning sun.

The other patio really sets the tone for this discreet hotel. Dispersed among the royal palms, figs, orange, banana and African tulip trees are dining tables, many with umbrellas. Weather permitting, all three meals are served here, and each time of day has its own captivating mood.

In the evening, small lights twinkle on the inside of each umbrella and indirect colored lighting dramatically underscores the trees and exotic tropical plants. As night falls the lights become more brilliant against the dark blue sky. Now add a three-piece orchestra playing softly in the background and you have the complete picture.

The BC is quite reminiscent of the Black Point at Prouts Neck and the Bethel Inn in Maine. And the climate brings to mind the Inn at Rancho Santa Fe, California.

Because there are many long-staying guests, the selections on the menu are numerous and varied. The broiled pompano amandine is delicious. The red snapper and Florida lobster Newburg

are very appetizing also. There are several dishes prepared with Florida fresh fruit available at each meal.

Although the BC is two blocks from the ocean, there's a special sun deck atop one of the buildings. As innkeeper Bright Johnson explained, "This is for people who don't want to go down to the ocean everyday to get a good tan."

The lodging rooms and suites are furnished with quiet elegance. They overlook the residential area of the town or the attractive inner patios.

The BC is basically a conservative resort-inn with quite a few of the amenities that guests find enjoyable. There's great emphasis placed on both the food and the service. The famous Worth Avenue shops of Palm Beach are just a few minutes away.

I'm happy to add the Brazilian Court to a select list of inns and hotels in larger cities. Like the Algonquin in New York and the Cheshire in St. Louis, I think they meet a need for personal hospitality.

BRAZILIAN COURT HOTEL, 300 Brazilian Ave., Palm Beach, Fla. 33480; 305-655-7740. A 125-room hotel in the heart of Palm Beach. A secluded patioed garden spot just a short walk from the ocean and Worth Avenue shops. All Plans available. Breakfast, lunch and dinner served to travelers daily. Open from mid-December to early April. No pets. Swimming, boating, fishing, tennis, golf and bicycles nearby. Bright Johnson, Innkeeper.

Directions: From Sunshine State Parkway, take Exit 40 to Okeechobee Blvd. Turn left and proceed 6 mi. to Royal Palmway Bridge. Cross bridge and take first right, then turn left after 1 block on to Brazilian Ave. Hotel is two blocks east on Brazilian Ave.

CHALET SUZANNE, Lake Wales

I sat next to the swimming pool at Chalet Suzanne among the fabulous flowers and trees, wondering where to begin describing this place.

I decided to start with the Great Depression of the 30's. At that time Bertha Hinshaw was a new widow with two children, $1700 from a cancelled insurance policy, two old cars, and a six-room house about a mile and a half from the main highway. She decided to open a restaurant. For ten days no one came, and then finally a family of five arrived and stayed for Christmas. Chalet Suzanne was in business.

A fire in 1943 turned out to be a blessing because Bertha

started all over again—this time with some pretty unique ideas. She created an atmosphere that looked like a set from a movie. There is a conglomeration of little houses, lodges and chalets that could belong in nearby Disney World. It's Oriental, Persian, Bavarian, Swiss and chocolate layer cake. There are little bridges, penthouses, cupolas, balconies, minarettes, peaked roofs, flat roofs, and here and there little tiny windows that lack only a Snow White peeking through them.

These are all connected by brick walks and cobblestone paths. Guests can choose accommodations for their moods—Byzantine or medieval, carpenter gothic or *Erehwon*.

Truly exceptional food is served at Chalet Suzanne in five different dining rooms, all in a sort of Hans Christian Andersen setting. The late Clementine Paddleford tasted the soups and wrote in her column in the New York Herald Tribune, "It's good! good! good!" In fact, the soup led to still another business and now Chalet Suzanne Soups including at least nineteen different kinds are available in food specialty shops and supermarkets all over the country. My favorite is "Romaine."

Bertha's son, Carl, is the major domo of the kitchen and the opening course for dinner at Chalet Suzanne is always an invention by Carl's wife, Vita, such as chicken liver canape centered in the original Chalet baked grapefruit. Among other specialties is their famous Chicken Suzanne glazed with its own natural juices to a beautiful amber color. Other main courses are lobster Newburg, lump crab and shrimp curry. Crepes Suzanne are served just before the dessert. These are rolled up tiny pancakes topped with one of Carl Henshaw's special sauces. Incidentally, Carl is also the operator of the Chalet Suzanne air field which is immediately adjacent to the inn.

One important further thought—children love Chalet Suzanne. After all, why not, All those funny buildings, a lake, a swimming pool, air planes arriving and taking off, and even a little golf cart to ride around on. It "out-Disneys" Disney World.

CHALET SUZANNE, Lake Wales, Fla. 33853; 813-676-1477. A 30-room phantasmagoric country inn and gourmet restaurant, 4½ mi. from Lake Wales. Near Cypress Gardens and Disney World. European and Mod. American Plans available. Dining room open from 8 a.m. to 9:30 p.m. daily. Closed Mondays in September and October. Pool on grounds. Golf, tennis, riding nearby. For nature lovers. The Hinshaw Family, Innkeepers.

Directions: From Sunshine State Parkway, exit at Yeehaw Junction and head west on Rte. 60 to U.S. 27 (60 mi.). Proceed north on U.S. 27 at Lake Wales. Inn is 4 mi. north of Lake Wales on Rte. 17A. From Interstate 4 turn south on U.S. 27 toward Lake Wales.

Louisiana

The early history of Louisiana is a little cloudy. The mouth of the Mississippi may have been discovered by Alonso de Pinneda in 1519. Probably Hernando de Soto entered the present State of Louisiana, and was buried there, but there is no proof of that. At any rate, Spain did not claim the region, and when la Salle came down the river in 1682 he took possession in the name of France.

In 1699, Pierre le Moyne d'Iberville made the first settlement, a fort about forty miles above the mouth of the Mississippi. This settlement did not prosper until John Law, the Scottish gambler and financier, got control of the colony. In 1718, New Orleans was founded and the settlers began to grow cotton in 1740, sugar cane in 1751.

However, in 1762, King Louis XV ceded all the territory of Lousiana to his cousin, the King of Spain. The colonists did not care to be ruled by Spain. In 1768 they attempted a revolt which was unsuccessful.

After 1765, hundreds of French exiles from Nova Scotia made their way to Louisiana. Descendants of these Acadians, known as "Cajuns" still live there.

LAMOTHE HOUSE, New Orleans

For the benefit of all her friends, let me share with you a letter that I received in December from Gertrude Munson of the Lamothe House.

"As you know, I was hospitalized for almost four months in April and am now progressing very nicely. I expect to be back at the Lamothe House in March.

"Mr. and Mrs. James Vink are now managing the inn temporarily. They are a young couple and carrying on with enthusiasm all the traditions that we have established over the years.

"We continue to have many charming guests because of *Country Inns and Back Roads* and we are especially delighted to see them.

"My best wishes to you for a successful and happy 1975."

Well, that tells part of the story about the Lamothe House. Another letter from Jim and Deborah Vink indicates that Gertrude's enthusiasm and deep-rooted hospitality are being well nurtured. Deborah tells me that they are looking forward to the happy day when Mrs. Munson will again be pouring the breakfast coffee.

Jim Mellow also has been at the Lamothe House recently and tells me that it is as beautiful and as accommodating as ever.

So much for the correspondence and details. The Lamothe House is one of my "country inns in the city." Others include the Algonquin in New York, the Cheshire in St. Louis, and the Brazilian Court in Palm Beach.

The Lamothe House has fourteen very pleasant rooms, most of which overlook an inner courtyard. Many of these lodging

rooms have four-poster beds and all of them have handsome antiques.

Among the flowers and trees which bring much joy to the inn guests are magnolia, banana, azalea, and night-blooming jasmine.

Because the French Quarter has so many restaurants and is only a few steps away, only one meal a day is served—petit déjeuner. Each morning in the elegant dining room the guests meet and discuss the sights of New Orleans and how to reach everything including the beautiful mansions and gardens which are within driving distance. Also helpful is a table of touring information includng a guide book prepared especially for Lamothe House guests by Jim Vink.

This quiet, conservative inn is a little jewel in the New Orleans crown. There is hardly a time when reservations are not needed well in advance.

I'm anxious to return again to have a long visit with Mrs. Munson and Jim and Deborah Vink and also to visit my good friends in New Orleans whom I haven't seen in quite some time, Bud and Genevieve Trimble.

LAMOTHE HOUSE, 621 Esplanade Ave., New Orleans, La. 70116; 504-947-1161. A small elegant 14-room inn in the French Quarter within walking distance of many fascinating New Orleans restaurants and attractions. European Plan with complimentary petit déjeuner. No other meals served. Open September 1 to August 1. No pets. Near Lake Pontchartrain and the Mississippi River, bayou and river cruises, plantations and mansions on the Great River Road. Golf, tennis, fishing and bicycles nearby. For history lovers. Mrs. Gertrude Munson, Deborah and James Vink, Innkeepers.

Directions: from the west or east on I-10, take the Orleans Ave. exit to Claiborne Ave. which runs under I-10 at that point. Proceed east for 7 blocks or until the intersection of Esplanade Ave. Turn right on Esplanade and proceed 10 blocks.

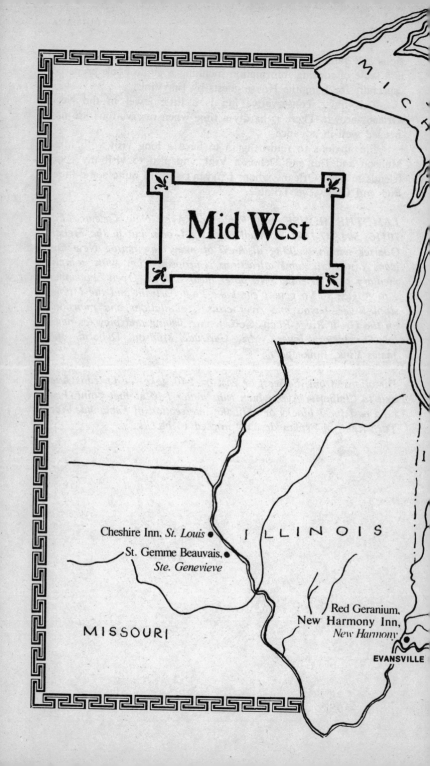

Mid West

MICH

ILLINOIS

Cheshire Inn, *St. Louis* ●

St. Gemme Beauvais, ●
Ste. Genevieve

Red Geranium,
New Harmony Inn,
New Harmony

MISSOURI

EVANSVILLE

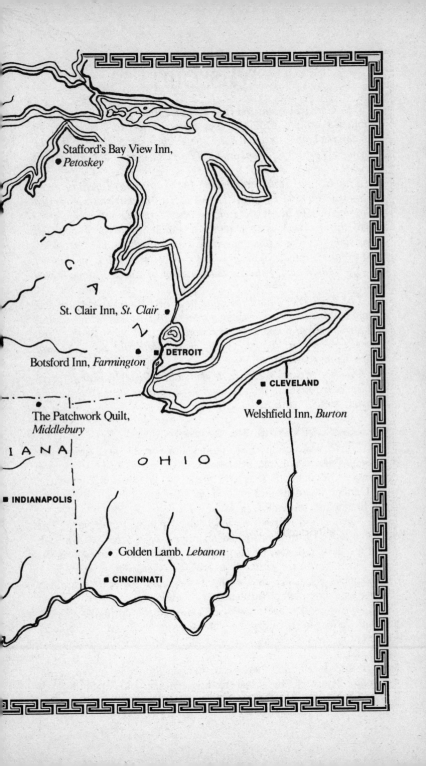

Missouri

Ste. Genevieve was the first permanent settlement in Missouri, established around 1732. At that time the territory was part of Louisiana which was owned by the French, later they ceded the Louisiana Territory to Spain. St. Louis started as a trading post in 1764.

The United States purchased the Louisiana Territory from the Spanish in 1803 and in 1817 the Territorial Legislature applied for permission to become a state. A considerable controversy grew out of the question as to whether or not it would be a so-called "slavestate" or free. The question was settled by the "Missouri Compromise" which allowed slavery in Missouri but prohibited it in the remainder of the nothern section of the Louisiana Territory.

The Civil War found the state divided between secession and Union sentiment. The governor departed in haste from the capital and signed an ordinance of secession and affiliation to the Confederacy. However, the pro-Union group, with the aid of federal troups removed the governor.

On this trip to Missouri, I visited Ste. Genevieve and found an impressive historic area as well as a country inn. In St. Louis I found another "inn in the city."

ST. GEMME BEAUVAIS, Ste. Genevieve

I love waking up in a country inn for the first time. Here in Ste. Genevieve I had set the alarm for an early hour because I wanted as much time as possible to get a full tour of the Inn St. Gemme Beauvais and to learn all I could about Ste. Genevieve, the first white settlement in Missouri.

My bed had a large, carved back in polished mahogony. The marble-topped bureau also had an impressive mirror with a 19th century carved frame. The flowered wallpaper, drapes, carpets and other furniture made it a realistic Victorian experience. I subsequently learned that each of the eight suites has at least two rooms completely furnished with antiques.

My day really started with breakfast in the dining room with walnut ladder-back chairs, Belgian lace curtains, marble fireplace, fine china, and graceful stemware—all reminders of elegant by-gone days.

I discovered that there were two meals a day served at St. Gemme Beauvais: breakfast to houseguests, and lunch by ad-

vance reservation. Anxious to preserve the true French heritage of the town, Frankye and Boats Donze, the innkeepers, put great emphasis on French cuisine for both meals. My eggs Benedict were very tasty, but I also found that there was something different each day, such as French crepes, French mushroom omelettes, and French toast with ginger fruit sauce.

The luncheons favored Quiche Lorraine, broccoli casserole, and other French specialties, such as stuffed chicken breast.

After breakfast Frankye took me on a tour of each room. I was particularly impressed by the bridal suite with an elaborate crystal chandelier, some handsome antique pieces, and two windows overlooking the Main Street. She also explained to me that each of the numbers on the lodging room doors were painted recently by her daughter-in-law. The inn is quite a family affair, I learned, with three sons and one daughter taking part in both the fun and responsibility. One of the rooms had an unusual bridal picture from at least a hundred years ago. Around the inside of the filigree frame there was material obviously from the bridal gown and preserved flowers from her bouquet. Frankye said that she and Boats have carefully collected as many regional antiques as possible for the inn.

Back downstairs in the tiny office, Boats, who grew up in the house, explained that the old-fashioned cubbyholes came from a post office in Illinois. I also noticed a little sign which best expressed the real philosophy of this home-like inn:

"There are no strangers here, just friends we haven't met."

ST. GEMME BEAUVAIS, 78 N. Main St., Ste. Genevieve, Mo. 63670; 314-883-5744. An 8-room village inn about 1½ hrs. from St. Louis. Mod. Am. Plan includes breakfast only. Breakfast served to house guests daily and to travelers only on Sunday. Lunch served by reservation only. Open year-round. Closed Christmas Day. No pets. Golf, hunting and fishing nearby. For history lovers. Frankye and Boats Donze, Innkeepers.

Directions: from St. Louis, south on I-55 to Hwy. 32. Exit east on 32 to Hwy. 61 to the Ste. Genevieve exit.

A MINI TOUR OF STE. GENEVIEVE

My tour of Ste. Genevieve with Frankye Donze really just scratched the surface, for there's so much to see and ponder. I learned that this unique town was the first settlement on the west bank of the Mississippi. It was founded by the French before 1735. Later on in the 19th century there were many German settlers.

As Gregory M. Franzwa says in his book *The Story of Old Ste. Genevieve,* which is available at the museum, "Ste. Genevieve is a sleeper. It isn't listed in most gazetteers, the pocket encyclopedias don't mention it, it gains only passing note in the national tourguides. Yet it has more historic integrity than many of the great national historic towns which attract millions of visitors each year."

During my tour with Frankye I saw more than twenty existing buildings from 150 to 200 years old. Quite a few of them have been restored as tour homes and museums but, happily, most of these 18th and 19th century structures are occupied today, maintained with pride by their owners.

Among those that I did visit was the Amoureaux House which has been restored by the Donzes. The keeping room dates back to 1770 and the furnishings mix various styles and modes indicating that a house does not remain static. It changes as new occupants and new furniture styles are added over the years. Most of the antiques have been collected in and around Ste. Genevieve, many of them tools and artifacts used by the settlers. The house construction is French Creole which is characterized by cedar logs set directly into the earth. The outer walls support the roof and the interior is then supported by huge beams.

Among other things, at the Amoureaux House there is a truly remarkable collection of antique dolls—literally a room full of them. Immediately next door is an old-fashioned country store with all kinds of candy, candles, jellies, soups and other similar articles on sale. The decorations include a very interesting display of old jars, an old talking machine, and a fancy old cake box.

We spent some time at the Beauvais House which was also built around 1770 and moved from an old village. It has huge ceiling beams and a great fireplace divides the two rooms. Henry Brackenridge, the noted historian, was a guest there in 1790. Frankye and Boats have also restored this house which ultimately led to the idea of restoring the inn.

I visited several other historic houses including the Mammy Shaw House and the Bolduc House which has a stockade fence.

Even in a short time I was prepared to agree with author Franzwa that Ste. Genevieve is well worth any traveler's visit, and it is most fortunate that it also has a graceful country inn to provide hospitality and lodging.

CHESHIRE INN, St. Louis

My good friend Jim Mellow from St. Louis has been telling me about the Cheshire Inn for at least two years. He sent me photographs, literature, and anything else that would help to explain it. But even with all of that, I still was amazed on my first visit. The entire atmosphere is highly reminiscent of half a dozen English country inns I have visited. The big difference is that this one is located in St. Louis, Missouri. It even has two red double-decker busses parked in front.

All the lodging rooms are done in an elegant Jacobean style, some with full canopied king-size beds. Many rooms have winged-backed chairs with rich brocade covers and wall tapestries. There are special rooms for prominent English literary figures such as Tennyson, Dickens, Samuel Johnson, and Galsworthy. The hallways are decorated with beautiful prints and oils of English kings and nobility. There is also a large collection of authentic Scottish badges and tartans. There's even a group of rooms on the top floor that share a small outdoor terrace.

The dining rooms at the inn contain one surprise after another. The first thing to greet me was a great slowly turning spit with a huge prime roast of beef emitting heavenly aromas. This is served with Yorkshire pudding and horseradish. The menu can best be described as formidable. It's jam-packed with hearty dishes from our English neighbors.

A dining room called the Great Hall looks for all the world like an English manor house hall with baronial flags and a huge fireplace. Each of the dining rooms is different but all feature an extensive collection of art and antiques. I was particularly impressed with the intimate, romantic atmosphere of a small pub in the lodge—the Fox and Hounds Tavern.

The inn is well known in St. Louis for its flowers and plants which are changed with every season. The proprietor's mother, Mrs. Florence Hulling Apted, maintains extensive gardens at her home for this purpose.

Things are so British here that even the public telephone booth is one of those red ones imported from England.

I understand from innkeeper, Mike Parker, that they've applied for admittance into the British Commonwealth of Nations. I thought that was a pippen!

CHESHIRE INN and LODGE, P.O. address: 6300 Clayton Rd., St. Louis, Mo., 63117; 314-647-7300. A 110 room English style inn, 1 block off Hwy. 40 near Forest Park. European Plan only. Breakfast, lunch and dinner served to travelers daily. Accommodations available every day of the year. Restaurant closed on New Year's Day, Memorial Day, July 4th, Labor Day, and Christmas Day. Pool, bicycles on grounds. Boating, golf, tennis and riding nearby. St. Louis Art Museum, zoo, Gateway Arch and opera nearby. Mike Parker, Innkeeper.

Directions: Just off Hwy. 40 at Clayton Rd. and Skinker Blvd. on southwest corner of Forest Park. From the east, take Clayton Rd. exit. From the west, take McCausland Ave. exit, north two blocks to Clayton Rd.

Indiana

A VISIT TO NEW HARMONY

I exchanged a few words of greeting with the man at the toll booth and crossed the Wabash from Illinois into Indiana. I had left St. Louis just a few hours earlier, and, with the directions provided by my friends Jim and Mary Virginia Mellow, I picked up Rte. 460, traversing the same prairies Abe Lincoln had crossed going West at an earlier time. The trip was punctuated by the appearance of several interesting towns involved in much farming activity. It was a pleasant drive between breakfast and lunch.

Just the name New Harmony promises hope, peace, and progress. I was to learn that these same values have played an important role in this pleasant community in the past and bid fair to play an even more important role in the future.

Perhaps a word of explanation is in order. In 1814, a group of religious dissenters from Württemberg, Germany who prospered under the leadership of George Rapp and his adopted son, Frederick, set up what was to be the first of two experiments in communal living in New Harmony. The Harmonists, as they were known, completely pooled their assets and then shared equally from the benefits derived from their activities. They were excellent farmers and craftsmen.

The Harmonists remained in the community until 1824, and during that short time constructed several enduring buildings.

When the cold whistled around the cabins of these early Indiana settlers, they were snug in their well-insulated, uniquely constructed houses. Twenty-five Harmonist buildings remain to-

241

day. More than ten are restored and not one leans with the West wind. They are scattered throughout the community and fortunately there is an excellent walking tour of the town which includes most of them.

The second experiment took place when a group under the leadership of Robert Owen, a Welsh social reformer, purchased the Community from the Harmonists in 1825. Owen's purpose was to create "universal happiness through universal education." They chose to establish their community in America where the expression of thought was free.

They succeeded in attracting to New Harmony leading scientists and educators from Europe and the educational centers of the United States. The achievements of the Owenites included the establishment of the first free public school system in America, the first free library, first free kindergarten, the first infant school, the first women's club with a written constitution, the first civic dramatic club, and was the seat of the first geological survey in the United States. Incidentally, in New Harmony in 1825, both boys and girls had equal access to education.

The Owenite social experiment lasted only two years but the society remained. New Harmony became the natural sicence center of America for the remainder of the pre-Civil War period. However, the basic philosophy of the community was now well established—it was the thrifty, hard work ethic of the Harmonists, combined with the intellectual and cultural objectives of the Owenites. Sounds like a real Utopia, doesn't it?

Some of the best of these two ideals is today evident in New

Harmony. Among the restored Harmonist buildings are the old Fauntleroy home which became outstanding during the Owen era as the birthplace of the Minerva Society; the Poet's House; the Thrall Opera House which was originally built by the Harmonists and converted to an opera house during the Owenite period, and several others.

There is a continuous program of restoration and development going on within New Harmony and among the most important of these will be the MacLeod Center, under construction on my last visit. It is dedicated to Lord George MacLeod who contributed so much to the field of working with youth. Lord MacLeod once said, "Peace is the only thing that is going to effect our total world, and if we can do something to bring these young people here together and channel their endeavors through housing, then we welcome them with open arms."

New Harmony has been designated as a National Historic Landmark, with world-wide recognition for its role in the preservation of Utopian communities.

One of the most remarkable phenomena in this community occurs when the Golden Raintree comes into bloom each June. The town is alight with the beauty of their blossoms and a festival is held by the townspeople each year to express gratitude.

The continuing search for the Spirit in New Harmony is strikingly shown in the famous Roofless Church. It is located right next to the Red Geranium and the New Harmony Inn. It was built in 1960 and designed by Philip Johnson. It has truly inspired sculptures by Jacques Lipchitz. The dome, shaped like an inverted rose bud, casts the shadow of a full blown rose. Services for churches of all denominations are frequently held within its walls.

Another indication of the continuing growth of New Harmony is the completion of the handsome New Harmony Inn.

NEW HARMONY INN, New Harmony

I saw remarkable progress at the New Harmony Inn on my last visit. The inn building, the Entry house and the year-round swimming pool, brilliantly designed by Woollen Associates of Indianapolis, were now completed. The surrounding grounds were beautifully landscaped with evergreen iberium, firethorn, Oregon holly, grape and chokeberry bushes. The red brick buildings seemed to interplay harmoniously with the adjacent Roofless Church, the Paul Tillich Park and the nearby restored Harmonist

243

buildings. The inn was built on the shores of a calm lake amidst forest and field where bicycling and walking paths abound.

My lodging room at the inn was also quite remarkable for its purity of design and uncluttered use of space. It was one of 45 individually styled rooms designed to provide what innkeeper Gene Kincheloe referred to as a "retreat" atmosphere. In addition to a wood burning fireplace (found in many rooms) it had rockers and chairs with the look of Danish Modern and a bed inspired by Shaker design. There was also a graceful circular staircase leading to a sleeping loft and a kitchenette if needed. Gene explained that there are a limited number of rooms with these available.

The design and feeling of the inn reflect contemporary influences. The generous use of stone and plaster as well as brick in the rooms, hallways, and reception areas indicate a great appreciation of natural wood as well as a blend of both muted and exciting colors. Extra large windows provide communication with the beautiful Indiana outdoors.

I found one particularly interesting feature in the Entry house when I first arrived. A non-sectarian chapel has been built off one corner. The room is nearly a complete circle with a skylight and an altar of natural wood has been built into one wall. The chapel is dedicated to Herbert Waddams, a Canon of Canterbury for ten years, and is used for quiet meditation and occasional weddings and baptisms.

The inn has provisions for many types of guests including

families with children. The swimming pool is a particularly happy addition with a sliding glass roof to bring summer inside and keep winter out. Because it's completely surrounded by glass walls, the trees are so close that it's like swimming in an old-fashioned Indiana swimming hole.

Meals are not served at the New Harmony Inn, but all three meals are available at the Shadblow restaurant, and lunch and dinner at the Red Geranium.

Just as the Harmonists and Owenites were both innovative groups who sought new horizons in this gentle farm community, so do the present owners of the New Harmony Inn seek new horizons in innkeeping and at the same time carry on a tradition that is centuries old.

NEW HARMONY INN, New Harmony, Ind. 47361; 812-682-4491. A 45-room village inn on the site of Harmonist and Owenite restorations. European Plan, no meals served; some rooms with kitchenettes. No pets. Open every day. Year-round swimming pool on grounds. Golf, boating, tennis and riding nearby. For history lovers. Gene Kincheloe, Innkeeper.

THE RED GERANIUM and SHADBLOW RESTAURANTS,
New Harmony

I had heard about the Red Geranium long before my first visit in 1972. Letters from avid enthusiasts praised the community, the Labyrinth, the Roofless Church, and especially the wonderful food at the Red Geranium.

One letter said, "By all means, be sure to have the spinach salad and the Shaker Lemon Pie," so I was prepared for something unusual on my first visit.

I poured some special Red Geranium dressing on the spinach salad, and my first bite made me a believer. This was accompanied by the warmest homemade bread I've ever eaten—the butter melted on it instantly.

I can also remember the main dish at that particular meal, it was char-prime steak. The entire prime rib is cooked rare in the oven and then sliced and put on the grill for the last few minutes. My slice was a half inch thick, and did the gravy ever taste good with that delicious bread!

As for the desserts, the strawberry pie, chocolate Bavarian Pie and Heaven cake all looked good, but for me a trip to the Red Geranium would not have been complete without some of that Shaker Lemon Pie.

Incidentally, among the other entrees which require a bit more time are Chateaubriand for two; Beef Wellington for two; a steak and lobster combination; veal Cordon Bleu and chicken a la Kiev.

Regular offerings include a surprising variety of seafood, as well as a variety of chicken and beef dishes.

My most recent visit to New Harmony gave me an opportunity to see the newest restaurant, the Shadblow, which is located in a well-preserved, 19th century block on Church Street (Rte. 460) known as the Mews. The restaurant is accessible not only through its own entrance but through a remarkably fine bookstore which features many books about the Owenites and the Harmonists.

The Shadblow is built around an open courtyard, in the center of which, to be sure, stands a shadblow tree. The restaurant was named for the tree, whose berries and fruit delighted the early New Harmony settlers. The Shadblow has a brick floor and green bentwood chairs. The menu is limited to items that can be quickly prepared. It offers tasty homemade soups and an assortment of salads and sandwiches for lunch, with most reasonably priced main dishes for dinner.

At the Shadblow the food is very "homey" and the service is deft. It is just right for the traveler who wants to spend his time experiencing the remarkable sights of the community.

Now New Harmony is coming into yet another era. The Red Geranium, of course, has been delighting lovers of good food for fifteen years. With the addition of the New Harmony Inn and its comfortable lodgings and the Shadblow restaurant, travelers now have even greater reason to visit this attractive, restored community.

RED GERANIUM RESTAURANT, New Harmony, Ind. 47361; 812-682-4431. No lodgings, guests accommodated at adjacent New Harmony Inn. Open 11a.m.—11p.m. Tues.—Sat.; 11a.m.—8p.m. Sunday. Closed Mondays. Closed July 4th, Christmas, and New Year's Day. Gary Gerard, Manager.

SHADBLOW RESTAURANT, New Harmony, Ind. 47361; 812-682-4463. No lodgings. Breakfast served from 5:30a.m.; lunch from 11a.m.; dinner 4-8p.m. Open every day except Christmas. Gary Gerard, Manager.

Directions: Located 30 mi. northwest of Evansville. Approximately 18 mi. on Rte. 460, south of I-64 (under construction).

PATCHWORK QUILT, Middlebury

Treva Swarm, our waitress, stopped in front of our table and with a warm smile gave us a rundown on the desserts offered at the Patchwork Quilt that evening.

"We have coffee toffee pie, grasshopper pie, cherry walnut torte, cheddar cheese cake, sugar cream pie, candied violet cake, apricot chiffon pie ... " she continued through a list of sumptuous offerings.

I was having dinner in the Wood Shed at the Patchwork Quilt where the barn board walls are mounted with antique wood tools. By this time I had struck up an acquaintance with several people at the adjoining tables. Quite naturally the topic that we kept talking about was the fabulous food at this farmhouse in the midst of acres of Indiana farmland. Incidentally there are no rooms available.

Everybody enjoyed the buttermilk pecan chicken. One man was very enthusiastic about the Hoosier baked ham, and still another raved about the barbecue-style chicken rodeo and the Indiana-raised duckling. His wife loved the homemade Dutch apple ice cream.

The Patchwork Quilt is a place where I would like to make a meal out of just the relishes, salads and vegetables. The salads in themselves are an impressive symphony. On that particular evening there were fifteen varieties. It would be impossible to sample all of them and still have room left to enjoy the main dishes.

"It's just good, Indiana down-on-the-farm cooking," explained Arletta Lovejoy. "We all grew up on it and serve this kind of food to our families. It's the thing that we all know how to do best."

Well, Arletta's very modest because, the fact is, she's added so many of her own original touches to those old farm recipies that Patchwork Quilt is well-known in big cities a considerable distance from the little farm community of Middlebury.

Speaking of Middlebury—it is also the shopping center for the Amish living in the surrounding farm country. One of the stores carries the simple materials and ready-to-wear clothing that are worn by this religious group. There are black hats, plain suits and unfrilly dresses. On a drive through the country with Arletta, I saw some of the Amish plowing behind horses in the old-fashioned way. "They believe that God rather than man should be glorified," explained Arletta, "I've lived out here all my life among these people and they make wonderful neighbors."

Well, I finished my meal and took the place card for a souvenir. The bill was handwritten on notepaper. A real friendly touch.

I must say that at the Patchwork Quilt it is very difficult to live up to one of the Amish admonitions, "Eat yourself full but clean your plate empty."

PATCHWORK QUILT COUNTRY INN, R.R. #2, Box 194, Middlebury, Ind. 46450; 219-825-2417. A working farm restaurant in the tradition of midwestern hospitality, about 20 mi. east of Elkhart. No lodgings. Dinner served daily by reservation only. Closed Sundays, Thanksgiving, Christmas and New Year's. Arletta Lovejoy, Innkeeper.

Directions: From east or west, exit Indiana Toll Road at Middlebury (Exit 10) and go north ¼ mi. to County Rd. #2 and proceed west 1 mi. to inn. From Middlebury follow Indiana Rte. 13 for 8 mi. north to County Rd. #2 and west 1 mi.

Ohio

WELSHFIELD INN, Burton

"Welshfield," said Polly Holmes, "has a history that is directly connected with New England. It was settled in 1811 by Jacob Welsh who came from Boston. The old boy gave the town land for churches and cemeteries providing they named it for him. Funny thing," she added, "when they read his will they discovered that he forgot his promise so they changed the name to Troy because a lot of early settlers came from Troy, New York. Years later the town was renamed Welshfield and now receives its mail through the Burton post office."

It was lunchtime at the Welshfield Inn and Brian Holmes, complete with chef's cap came in with some chicken a la king on homemade biscuits that captured my attention immediately. He dropped a nickel in the nickelodeon and the combination of sounds resembling a piano, violin, mandolin and flute gave forth with "After the Ball Is Over".

"I certainly know the words to that one," I said. Brian laughed, "Well, after you wrote about 'Barney Google' people almost wore it out." The nickelodeon, in its way, is one of the main reasons why the Welshfield Inn is so popular with people from Cleveland and Youngstown, as well as Berkshire Travellers who make a special point to stop off for lunch or dinner.

Of course, much of its popularity can also be attributed to the specialties of the inn: chicken fried in a heavy cast iron skillet, turkey, baked acorn squash, stuffed zucchini, hot apple pie, strawberry shortcake, and turtle soup.

"Many people come in for Sunday dinner," explained Polly. "They love our casseroles of vegetables, mashed potatoes, gravy, rolls, relishes, salads, and homemade apple pie with ice cream. They also like to look around at all the bric-a-brac and antique relics which we have collected. We try to give as many as possible a complete tour of the inn."

The inn was built in 1842, and was known for years as the

Nash Hotel. During the Civil War, it was an underground railway station.

In those years, just as today, the inn was the center of social affairs. At one time the ballroom was changed into bedrooms, but the inn has no lodgings today.

I had finished my lunch and was looking longingly at a creamy baked French pudding which was coming my way, when Brian said, "Something quite interesting happened a while ago. A man chartered a helicopter from Akron and brought his wife here to celebrate their thirtieth wedding anniversary. He said he read about us in *Country Inns and Back Roads*.

I wondered which of the many music rolls he played on the nickelodeon.

WELSHFIELD INN, Rte. 422, Burton, Ohio 44021; 216-834-4164. A country restaurant on Rte. 422, 28 mi. east of Cleveland. No lodgings. Lunch and dinner served weekdays. Dinner only served on Sundays and holidays. Closed one week over July Fourth and three weeks after January 1st. Open Labor Day. Near Sea World and Holden Arboretum. Brian and Polly Holmes, Innkeepers.

Directions: On U.S. 422 at intersection of Ohio 700, midway between Cleveland and Youngstown, Ohio.

GOLDEN LAMB, Lebanon

Jack Reynolds and I were enjoying dinner in the Shaker Dining Room at the Golden Lamb. Seated as we were among all the Shaker memorabilia, the talk naturally turned to Mother Ann's communities.

"Three miles west of here, where the Otterbein home is located there was once a very large Shaker settlement," Jack explained. "As a matter of fact, the three Shaker missionaries who came here were originally from the Ann Lee sect at New Lebanon, New York. That's just over the line from Stockbridge, isn't it?"

I nodded in agreement.

"Apparently they were successful because there was a Shaker society here at Union Village which grew to more than 4,000 acres. It disbanded in 1915.

"Mr. and Mrs. Jones, the previous owners of the Golden Lamb collected Shaker furniture and artifacts, and as a result, I think we have one of the best private collections in the country.

The Warren County Museum, which is just up the block from the Lamb, has an outstanding Shaker exhibit on the second floor."

My eye traveled around the dining room and noted so many Shaker things—boxes, dowels, chests, tables, and bentwood chairs. I asked Jack whether they also made a special effort at the Golden Lamb to put Shaker recipes on the menu.

"Oh, yes," he said. "Besides the Shaker beef stew with herb dumplings, we have Brother Ricardo's favorite chicken pudding, Shaker string bean salad with herb dressing, corn oysters, carrot marmalade, Shaker pork steak with winter cabbage, a potato and turnip dish from Mt. Lebanon and North Union pease porridge. Among the desserts are Sister Lizzie's Shaker Sugar Pie, and Ohio Shaker Lemon Pie."

Lest I leave the reader with the impression that only Shaker food is served at the Lamb, let me add that the menu includes great American dishes associated with the farm country of the Midwest including pork chops, lamb chops, steaks, fowl, and dozens of fresh countryside vegetables.

I believe it's justly well-known as one of America's great inns.

GOLDEN LAMB INN, 27 S. Broadway, Lebanon, Ohio 45036; 513-932-5065. A historic 20 room village inn in the heart of Ohio farming country on US Hwys. 63, 42 and 48. European Plan. 12 rooms with private bath. No pets. Breakfast served only on Sunday. Lunch and dinner served daily except Christmas. Golf and tennis nearby. For antique lovers. Jackson Reynolds, Innkeeper.

Directions: From I-71, exit Rte. 48 N, 3 miles west to Lebanon. From I-75, exit Rte. 63 E, 7 miles east to Lebanon.

Michigan

Michigan was the land of Hiawatha—that is, of the legendary Hiawatha of whom Longfellow wrote in his poem. From 1618 on, various French explorers visited the area, the first of them looking for a passage through the lakes to the Orient, and in 1701 built a fort at Detroit. Despite later English and American rule, French remained the common language of the Detroit waterfront until nearly a hundred years ago.

In 1763, the English took over Michigan from the French. At least, they thought they had, but an Ottawa chief named Pontiac had other ideas. He took most of the Michigan forts and their defenders, only the one at Detroit holding out until Pontiac was at last defeated. And as late as 1772, such few white settlers as there were in Michigan worried more about Indians than about the British King and Parliament.

Incidentally, the Great Lakes were dug by Paul Bunyan. He piled the dirt from them up into mountains. All with his shovel.

STAFFORD'S BAY VIEW, Petoskey

Kathy Hart, the very personable manager at Stafford's Bay View, met me as soon as I reached the top of the steps and headed toward the ornate old front door.

"Stafford is at a meeting of the Rotary Club. He wondered if you would mind coming in to join them and, perhaps, speak a few words about country inns."

Of course, I was delighted. The only problem is that I've never been known to limit myself to just a few words on country inns.

The luncheon was really great fun. There was a lot of ribbing and goodnatured joshing; however, quite a few serious subjects were discussed, many concerning community projects. A great many of the members were summer visitors at Bay View, which I think is unique among American communities.

The Bay View Association is a summertime religious, music, art, and recreation center. It started in the 19th century when northern Michigan was discovered as a summer resort, and so many of the beautiful Victorian cottages were built.

Stafford's with its mansard roof is a landmark right on the edge of the Bay View section.

After the meeting Stafford and I walked down to the lakeshore. He was filled with enthusiasm: "This year is the centennial anniversary of the Bay View Association. There are lots of unusual events planned for the entire summer and many people have already made their plans to be with us at that time."

The inn was established in 1886 which makes it about eleven years younger than the Association. It was originally known as the Woodland Avenue House, then shortly the Howard House and that name, etched in glass, remains over the front door.

Stafford and Janice met at the hotel in 1960 when he was the assistant manager and she was the hostess. They were married and since that time the inn has been their life.

"Janice and I always wanted to keep the inn as a period piece," he explained. "We were inspired by a great many inns in the New England area. Maybe you noticed that tall, black walnut sideboard and the bookcase. They came from the first governor's mansion in Vermont."

Stafford's Bay View is well-known for many things, but first and foremost, is good food. There's particular emphasis on regional dishes including white fish and lake trout which are caught right out in front in Little Traverse Bay. There are also other dishes from northern Michigan including baked apples, baked

cherries (this is great cherry country), corn pudding, buttermilk pancakes and biscuits, carrot cake and Michigan pea bean soup. The smorgasborg which is served every day during July and August is very popular.

Another special feature of Stafford's is that people in their retirement years are made especially welcome. "We love them," said Stafford. "We just mix them in with all of our guests and everybody seems to have a wonderful time. There always seem to be a few surrogate grandparents around here."

STAFFORD'S BAY VIEW INN, Box 3, Petoskey, Mich. 49770; 616-347-2771. A 21 room resort-inn on Little Traverse Bay in the Bay View section of Petoskey. Mod. American Plan omits lunch. Breakfast, lunch and dinner served daily to travelers. Open daily mid-June to mid-September, Christmas week and long weekends during the winter sports season. Lake swimming and xc-ski on grounds. Boating, fishing, bicycles, hiking and Alpine ski trails nearby. Stafford and Janice Smith, Innkeepers.

Directions: From Detroit, take Gaylord Exit from I-75 and follow Michigan Rte. 32 to Rte. 131, north to Petoskey. From Chicago, use U.S. 131 north to Petoskey.

ST. CLAIR INN, St. Clair

The long boardwalk, which extends along the waterfront of the town of St. Clair next to the river, had been thoroughly washed by the crashing thunderstorm of the previous night. It gleamed in the morning sun. A young man was mowing the lawn which extends down to the edge of the boardwalk in front of the St. Clair Inn. The terrace furniture was already out and the morning river traffic was already in full motion.

The first boat to heave into sight was a power-driven sail-boat on the way north into Lake Huron. This was followed in a few moments by the ore boat "John Hulst." I waved at the ore boat and the captain sounded his deep-throated whistle twice in an answering signal. Then, for just a few moments, the St. Clair River, directly in front of the inn, was quiet, and I could see the houses and automobile traffic in Canada just across the river.

I walked down the boardwalk and recalled earlier visits to this community, which is a model for towns and villages who feel the need to raise themselves up by their bootstraps.

On my first visit, in 1968, the buildings were ramshackle,

unpainted and most uninspiring. The waterfront was a shambles. Now, the entire business section of the town was completely transformed with attractive business blocks and parking spaces tastefully arranged. The waterfront was almost completely clear from one end of town to the other. It was a total transformation in just a few years.

Since I've discovered that all country inns have their own personalities, I reflected that the St. Clair has its own as well. In many respects it's more sophisticated than some of the others. This is partially explained by the fact that, not only does it provide lodgings and recreation for the traveler and holiday-seeker, but it is very popular with people from Grosse Pointe and Detroit.

Evidence of this sophistication can be found in the interior which is lavishly furnished in carved chairs and large upholstered sofas. The furnishings are almost ornate and there is a most impressive collection of oil paintings. In some respects it resembles a fashionable private club.

If the decor and furnishings of the St. Clair bespeak a certain amount of sophistication, the menu says, "We're just folks." Always featured is the famous St. Clair River pan-fried pickerel. I also found barbecued lamb shank, calves' liver and bacon, lamb and pork chops, baked potatoes, Virginia ham and other hearty foods associated with country inns. There's always fresh strawberry pie on the menu. All the pies have that old-fashioned flaky crust that means they're homemade.

In the past I've tried to stay for at least two days at the St. Clair and spend part of one day at the St. Clair Country Club, getting in at least 18 holes of golf and maybe a dip in the pool. Now, since the addition of tennis courts, I may have to make it three days at this beautiful river inn.

255

ST. CLAIR INN, St. Clair, Mich. 48079; 313-329-2222. A 75-room river inn with many resort features, 50 mi. north of Detroit on the shores of the St. Clair River. Well-known for the Great Lakes water traffic passing directly in front. European Plan. Breakfast, lunch and dinner served daily except Christmas. Golf course and swimming pool. Creighton Holden, Innkeeper.

Directions: Take I-94 East from Detroit for 40 mi. Take St. Clair Exit and go 7 mi. to St. Clair.

BOTSFORD INN, Farmington Hills

I go back a long time with the Botsford Inn, not way back to 1836 when it was first built by Orrin Weston as a home, or to when the famous Botsford family took it over and converted it into an inn. But I have been visiting it for quite a few of the more recent years.

I can remember when I first heard of it, my reaction was: "Who would expect to find a New England country inn in Detroit?" I soon learned that it wasn't really in Detroit, but Farmington, and the people in Farmington Hills will tell you that there's quite a difference. It's a very pleasant residential town. The inn was a stagecoach stop on the road from Detroit and, in fact, at one time the Grand River plank road followed an Indian trail that went on to Lake Michigan.

Strolling around the surprisingly spacious grounds, including the rose garden which was originally created by Mrs. Henry Ford, and admiring the towering pine, maple, and elm trees, I realized that some of the more elegant features of the 19th century have been preserved at the Botsford, many by Mr. Henry Ford, who restored it in the 1920's. I think it is remarkable that such a valuable piece of property has not gone the way of the wrecking ball and bulldozer long before now.

One of the principal reasons for this must be attributed to the devotion of the present innkeeper and owner, John Anhut, who has a weakness for country inns. Following Mr. Ford's example, John has succeeded in holding back time. For example, in two sitting rooms there are many furnishings from Henry Ford's house including a beautiful little inlaid spinet, a horsehair sofa, music boxes, inlaid mahogony tables, and spinning wheels.

The older sections of the inn have very low ceilings, huge beams, and handsome fireplaces with big andirons. One of the more celebrated features of the inn is the second floor ballroom,

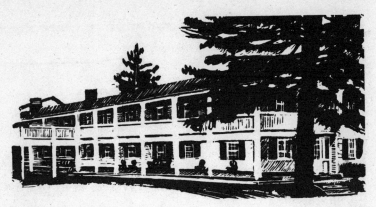

where, at a country dance, long ago, Henry Ford first met the young lady who was to become his wife.

I'm certain that innkeeper Botsford and preserver Ford would approve of the contemporary changes that innkeeper Anhut has made, including a welcome swimming pool, air conditioning against the Detroit summer heat, and lodging rooms with reproductions of colonial furniture.

It's also certain that the farmers, drovers, and traveling men of the past century would nod their heads in approval at the hearty offerings from the Botsford kitchen today. These include: Braised Short Ribs of Beef with Jardiniere Sauce, Frogs Legs Sauteed in Chablis, Botsford Old Fashioned Chicken Pot Pie Topped with Flaky Buttered Crust, and Roast Prime Rib of Western Beef, Au Jus.

There's another thing that appeals greatly to me about this inn, and that is about John Anhut himself. As busy as he is, he makes a concerted effort to meet every one of his guests. "Some of them have really become old friends to me," he said. "I think it's the best part of having a country inn."

BOTSFORD INN, 28000 Grand River Avenue. Farmington Hills, Michigan 48024; 313-474-4800. A 62 room village inn on the city line of Detroit. European Plan. Dinner served daily except Monday, continental breakfast and lunch Tuesday thru Saturday. Sunday brunch. Closed Christmas and New Year's Day. Pool on grounds. Greenfield Village nearby. Skiing and state parks nearby. John Anhut, Innkeeper.

Directions: Located in Farmington Hills on I-96 which is easily accessible from major highways in Michigan.

257

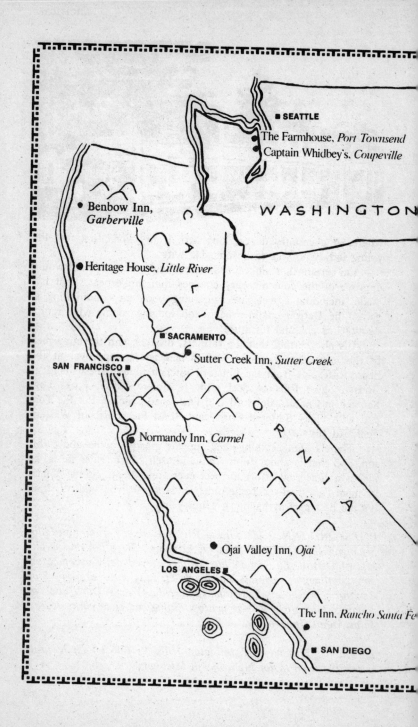

SEATTLE

The Farmhouse, *Port Townsend*
Captain Whidbey's, *Coupeville*

WASHINGTON

Benbow Inn, *Garberville*

Heritage House, *Little River*

SACRAMENTO

Sutter Creek Inn, *Sutter Creek*

SAN FRANCISCO

CALIFORNIA

Normandy Inn, *Carmel*

Ojai Valley Inn, *Ojai*

LOS ANGELES

The Inn, *Rancho Santa Fe*

SAN DIEGO

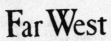

Far West

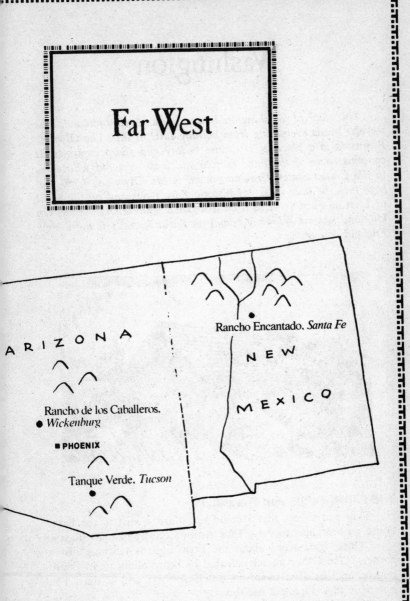

A R I Z O N A

Rancho Encantado, *Santa Fe*

N E W

M E X I C O

Rancho de los Caballeros,
● *Wickenburg*

■ PHOENIX

Tanque Verde, *Tucson*
●

Washington

The state of Washington is a year-round vacationland. The traveler needs everything from bathing suits to skis. The Olympic Peninsula is a place of awesome beauty and sharp contrasts. It contains some of the most remote and least explored wilderness in the United States. Crowning it all is Mt. Olympus, 7,960 feet high into the blue skies. At historic Port Townsend on the Strait of Juan de Fuca I found a most unusual gourmet restaurant. On long and narrow Whidbey Island on Puget Sound I found a New England country inn.

THE FARMHOUSE, Port Townsend

This was a year that I could not make a visit to the Farmhouse, so I'm going to share John Ashby Conway's letter with you:

"Once again word about the Farmhouse is reaching distant corners. One of our guests said that he heard about us in Copenhagen; another first heard in Saudi Arabia; and a third read about us in a Japanese cookbook.

"Here on the Strait of Juan de Fuca, hidden behind our 100-year-old holly tree almost three stories high, the world seems to be coming to us—along with an increasing number of people who enjoy well-prepared good food.

"In June, July and August we'll be back on our summer schedule. Dinners on Thursdays will feature an entree of ham cooked in champagne; on Fridays it will be seafood direct from the fishing boat. Saturday's entree is red meat, and the Sunday entree is usually chicken cooked in an Oriental manner. Reservations are absolutely always necessary. I do hope you'll tell all your readers how to get in touch with us.

"We serve one meal at a time, a practice which permits us to prepare everything from scratch. Our patrons have a choice, of course, by choosing the day or month we serve the food they like to eat. For example: in September, we serve classic Japanese food; in October, we serve food from Tuscany; November is Hungarian month, and so on.

"Our little shop is filled with interesting things including camel hair blankets from Austria, puffs and pillows of German goose down, washable acrylics, and blankets from Germany. We have Persian copper and Russian samovars.

"Some of your readers would be interested to know that four forts were built in our area to protect us from a Spanish invasion in 1898 that never actually happened. The forts remain as cultural centers.

"I'm sorry that you were unable to be with us this year, but we've had visits from our mutual friend, Joan White.

"Do try to come this year. We've had a great many people stop because of your book, and they all seem to enjoy our modest offerings. Keep up the good work."

THE FARMHOUSE, North Beach, Port Townsend, Wash. 98368; 206-385-1411. (Seattle Number: 206-LA3-4625.) A unique gourmet country restaurant, 50 mi. from Seattle. Meals by reservation only. Dinner served Thursday through Sunday in June, July and August; lunch served Saturday and Sunday in July and August. Dinner served Saturday and Sunday from September through May. Brunch served on Mother's Day, Father's Day and Easter. Closed month of January, except New Year's Day. For nature and history lovers. Dorothy and John Ashby Conway, Innkeepers.

Directions: From Olympic Highway 101, exit at Pt. Townsend. About 10 mi. after crossing the Hood Canal floating bridge. Coming east on #101 around the Olympic Peninsula take the Port Townsend exit.

THE CAPTAIN WHIDBEY, Coupeville

This year, I wasn't on Whidbey Island near Seattle visiting with Steve and Shirlie Stone at the Captain Whidbey Inn. Instead, I was having a long conversation with their son, John, on Nantucket Island in Massachusetts.

"Yes, Dad is from Nantucket," John affirmed, "and I've been back here before to visit my grandparents who still live on the Island. This time your meeting coincided with the trip so I decided that I would come and represent us." The occasion was the annual meeting of innkeepers included in *Country Inns and Back Roads*. This year it was being held at the Jared Coffin House in Nantucket.

John Stone, who has spent at least ten years at the Captain Whidbey, proved to be a personable young man and we were delighted to meet him. He was asked when the Captain Whidbey was built. "About 1907," he said. "I wish all of you could see it. It is made from Madrona logs with a sort of polished, rustic look. We are located on the part of Puget Sound known as Penn Cove. There are usually quite a few boats around, and occasionally a few whales.

"It originally started as a family inn—a retreat for people to get away from the cares of the city. Steamers used to bring folks from Seattle, and the inn had its own pier in those days. Today we have a floating dock in the summer for boaters. Mom and Dad entered the picture about ten years ago.

"It hasn't changed very much. We have added several cottages which are more modern than the main part of the inn. Many have woodburning fireplaces. People also seem to really like staying in the old inn."

Someone asked John if he was doing any cooking. "Oh yes, I really enjoy it. I prepare many of the things like the Dungeness Crab and our homemade French bread. We also have the Captain Whidbey Bleu Cheese Ball that everybody likes. The grilled salmon which comes from Puget Sound is one of our most popular items. I've learned how to cook all of them."

One of the innkeepers at the table asked John what guests did for entertainment on the island and he replied, "Well, there is boating and fishing. Have you ever been salmon or steelhead fishing? Another thing that our guests enjoy is walking along the beach and picking up the agates and driftwood, or sitting by the fireplace reading a book from our extensive library.

"Lots of people come to see us just to be in a quiet atmosphere on the water. Most of our rooms have a water view."

Well that's part of the story of the Captain Whidbey Inn told by a very enthusiastic young man who has grown up in the innkeeping tradition.

We all hope that he remains in it, because we think he'll do very well.

THE CAPTAIN WHIDBEY, Rte. 1, Box 32, Coupeville, Wash. 98239; 206-678-4097. A 17-room country inn, 50 mi. north of Seattle, 3 mi. north of Coupeville. European Plan. 8 cottages with private bath; 9 rooms with shared baths. Breakfast, lunch and dinner served daily to travelers. Open year-round. Pets allowed in cottages only. Boating and fishing on grounds. Golf nearby. Steve, Shirlie and John Stone, Innkeepers.

Directions: Whidbey Island is reached year-round from the south by the Columbia Beach-Mukilteo Ferry, and during the summer by the Port Townsend-Keystone Ferry. From the north (Vancouver, B.C. and Bellingham), take the Deception Pass Bridge to Whidbey Island.

California

Recent findings estimate that Indians may have been in California as many as 100,000 years ago. A Spanish captain named Cabrillo explored some of the coast in 1542 and hot on his heels came Sir Francis Drake in 1579. He claimed the land for England. Drake's stopover caused the Spaniards to get busy and send more expeditions. In 1769 Captain Gaspard de Portola set up forts at what are now San Diego and Monterey. After that came the Franciscan missionaries.

BENBOW INN, Garberville

The bid was four hearts. My partner did not double and I had no count in my hand. I passed. The dummy laid down his hand and the lady from Red Bank, New Jersey, began to play.

We were in one corner of the sumptuous lobby of the Benbow Inn, which is located in the heart of the big Redwood country of northern California. Other guests were also playing cards; some were enjoying a game of cribbage, and a father was teaching his son to play chess. Our table was a few feet from the large fireplace which had a cheery blaze, and we had a chance to say hello to many people who came up to share its warmth.

My partner was a man from Sacramento whom I'd met on the inn golf course earlier that afternoon. He had visited the

Benbow quite a few times with his wife. "I like this golf course," he said, "because it's seldom crowded and the scenery is fantastic. My wife loves the food here at the inn."

The lady from Red Bank, who was busy making six hearts instead of four, paused for a moment to tell me that she was touring the west coast and looking for other country inns. "I wish they were all like this one," she said. I mentioned the names of some other inns that I knew of in both California and Washington. She was delighted.

The other bridge player was from Kankakee, Illinois. His wife sat nearby doing needlework. This was their first trip to California and like everyone else, they marveled at the tremendous beauty, size, and scope of the giant trees and tumultuous rivers.

We all agreed there was simply no way to adequately describe the grandeur of these forests. "I hate to think of leaving tomorrow," was one comment.

Innkeeper Art Stadler and his wife Claudia have been operating the Benbow since 1962. It was built during the early twenties and is enjoying great popularity under their direction. The emphasis is on easy California informality. All the children I observed appeared to be having a wonderful time.

In addition to the overnight vacationing guests at the inn, there were quite a few travelers who stopped in for dinner.

"Yes," explained Art, "we're right on Route 101. Many folks driving north into Oregon and Washington stop to eat along the way. Then we find them coming back for a longer stay on the return trip."

The dinner menu at the inn includes some very hearty offerings such as Beef Stroganoff, shish kabob and Abalone steak—good sustenance for a rigorous evening of bridge. My partner's next bid was four no-trump!

BENBOW INN, Garberville, Calif. 95440; 707-923-2124. A 58-room inn in the heart of redwood country on Rte. 101, 2 mi. from Garberville, near Benbow State Park. European Plan. Breakfast, lunch and dinner served to travelers daily. Open from April 1 through November 1. Golf and swimming on grounds. Hiking and bicycles nearby. For nature lovers. Arthur and Claudia Stadler, Innkeepers.

Directions: From San Francisco, follow Rte. 101 200 mi. north and exit at Benbow.

HERITAGE HOUSE, Little River

I set my alarm for six a.m. because I wanted to see the sun rise over the Pacific. Innkeeper Don Dennen couldn't have chosen a better room for this purpose, for when I opened the drapes on the glass wall, I felt as if I were isolated on a point of land. There was water literally on three sides.

I stepped out on the covered deck and a fresh clean wind caught me full in the face. I could hear the whistling buoy, and the light from the channel marker was clearly visible in the semi-darkness.

The first streaks of light were now appearing, and I was aware of the chill morning air since I was only wearing pajamas. I returned to the warmth of the bed and propped myself up to watch this drama unfold.

The previous afternoon I had driven over from Sutter Creek through Sacramento and Woodland, via Routes 16 and 20 through Lake County. I drove up to Fort Bragg and down the coast a few miles to Mendocino and then to Little River and the Heritage House.

The inn is very difficult to pin down in one paragraph. The Main House, with its New England doorway, sits among the high Eucalyptus trees. However, most of the lodgings are in unique little buildings, some of which were moved from other parts of Northern California. They reflect the atmosphere of things past.

As the light became stronger I could see a few of them from my terrace. Some were sod-roofed houses in the style of the early settlers. Other guest houses had furnishings and wallpaper that would be appropriate for an apothecary shop, a post office, the town hall, a country store or a bonnet shop, and these, incidentally, are their names. Many have fireplaces.

All of these elegantly restored cottages are tucked unobtrusively into the landscape. The plantings, flowers, bushes and trees have been planned to blend with the slope of land toward the cliffs which border the ocean.

Heritage House is different. It's a pleasant, peaceful, intimate atmosphere without television or room telephones. There are no planned activities, just the many paths through the forest and along the beaches next to the ever-changing ocean.

HERITAGE HOUSE, Little River, Cal. 95456; 707-937-5885. An elegant 45-room oceanside inn on Coast Highway #1, 144 mi. north of San Francisco, 6 mi. south of Mendocino. Mod. American Plan omits lunch. Breakfast and dinner served to travelers daily by reservation. Open from February through November. For ocean lovers. Don Dennen, Innkeeper.

Directions: From San Francisco, follow Rte. 101 to Cloverdale, then Rte. 128 to Coast Highway #1. Inn is 5 mi. north of this junction on Hwy. #1.

SUTTER CREEK INN, Sutter Creek

It was 1967 when I first flew to the West Coast in search of country inns. I had been persuaded by Jane Way at the Sutter Creek Inn to visit the gold fields of California. She was sure that I would love it. Well, Jane was right, and I have been visiting California and writing about the Sutter Creek Inn ever since.

It is, in fact, an inn with its New Hampshire heritage much in evidence in the porches and high pointed roof. There are grape vines, tomato plants, gardinias, trumpet vines, Virginia creepers, hollyhocks, chrysanthemums, gooseberries, zinnias, and roses in abundance.

On that first visit and every time since, I have joined the other guests on the porch at the end of the day to watch the huge, old white owls that live in the barn circle over the backyard and fly over to the redwood trees to spend the rest of the night.

The only meal served at this inn is breakfast, but this is really an experience. When the bell rings at 9 A.M., everyone sits at long, family-style tables. "Our breakfasts are big and hearty," says Jane. "It's a good basis for a full day of exploring the Mother Lode country."

In the evening, Jane is apt to join her guests at dinner across the street at a restaurant which serves delicious Mexican food. There are also Italian restaurants and Serbian boarding houses nearby which have very special dishes.

The rooms in the Sutter Creek Inn have, what Jane calls, "great vibrations." They're all different. Some have beds hanging from the ceiling on chains, and others have fireplaces or Franklin stoves.

The principal diversion of guests here is, of course, to tour the gold fields and old towns in the foothills of the Sierras. Some energetic souls even try panning for gold.

By the way, the next time you visit the Sutter Creek Inn, ask Jane to tell you the story about Old Abe, the canon, delivered to the gold fields by a horsedrawn hearse during the Civil War.

SUTTER CREEK INN, 75 Main St., Sutter Creek, Calif. 95685; 209-267-5606. A 16-room New England village inn on the main street of a historic Mother Lode town, 35 mi. from Sacramento. Lodgings include breakfast. No meals served to travelers. Closed first 2 weeks in January. No children under 10. No pets.

Water skiing, riding, fishing and boating nearby. For history lovers. Mrs. Jane Way, Innkeeper.

Directions: From Sacramento, travel on the freeway toward Placerville and exit at Power Inn Rd. Turn right, drive two blocks, then turn left onto Fulsom Rd. In less than ¼ mi. turn left on Hwy. 16 toward Jackson and travel 45 min. to Hwy. 49. Turn right to inn. From San Francisco, drive through Stockton or Sacramento toward Jackson. Inn is 4 mi. north of Jackson on Hwy. 49.

NORMANDY INN, Carmel

A few weeks before this edition went to press I was looking through some photographs that Jim Mellow had taken of the Normandy Inn when he stayed there last year.

The first one showed the front entrance to the inn and that marvelous old tree that twists around like a boa constrictor.

The next one had the inner court, with the patio of fitted flat stone and the second floor gallery. The third photograph took me right back to a sunny afternoon I had spent around the swimming pool, which is in the rear of the inn in a little sylvan hideaway.

It was an interesting coincidence that I ran across a letter from a man in Atlanta. "Having twice benefited from your recommendations, I wanted to write and inform you how much my wife and I enjoyed the Whitehall Inn in Camden, Maine, and the Normandy Inn in Carmel.

"To our delight, your description of the Normandy Inn was most accurate. Rarely before have we been so absolutely charmed by an inn, especially our quarters—a twin-bedded square room with a fireplace, a vaulted ceiling, and an ocean view over the courtyard. The continental breakfast was not only tasty but plentiful. The Sunday papers on the table were a nice treat. At the front desk the people were cheerful and helpful in suggesting a good restaurant in Monterey."

To visit Carmel is to visit its fascinating shops. It's also to spend a great deal of time walking about the town and on the beach. For the golfing enthusiast, the golf courses in this part of California are some of the best-known in the country.

Those photographs certainly put me in the mood for reserving a seat on the next plane to California. I think that the best time to visit Carmel is beween October and May. And the place that I enjoy the most is the Normandy Inn.

NORMANDY INN, Carmel, Cal. 93921; 408-624-3825. A 48-room French Provincial inn in the heart of Carmel, on Ocean Ave. between Monteverde and Casanova. Within walking distance of beach, shops and restaurants and near Point Lobos State Park. European Plan includes continental breakfast served to inn guests only. No other meals served. Open from May 15 to November 1. No pets. Tennis, golf, fishing, bicycles nearby. Mike Stanton, Innkeeper.

Directions: Follow Rte. 101 to Salinas, then Rte. 68 into Monterey Peninsula. Or, follow Coast Highway #1 which travels through Carmel.

OJAI VALLEY INN, Ojai

It was early March in Ojai which is springtime in Southern California. The robins were nesting in the oak trees. The plantings on the patio of the Ojai Valley Inn were in early bloom, and the golf course and tennis courts were in readiness. The putting green had already been swept free of the dew, and the air was so clear and dry I felt as though I could drive every green or ace every serve.

The native Indians named this sunny valley which is pronounced "o-hi." It means "the nest." It is most aptly named for it sits in the center of a vast amphitheatre of towering mountains. These mountains create an ideal climate year-round, and I understand that the average summer temperature is between 70 and 90 degrees. Winter daytime temperatures range from 60 to 85 degrees. There is no fog or smog or dampness because everything is 1000 feet up in the dry, invigorating air. The days are warm and brilliant with sunshine and the nights are cool. I've slept under a blanket even after the warmest days.

This inn is one of the very few American resorts where guests can enjoy the four major outdoor playtime activities—golf, tennis, riding, and swimming throughout the year.

The championship golf course, designed by Billy Bell, is 6,800 yards. "Tricky, but fair" is one description. There's a heated swimming pool with cabanas and terraces for sun bathing, and luncheon and refreshments are served at poolside. There are hundreds of miles of riding trails in the mountains, valleys, and canyons surrounding Ojai. Horses are available at the inn stable. The tennis pro is always glad to arrange games, and I've already made quite a few tennis friends among the regular residents of this attractive town.

One other important feature that delights me at this inn is that there's plenty of fun for children. There's even a playground

for them, and babysitters can be arranged.

The architecture of Ojai Valley Inn is Spanish Mission-style. It is surrounded by beautiful oaks, evergreens, Eucalyptus and an occasional palm tree. There are more varieties of birds than I could possibly count.

Golfers were already getting ready for the morning round. As two of them passed on their way to the first tee, I heard one say, "Do you realize that we're only an hour and a half from L.A.?"

OJAI VALLEY INN & COUNTRY CLUB, Ojai, Calif. 93023; 805-646-5511. A 100-room resort-inn with its own championship golf course, 19 mi. northeast of Ventura on U.S. 33. American Plan. Breakfast, lunch and dinner served to travelers daily. Open year-round. No pets. Tennis, riding, heated pool, golf and bicycles on the grounds. For golf lovers. Bill Briggs, Innkeeper.

Directions: From the Ventura Freeway, exit at Highway 33.

THE INN AT RANCHO SANTA FE, Rancho Santa Fe

The town of Rancho Santa Fe, California, is one of the most attractively designed that I have ever visited. It has been well-described as a "civilized planned community." The homes and estates have been created in perfect harmony with nature's generous endowment of climate and scenery. One of the dominating factors is the presence of the gigantic eucalyptus trees.

Innkeeper Dan Royce told me the story. "It's hard to imagine this place without these great trees, but back in 1906 it was nothing but an area of sand and occasional low trees and brush. At that time the Santa Fe Railroad purchased the land for the purpose of growing eucalyptus trees for railroad ties. About three million seedlings were planted, but the project failed when it was discovered that the wood was not suitable. Fortunately, the trees were left to flourish and today we have glorious shade and beauty. They provide homes for literally thousands of birds.

"The first building of the Inn was constructed in 1923 and is now a part of the main building of today's inn. Beginning in 1941 it was expanded into a quiet resort where guests could enjoy the truly beautiful surroundings.

"In 1958, my father, Steve, acquired the property, and it's been a family operation ever since."

On my first visit to Rancho Santa Fe, I had the pleasure of enjoying a tour of the entire community and the Inn with Steve Royce, the dean of California hotelmen.

Although the Inn is a luxury resort-inn, Dan makes it a point to meet personally every guest in the inn during their stay.

Cottages are scattered among the towering trees, and there's recreation for everyone here, including the younger set. The inn has membership in several nearby private 18-hole golf courses and there are three tennis courts and a putting green on the grounds. The swimming pool has an outdoor terrace where luncheons and refreshments are available. Also the Inn has a beach cottage at nearby Del Mar for use during the summer months.

Part of the pleasure of staying at the Inn is the opportunity to visit the shops in the village. They are all designed to be attractive but unobtrusive. I stood in front of one building for three minutes without realizing that it was a supermarket!

All of this is happening today at Rancho Santa Fe because eucalyptus trees could not be used for railroad ties!

THE INN, Rancho Santa Fe, Calif. 92067; 714-756-1131. A 75-room resort-inn, 27 mi. north of San Diego Freeway #5, 5 mi. inland from Solana Beach, Del Mar. European Plan. Breakfast, lunch and dinner served to travelers daily. Open year-round. Pool, tennis, putting green and bicycles on grounds. Golf and ocean nearby. Airport transportation provided. Daniel Royce, Innkeeper.

Directions: From I-5, take Exit S8 and drive inland about 6 mi.

Arizona

Arizona is a state of many contrasts. It has some of nature's most scenic attractions including the Grand Canyon, the Painted Desert and the Petrified Forest. One seventh of the Indian population of the United States lives here and there are 19 Indian reservations that comprise one quarter of the state's area.

I found a prestigious ranch-inn north of Phoenix in Wickenburg in the high plains country at 2000 feet altitude. Just outside Tucson there is another fine ranch-inn not far from the Saguaro National Monument, an excellent example of Sonoran Arboreal Desert.

RANCHO de los CABALLEROS, Wickenburg

I found myself with an interesting group. There was a gentleman and his wife from Illinois who had been coming to the Rancho for at least ten years. They had become so attached to the high desert country in Wickenburg, that during the previous year they had purchased one of the beautiful houses adjacent to the ranch property and were now part-time residents. Sometime during the last two or three years, they had met a second couple also staying at the ranch and found that they all liked tennis. This was actually a reunion for them.

We were all sitting in the lounge overlooking the tennis courts, swimming pool and the Bradshaw Mountains. The clarity of the air made them appear to be about 25 miles in the distance, but I was surprised to learn that they were at least 50 miles away! The sun was going down behind Vulture Peak and the convolutions and gradations of the mountains across the valley were constantly changing until they melted into one black silhouette against the night sky.

More people joined our circle and we talked about the day's activities. The newcomers who had been out on one of the trail rides were being kidded about feeling a bit stiff. The "old hands" enjoying their third or fourth day were comparing the personalities of the different horses. All of this "horsey" talk caused me to change my mind, and instead of more tennis the next morning, I told the head wrangler that I would be on the slow ride, at ten o'clock.

Rancho de los Caballeros is a most impressive ranch-inn. A great deal of care is taken with plantings, gardens and lawns around the Main House and the beautiful cacti and trees are filled with birds (at least 45 varieties), particularly in early morning.

The decor and furnishings are those of a luxurious, large hacienda and the individual lodgings are all done in an Arizona-Indian motif.

Many families have been returning for years, and there is a children's counselor to keep young people entertained. I'm always amazed at how the children take immediately to ranch life. They are the first ones out and the last to come in.

Our little group broke up in order to be ready for dinner. We arranged for a large table to accommodate all of us, and it looked like it would be another fine evening at the Rancho de los Caballeros.

RANCHO de los CABALLEROS, Wickenburg, Ariz. 85358; 602-684-5484. A luxury 52-room ranch-resort, 60 mi. north of Phoenix in the sunny dry desert. American Plan. Rooms with private baths. A few with shared baths. Breakfast, lunch and dinner served to travelers daily. Open from mid-October to early May. No pets. Pool, corral of 75 horses, hiking, skeet shooting, putting, tennis on grounds. Golf nearby. For nature lovers. Dallas Gant, Jr., Innkeeper.

Directions: Rtes. 60, 89 and 93 bring you to Wickenburg. Ranch is 2 mi. west of town on Rte. 60 and 2 mi. south on Vulture Mine Road.

TANQUE VERDE, Tucson

Driving out Speedway Road from Tucson to Tanque Verde, I felt exhilerated to be in this high country once again. As the sun dipped lower, the sharp-toothed mountains were taking on new hues with each passing moment. Here were my old friendly cacti, particularly the stately saguaros, with their thick branches pointed in semaphore fashion into the Arizona sky.

My reunion with Bob and Dee Dee Cote took on added zest because I had my first visit with their son, Brett, who by now was quite a young armful.

I asked Bob if the bird banding was still going on and he replied that it was even more exciting than ever.

"Since you are going to be here on Thursday morning why don't you get up early and help us set up the nets. The desert is gorgeous at dawn."

The last time I looked, The Tanque Verde bird list numbered 174. For the benefit of the many bird enthusiasts, there is a complete list available.

Dinner that night was in the new dining room at the long ranch-style tables with a view of the fading light through the big picture windows. Everyone gets acquainted very quickly, and newcomers are carried right along with the people who have been here three days, three weeks, or even three months. It's easy to tell the length of the guests stay by the faded quality of their blue jeans. I always take an old pair so I won't look like a tenderfoot.

Speaking of dinner a day on the desert seemed to produce voracious appetites. The steak roasts in the cottonwood grove every week are great fun with everyone singing around the campfire.

There was square dancing after dinner. While I was trying out my rather rickety style with Dee Dee, she suggested that what I really needed to loosen me up was the morning ride. "Bob tells me that you have been riding eastern style up in Vermont at the Kedron Valley Inn," she said. "I think you should get into one of our western saddles."

Tanque Verde, with its real western home flavor is a most enjoyable ranch-inn experience. Besides the desert rides, there are a swimming pool and sauna. Recently installed lights allow guests to play tennis at night. It's a wonderful place to bring children on a vacation even if they've never been on a horse. The head wrangler tells me they learn very quickly.

The ranch has a 100-year-old history as one of Arizona's pioneer guest and cattle ranches and even has tales of Apache raids.

Lodgings are in an assortment of *casitas,* some with their own patios and fireplaces.

By the way, my breakfast ride the next day was a huge success—except this time I forgot to pack my old blue jeans.

TANQUE VERDE RANCH, Box 66, Rte. 8, Tucson, Ariz. 85710; 602-296-6275. A 65-room ranch-inn, 10 mi. from Tucson. American Plan. Breakfast, lunch and dinner served to travelers by reservation. Open year-round. Riding, indoor and outdoor pool, tennis, sauna, exercise room and whirlpool bath on grounds. For nature lovers. Robert and Dee Dee Cote, Innkeepers.

Directions: From U.S. 10, exit at Speedway Blvd. and travel east to Dead End.

New Mexico

New Mexico was the land of the cliff dwellers when the first Spaniards arrived, and it soon became "the land of fabled treasure." One of the stories was of the "Seven Cities of Cibola" with walls made of precious metals and streets full of busy silversmiths. Many people sought these seven cities but the precious metals were nothing more than the bright sun shining from the adobe walls. The real treasure was for the archeologists to find—thousands of relics of a civilization that had existed as much as 15,000 years ago, buried layer upon layer beneath the floors of the cliff dwellings.

RANCHO ENCANTADO, Santa Fe

The little note on the bureau of my lodging room was handwritten. It read: *"Mi casa es su casa!"* It is a simple Spanish statement that succinctly expresses Betty Egan's philosophy of innkeeping. Translation: "My home is your home."

Betty and I were enjoying a New Mexican breakfast in the impressive dining room at Encantado. I had ordered huevos rancheros, a Mexican breakfast dish of eggs, chili and cheese. They were served with good, crisp, hash browned potatoes. The room had very high ceilings of cream plaster and massive exposed rafters. The tables were placed on different levels and there was one particularly intriguing balcony which was set for two and was reached by a narrow stairway.

The full length windows led to a terrace and a fountain. The view of the distant Jemez Mountains shining in the morning sunlight was a setting worthy of a movie.

I remarked as much to Betty and she said, "You'll never believe this, but the man who is walking across the terrace right now is a movie producer. He is coming here to take a look at the dining room because it may be just the set they need for a movie he is doing."

There is certainly ample background material for a movie in this luxurious ranch-inn. For example, any one of the lodging rooms would be ideal for an interior scene. Almost all have fireplaces and each one is enchantingly decorated with various furnishings of Spanish missions. Some of the accommodations have a bunkhouse atmosphere.

Betty explained that the ranch is a "quarter section" entirely surrounded by Indian land. There are literally thousands of acres of colorful chapparal country, crisscrossed by riding trails.

Besides riding there are innumerable forms of ranch recreation at Encantado. These include the swimming pool, tennis, target and trap shooting, fishing, golfing, skiing, and art gallery. I have always been impressed by the sense of style and taste which has been projected into everything.

I am most enthusiastic about the high country of New Mexico. There are Indian pueblos, ancient Spanish villages, museums of Navajo and Spanish culture and many unusual shops. The Santa Fe Opera House is just minutes from the ranch.

As far as Betty is concerned, the Spanish motto about sharing a home is indeed a sincere wish. This is her home and guests at the ranch are literally her house guests. Her ideas of what a home should be like have simply been projected into a larger dimension.

One interesting touch is that on Christmas Eve, a time when there are a great many children in residence, there is a special dinner with twenty-five orphans as guests. And Santa Claus comes down the chimney with presents for all.

I found Rancho Encantado indeed enchanting.

RANCHO ENCANTADO, Rte. 4, Box 57C, Santa Fe, N.M. 87501; 505-982-3537. A 28-room luxurious ranch-inn, 8 mi. northwest of Santa Fe. European Plan. Breakfast, lunch and dinner served to travelers daily. Closed for 3 mos. in winter. Tennis, swimming, riding, rifle range, trap shooting on the grounds. Golf, hunting, fishing, skiing and bicycles nearby. Betty Egan, Innkeeper.

Directions: From Santa Fe, travel 8 mi. north on I-25 and exit at Tesuque. Drive 3 mi. to State Road 22 (Rte. 4), then 2 mi. to inn.

NEWFOUNDLAND (continued from page 118)

A country inn it isn't. But it is clean comfortable accommodations, a clean dining room and pleasantness and courtesy.

Bonavista is the place where John Cabot first landed in North America. There's a larger-than-life statue of him on the cliffs. There are many houses on the relatively treeless meadows with picket fences, and a conversation with a local fisherman confirmed that the fences keep the valuable vegetable gardens from being raided by stray cattle.

I went out to the very tip of the peninsula, where there is an old lighthouse. It was from the cliffs out here that I saw another awesome sight, an entire ice field. Not just icebergs, but almost solid ice, as far as the eye could see. It looked like a ghostly white desert. Mr. Abbott, the fisherman that I spoke with, explained that the ice pack had been there since the middle of May and it kept the fishing boats from coming in or out. As he said, "Some boats go out just so far, but they have to turn back. The fishing season is from May to November, but it's June and we're all locked in here now."

It was while I was talking with Mr. Abbott that I became aware of a series of sounds that resembled several rifles being fired at random. He explained that it was the huge sheets of ice breaking up from the action of the tide.

We walked back to the road and I noticed little flowers growing among the moss on the rocks and in sheltered places. They were like miniature daisies, and even as I stood there more colors seemed to be emerging in the sunshine and warmth of late June. The season was before them. Their hour of glory was dawning, but it was to be short-lived.

I left Bonavista and headed back inland, however this time I decided to follow a country road and see some of the out-of-the-way guest houses.

My first stop was at Mrs. Reader's Guest House in Bloomfield, a small cluster of houses on a secluded inlet. It was typical. There was a huge pile of wood in the front yard and some stray chickens. I entered through the kitchen and there was Mrs. Reader, her daughters and grandchildren. She showed me two rooms which she said were occupied most of the summer. It's a warm comfortable and natural atmosphere, and if you happen to be there at mealtime you'd probably be invited to sit down with the rest of the family. It is informal to say the least.

Mrs. Reader's sister runs Bessie's Tourist Home in nearby Musgravetown, but she told me that her sister is a little more strict. he "doesn't allow smoking in the rooms or beer upstairs and no television on Sunday." Although quite tempted to stay the night, it was still too early to stop, so I moved on.

I entered Terra Nova National Park and spent about an hour in the observation tower which has a tremendous view in all directions. There were bays on three sides, and I could see thousands of icebergs and the tremendous ice pack.

Here in the park, I found some accommodations at the Terra Nova Park Cabins. They were clean and neat with housekeeping facilities.

I left the park and drove out the Eastport Peninsula. It was a beautiful afternoon with a blue sky and billowy clouds. The landscapes and water views were gorgeous. In Eastport I found the *White Sails Inn*.

It is a white house surrounded by a picket fence with a sandy beach on the bay side. Guests were in wading even though there were icebergs 50 yards offshore. They have several housekeeping cabins and a few rooms available at the main house. Meals are served to house guests only. The owners are Mr. and Mrs. Les Dawe. He is a fireman on a fireboat in Toronto. They are here for two months of the summer. I still can remember the delicious smell of rhubarb pies and cakes being made in the kitchen. Reservations must be made in advance.

After leaving Eastport, I decided that since I had one more night to spend in Newfoundland, instead of going north, I would head back and go out the Burrin Peninsula towards Marystown.

This peninsula has some really remarkable scenery. I was impressed by the unusual massiveness of the bare hills. The jagged tops reminded me a great deal of southwest Arizona. There are many swift flowing creeks and rivers, and the highway runs over and around them, and between ponds and lakes. There's also a considerable section of raw barrenness. All the trees were gone. Perhaps there was a burn-off in some earlier year.

The sun was still high in the sky, but the hour was getting late. Again I found that I had waited too long, and the infrequent accommodations on this road were either filled or closed. I called ahead, using the "where to stay" booklet, but to no avail. I even tried places 30 miles off the main highway. Finally I did find some unlisted accommodations, which were clean and comfortable although, once again, quite austere. The owners invited me to share their bathroom instead of the public bathroom which had been set aside for eight rooms. I'll always remember their concern and hospitality.

The next day at noon, I was back in St. John's in time to watch the Dominion Day ceremonies in 80-degree heat. Even the usually imperturbable "Mounties" in their winter uniforms looked uncomfortable.

As the plane took off for Montreal, I had a few moments for reflection. My three days had provided excitement and novelty. Of course I had barely scratched the surface, nor have I been able to report more than a third of the events of this trip. There are literally thousands of adventures awaiting travelers in this Canadian province. I found the people cheerful, helpful and generous. I was fortunate, so I was told, to have had three days of ideal weather, since Newfoundland is at the apex of 3 storm tracks.

On the next visit, I will spend at least a week, and search for personal accommodations in even more remote locations, this time with a camper, lest I be beguiled again to travel too late in the day. And next time ... it's on to Labrador!

N.F. ACCOMMODATIONS (continued from page 120)

ARCHIBALD'S INN, Harbor Grace, Route 70. 9 rooms. Restaurant. Open all year. 709-596-5156.

READER'S TOURIST HOME, Bloomfield, Route 233, 2 rooms. Meals available to houseguests. (Almost like living with a family of fishermen.) Open all year. 709-467-2697.

These I did not see, but they were recommended:

HOTEL PORT-AUX-BASQUES, Port-aux-Basques. 50 rooms, private baths. Restaurant. Open all year. 709-695-2171.

GALLANT'S HOTEL, Stephenville, Route 460. 23 rooms, private baths. Breakfast and dinner available. Open all year. 709-643-2406.

GLYNMILL INN, Corner Brook. 66 rooms with private baths. Restaurant. Open all year. 709-634-5181.

CARMELITE HOTEL, Grand Falls. 26 rooms with baths. Restaurant. Open all year. 709-489-2271.

WOODSTOCK COLONIAL INN, St. John's, Topsail Rd. Restaurant. Open all year. 709-722-6933.

RAMBLER INN, Baie Verte, Route 410. 14 rooms. Restaurant. Open all year. 709-532-4245.

INDEX

The author of this book, Norman Simpson, is recognized as the foremost authority on today's country inns. Besides visiting literally dozens of inns for the first time each year, he also makes yearly visits to almost every inn already included. The result is a completely new book each year, entirely rewritten with a fresh viewpoint. Thousands of people have used this book for the past eight years to plan everything from a one-day excursion to a two-month vacation. The 1975 edition with the account of visits to over 140 country inns from Newfoundland to the Pacific Coast has newly discovered inns in many areas.